Counterterro_____

RONALD CRELINSTEN

polity

First published in 2009 by Polity Press

Polity Press
65 Bridge Street
Cambridge CB2 1UR, UK

Polity Press
350 Main Street
Malden, MA 02148, USA

ISBN-13: 978-0-7456-4293-2
ISBN-13: 978-0-7456-4294-9 (paperback)

A catalogue record for this book is available from the British Library.

Typeset in 10.25 on 13 pt FF Scala
by Servis Filmsetting Ltd, Stockport, Cheshire
Printed and bound in Great Britain by MPG Books Ltd, Bodmin, Cornwall

The publisher has used its best endeavours to ensure that the URLs for external websites referred to in this book are correct and active at the time of going to press. However, the publisher has no responsibility for the websites and can make no guarantee that a site will remain live or that the content is or will remain appropriate.

For further information on Polity, visit our website: www.polity.co.uk.

Contents

Acknowledgments

I would like to thank Louise Knight, commissioning editor at Polity Press, who invited me to write this inaugural book for Polity's new series, "Understanding Terrorism." Thanks, too, to Emma Hutchison, who took over from Louise when she went on maternity leave; Clare Ansell, production editor; and Leigh Mueller, copy editor; as well as the entire Polity team.

Anonymous reviewers, both at the proposal stage and at the manuscript stage, provided very useful comments and suggestions that helped me improve the focus, the structure, and the content of the present work. Of course, all errors or omissions are my own.

Portions of the following works were revised, updated, or expanded for use in this book:

Ronald D. Crelinsten, "Counterterrorism as Global Governance: A Research Inventory," in Magnus Ranstorp (ed.), *Mapping Terrorism Research: State of the Art, Gaps and Future Direction* (London: Routledge, 2007), pp. 210–35.

Ronald D. Crelinsten, "Analysing Terrorism and Counterterrorism: A Communication Model," *Terrorism and Political Violence* 14(2) (2002): 77–122.*

Ronald D. Crelinsten and Iffet Özkut, "Counterterrorism Policy in Fortress Europe: Implications for Human Rights," in Fernando Reinares (ed.), *European Democracies Against Terrorism: Governmental Policies and Intergovernmental Cooperation* (Aldershot, UK: Ashgate, 2000), pp. 245–71.

Ronald D. Crelinsten, "The Discourse and Practice of Counterterrorism in Liberal Democracies," *Australian Journal of Politics and History* 44(3) (1998): 389–413.

Ronald D. Crelinsten, "Television and Terrorism: Implications for Crisis Management and Policy-Making," *Terrorism and Political Violence* 9(4) (1997): 8–32.*

Ronald D. Crelinsten and Alex P. Schmid, "Western Responses to Terrorism: A Twenty-Five Year Balance Sheet," in A. P. Schmid and R. D. Crelinsten (eds.), *Western Responses to Terrorism* (London: Frank Cass, 1993), pp. 307–40.

* The periodical *Terrorism and Political Violence* can be accessed at the publisher's website, www.informaworld.com.

Introduction. Terrorism and counterterrorism before and after 9/11

Terrorism is a specific form of violence, one that is character-ized by its communicative function.[1] Whether used by state or nonstate actors, in the interests of government or against the interests of government, the victims of terrorism function as signs in a propaganda war. The bomb attacks, the hijackings, the assassinations, the torture, the disappearances, the mas-sacres, all function to convey messages to audiences beyond their immediate victims. The selection of victims is both sym-bolic and instrumental. In the case of selective assassination, kidnappings, or bomb attacks, the victims are often repre-sentatives of the State or some power elite. In the case of disappearances or torture, they are often members of social or political movements that are dedicated to reforming the State or altering the power structure. In the case of international ter-rorism, they are often citizens of states that are power-brokers within the world order or some smaller sphere of influence, or representatives of their governments. In all these cases, the victim is chosen because of whom she or he represents and because their victimization will resonate with specific audi-ences, either in generating fear or exhilaration, or in affecting allegiances and behavior. Even in the case of the most indis-criminate violence, such as machine-gunning of tourists in airports, the car bomb in city streets, the suicide bomber in a mass transport system, the massacre of villagers, or the attacks of September 11, the lack of discrimination between combatant and noncombatant, between involved and uninvolved, between active supporter and passive sympathizer, between innocent and guilty, has a symbolic function. What one analyst has called the "politics of atrocity"[2] is designed to attract widespread attention through the shock value of the attack. The gruesome beheading of hostages in Iraq is a more recent example of this kind of shock terrorism.

This victimization of noncombatants or innocents for the purposes of gaining public recognition for particular causes or imposing specific demands on third parties has been a feature of political life at various times and in various places for centuries, although it has not always been called "terrorism." While originally linked with the revolutionary terror of the French Revolution, and therefore the action of states, in its modern variant "terrorism" became a common word in public discourse in the late 1960s, when Palestinians turned to hijacking airplanes and Latin American guerrillas turned to kidnapping diplomats. In the ensuing decades, terrorism has been used by nationalists seeking new nations or wishing to secede from existing ones, by revolutionaries seeking to overthrow governments and to establish new regimes, by governments seeking to destabilize other governments or to control their own nationals either at home or abroad, and by fanatics and zealots pursuing a variety of social and religious causes. In the 1990s and culminating with the September 11 attacks in 2001 by Al Qaeda, terrorism has become a global phenomenon that transcends national and even hemispheric boundaries. The US-led war in Afghanistan destroyed the command and control center of Al Qaeda and led to its decentralization and dispersion. This, in turn, led to the outsourcing of terror attacks to sympathetic or like-minded affiliates in countries throughout Southeast Asia, North Africa, and the Middle East, including Indonesia (Bali), Morocco, Saudi Arabia, and Turkey. With the US invasion of Iraq in 2003, a lightning rod for terrorists and extremists was created in the center of the Middle East, and with the 2004 Madrid bombings and the 2005 London bombings, Europe became a major staging area for Al-Qaeda-inspired attacks by disgruntled or alienated citizens inflamed by internet images and propaganda.[3] The US-led "war on terror" has also become a master narrative that subsumes and simultaneously disguises many other conflicts, both domestic and international, whether Israeli/ Palestinian, Russian/Chechen, Chinese/Uighur,[4] Kashmiri (India/ Pakistan), or Spanish/Basque. One analyst argues that Central Asian states "have exploited the context of the global 'war on terrorism,' as well as the fear of Islamic extremism,to justify and intensity their suppression of dissent,without much concern about international condemnation."[5]

Used as a stand-alone strategy, terrorism is often considered the weapon of the weak: the insurgents or nation-builders who lack the material resources and the mass support necessary for sustained guerrilla warfare, armed insurrection, or a full-scale war of national liberation, or the government that lacks the necessary legitimacy to govern within the rule of law and the democratic forum of public debate and open dissent. Used as one tactic in a larger strategy of armed conflict or within a wider array of violent and nonviolent political action, terrorism is prized for its economy: kill one, frighten 10,000; actions speak louder than words; propaganda by the deed. Because its aim reaches beyond its immediate victim and because it is planned in secret and enacted without warning, terrorism commands attention while demanding few resources and manpower. Even what one analyst calls the "wholesale terrorism" of states[6] requires less infrastructure, management, and resources than do police forces and military organizations which follow the rule of law, whether domestic or international, and remain accountable to political authority and, in the case of excesses or systematic abuses, to criminal justice.

The definition of terrorism is fraught with difficulties.[7] There is no universally accepted definition of terrorism, although the United Nations has tried for a long time to achieve consensus among its Member States. One of the main sticking points has been the resistance by post-colonial states and other Third World states, including many Arab ones, to universally condemning the practice when conducted by groups resisting oppression or occupation. The well-known cliché, "one man's terrorist is another man's freedom fighter," encapsulates the problem. A common approach in international legal conventions has been to avoid defining terrorism altogether and to focus on terrorist tactics alone (see chapter 2). Former UN Secretary-General Kofi Annan has proposed a definition that confines terrorism to acts against civilians and noncombatants.[8] The problem here is that this merely shifts the debate from what constitutes terrorism to what constitutes innocent civilians and noncombatants. One analyst has suggested, for example, that "in societies highly integrated with reciprocity, . . . there is no accepted notion of individual innocence. All in-group members are responsible to the group, and share responsibility for the actions of others within it. . . . If there is conflict, all members of the out-group are enemies worthy of discrimination."[9]

In this volume, and in accordance with the centrality of communication in terrorist threat and violence, terrorism will be conceived as a form of violent communication or coercive persuasion. In defining terrorism, therefore, a behavioral approach will be taken rather than a motive-based or perpetrator-based approach. A "behavioral approach" means that terrorism will be conceived as a tool of coercive persuasion in a wide variety of power relationships, not just that of the insurgent who contests the power of the State. The definition will focus on what terrorists *do*, rather than who they are (perpetrator-based approach) or why they do what they do (motive-based approach). This is because defining terrorism in terms of who is acting or why they are doing so opens the way to selective definitions that are truncated for ideological, political, or epistemological reasons. The bulk of the terrorism literature focuses exclusively on insurgent terrorism and many works, though admitting that state terrorism exists and may even be the more pervasive and the more deadly form of terrorism, then proceed to exclude state terrorism from their object of study.

> A narrow focus on insurgent forms of terrorism separates the nonstate actor from the larger context within which he acts and, in particular, from the behaviour of state actors. Moral condemnation of outrageous acts of violence can blind the researcher and the policy maker to the place of terrorism in a wider range of options available to the non-state actor. Because other options exist, the choice of terrorism is viewed as an irrational choice, a symptom of pathology. What then passes as scientific discourse is really polemics, where conceptual typologies become catalogues of pejorative labels. The muddled state of definitions in the field of terrorism stems directly from this narrowing of conceptual frameworks to just those actors whose goals we find unacceptable. By defining terrorism by the context in which it occurs rather than as a tool of political communication which can be used in a wide variety of contexts, we preclude the possibility of anything more than a superficial understanding of a narrow aspect of the phenomenon.[10]

Viewed as a particular kind of coercive/persuasive tool, it becomes apparent that terrorism can occur in the context of criminal activity (crime), as much as within a political or a war context (insurgency/revolution). It can also be committed by state agents as much as by insurgents or political criminals. In fact, the use of torture has often been justified as a necessary weapon *against* insurgents and terrorists and has played a central part in terrorist regimes that have evolved from counterterrorism or counterinsurgency campaigns.[11]

Using this behavioral approach, terrorism will be defined as:

the combined use and threat of violence, planned in secret and usually executed without warning, that is directed against one set of targets (the direct victims) in order to coerce compliance or to compel allegiance from a second set of targets (targets of demands) and to intimidate or to impress a wider audience (target of terror or target of attention).

What this definition makes clear is that there are multiple audiences to the terrorist act and that not all these audiences experience fear or terror. The act of victimizing captures the attention of a variety of audiences and allows the terrorist to communicate more specific messages tailored to each one. The message need not be articulated in words; it can be symbolic (conveyed by the target selected, for example) or simply shocking (conveyed by the indiscriminate nature of the attack or the importance of the person targeted). This is classic propaganda by the deed. The attacks of September 11, for example, were not accompanied by any specific demands, though some were articulated later in the videotaped statements of Osama bin Laden and other Al Qaeda leaders, but the symbolism of the World Trade Center and the Pentagon being struck – and possibly the US Capitol – and the horrific toll of lives lost, including the passengers and crews of four planes, conveyed a complex set of messages that were clear to everyone. If terrorism is seen as a particular form of violent, coercive communication, then one can escape the ideological trap surrounding its definition. If freedom fighters use terrorism as part of their strategy, then they are terrorists; if counterterrorists use terrorism as part of theirs, then they are terrorists as well. The question then turns to why different actors, nonstate or state, use terrorism, and this leads, in turn, to a consideration of context.

To fully understand terrorism and how it emerges and develops within a society, however defined, it is important to analyze the targets, tactics, motivations, and modus operandi of terrorist groups. This is the who, what, why, and how of terrorism. It is also important to look at those people, groups, communities, or institutions – whether subnational, national, international, or transnational – with which the group interacts. This is one aspect of the wider context within which such groups operate. It is also imperative to look at what the members of the group were doing before they got into terrorism, what social and political climate existed then, and what kinds of control measures were used to deal with social and political protest during that time. This is the temporal dimension of that wider context within which any group operates. In other words, the spatial and temporal background of terrorist activity must be analyzed in order to fully grasp the context from which any terrorist group emerges and within which it operates. Part of this spatial and temporal background is the set of institutional measures taken in response to ongoing or previous social and political activity, including violent forms such as terrorism. An important element, therefore, in understanding terrorism is an appreciation of the forms that counterterrorism takes. This includes understanding how particular forms of terrorism can lead to the emergence of particular forms of response.

The danger that terrorism poses to democratic values and the way of life that they permit stems not just from terrorist threats and violence and the vulnerabilities that terrorists exploit, but from the ways in which societies think about them, talk about them, prepare for them, respond to them, and recover from their impact. One analyst goes so far as to suggest that the US "war on terror" poses a greater threat than the terrorism it is trying to combat.[12] This striking assertion highlights the fact that discourse and action are intimately related. How people talk about problems, frame them, and conceptualize them often determines what they do about them. Conversely, the way people deal with problems can often limit

the ways in which they perceive them, restricting their imagination and narrowing their options. These conceptual and
ideological filters can make it more difficult to understand a
problem in all its facets.

For example, since the attacks of September 11 and the ensuing "war on terror," counterterrorism has come to be viewed
primarily in military terms. This has led to emotional and
polemical debates about the very fundamentals of democratic
life as they relate to the nature of the terrorist threat and how to
deal with it.[13] When critics of this militarized approach to counterterrorism voice concerns about the rule of law and protection of human rights, they are often met with the disdainful
reproach: "you're so September 10!" This is sometimes coupled
with the remark, "you just don't get it." What critics of the "war
on terror" supposedly "don't get" is that "we are at war" with an
"implacable foe" who cannot be reasoned with or deterred by
threat of retaliation, who is out to kill as many of us as possible,
and who must be eliminated in order for victory to be achieved.
This might take a very long time, even generations, and until
we succeed, things like due process, rights for detainees, limits
to interrogation techniques, judicial control and oversight, and
counterweights to executive power are luxuries at best, and
serious impediments to the effective prosecution of the war on
terror at worst. In the words of US Justice Department spokeswoman Kathleen M. Blomquist, "The United States cannot
afford to retreat to a pre-September 11 mind-set that treats
terrorism solely as a domestic law enforcement problem."[14]
During the 2004 US presidential campaign, Democratic
candidate John Kerry was excoriated for suggesting that counterterrorism is primarily a question of law enforcement. After
the 2006 London bomb plot to explode airplanes with liquid
explosives was exposed, an anonymous Bush Administration
official continued to argue that the Democrats "do not have the
understanding or the commitment to take on these [jihadist]

forces. It's like John Kerry. The law enforcement approach doesn't work."[15]

The idea that "September 10 thinking" "treats terrorism solely as a domestic law enforcement problem" can be considered a discursive tactic similar to the rhetorical device of setting up a straw man. Counterterrorism before the 9/11 attacks was actually not confined solely to domestic law enforcement. The argument that "we are at war" reflects the "new terrorism" thesis[16] which suggests that terrorism today is fundamentally different from what it was previously.[17] Before 9/11, terrorism was primarily seen as a form of crime; after 9/11 it has been transformed into a new form of warfare. This war discourse can be called "September 12 thinking" to distinguish it from the "September 10 thinking" that it invents as a foil for its arguments. "September 12 thinking" views terrorism and counterterrorism post-9/11 from within a particular framework, but it also confines pre-9/11 thinking about terrorism and counterterrorism within a different framework that is seen to be passé, obsolete, and out of date. As such, "September 10 thinking" is an invention of "September 12 thinking" – a kind of projection which creates a straw man to argue with and criticize. They are two sides of the same coin, which represents narrow, conceptual models that distort the nature of the phenomenon to be dealt with and limit policy options.

It is true that counterterrorism before September 11 did privilege the rule of law, but it also emphasized international cooperation, policy harmonization across domestic *and* international jurisdictions, and, indeed, the rule of law, respect for human rights, and the primacy of law enforcement over the military option.[18] The latter was always included in the counterterrorism toolbox, but usually as a last resort and, in the case of aid to civil power, under the control of civilian authority. The use of force was often a tool of last resort in prolonged hostage sieges, for example.[19] International humanitarian law, including the Geneva Conventions, was not usually a part of the discourse since a war model of counterterrorism was not the norm. When international humanitarian law was discussed, it was usually in the context of explicitly *excluding* it as irrelevant to counterterrorism.[20] Since 9/11, international humanitarian law has come under increasing scrutiny as critics of the "war on terror" attempt to develop a legal framework for a primarily military approach to counterterrorism.[21] It is true that during the 1980s and, in particular, the Reagan years, a precursor of "September 12 thinking" did exist[22] and sometimes prevailed. An example was the 1986 US bombing of Libya. However, its military character was limited in scope and usually was a part of an overall "hard-line" approach. A common characteristic of this early discourse, for example, was an insistence on no negotiations with terrorists under any circumstances.[23]

Despite the militarized discourse and practice associated with the post-9/11 "war on terror," counterterrorism can actually take many forms. The polarization between "September 12 thinking" and "September 10 thinking" is a shortcut representation of the ideological divide that characterizes much contemporary discussion of counterterrorism. This ongoing ideological debate forms a kind of backdrop to any attempt to understand the complexities and challenges that countering terrorism faces in today's world. Each side highlights the strengths of their favored approach, while emphasizing the weaknesses of the other side. This introduces a background of distortion – a kind of white noise – for anyone attempting to understand counterterrorism and to formulate policy in this important domain. Figure I.1 depicts this by presenting an adaptation of the classic illusion of the vase and two faces that alternate as each other's backgrounds. The vase represents our understanding of counterterrorism in all its facets, while the

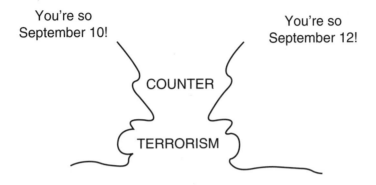

Figure I.1   Seeing counterterrorism through ideological filters: the polarized discourse revolving around 9/11

two faces represent the polarized discourse on the nature of terrorism and how to combat it, as represented by the dichotomy between "September 10 thinking" and "September 12 thinking." As we focus on the counterterrorism vase, our mind's eye suddenly becomes aware of the polarized discourse in the background (the faces). This then becomes the focus of attention for a while, only to be supplanted once again by the vase as one continues to try and comprehend the complete picture. Many assumptions about the subjects that people study are not really conscious, even though they inform the way they talk about them and the way they define and conceptualize them. Although the goal of social science is to be objective, even scientists and researchers cannot always prevent their feelings and emotions from affecting how they think about difficult issues and challenging problems. This is certainly true of the study of terrorism and counterterrorism.

Not all counterterrorism experts or terrorism analysts fall on one side of the divide depicted in figure I.1, and both kinds of thinking existed before the attacks of 9/11 and persisted thereafter. The dichotomy between "September 10 thinking" and

"September 12 thinking" can be characterized as another version of the more traditional dichotomy between hard-line and soft-line counterterrorism policies. Policy disagreements before 9/11 were certainly intense at times. Yet the post-9/11 period and the ensuing "war on terror" have been characterized by profound disagreements over the kind of threats we are faced with, the kinds of responses required, the institutions which should be responsible for this response, and the time-frame within which an effective response can be accomplished. Table I.1 summarizes the main differences across the most important variables.

"September 10 thinking" emphasizes legal approaches to counterterrorism, privileging the rule of law, international cooperation, and understanding the root causes of terrorism. While the military option is considered an indispensable part of the overall counterterrorism arsenal, it is seen as a tool of last resort, whose use must be legitimized and carefully controlled. The range of terrorist threats is seen as wide and diverse and the importance of understanding root causes and local contexts is recognized. Diplomacy and negotiations are considered important counterterrorism tools, particularly in the international arena. As far as state sponsors of terrorism are concerned, the preferred strategy is deterrence and containment. "September 12 thinking" emphasizes the military approach to counterterrorism, privileging the use of force and legitimizing it by changing the legal rules of the game if necessary, unilateral action by those capable of acting if others refuse or are incapable of cooperating, a heightened focus on state sponsorship of terrorism and weapons of mass destruction (WMD) / chemical, biological, radiological, nuclear (CBRN) terrorism, particularly in the context of identifying rogue (axis of evil) and failed states, the supplanting of deterrence and containment by a doctrine of preemptive defence, and a singular emphasis on one form of globalized

Table I.1 "September 10 thinking" and "September 12 thinking" compared.

	September 10 thought	September 12 thought
terrorist threat perception	- terrorist threat is diverse (domestic; transnational; international) - terrorist threat is evolving - terrorism is primarily a crime	- terrorist threat is uniform and primarily global (Salafist–Jihadi) - terrorist threat is new - terrorism is a new form of warfare
terrorist use of WMD/CBRN	- unlikely	- likely
importance of state sponsorship	- not a primary focus	- a primary focus (axis of evil)
importance of root causes	- a primary focus	- not a primary focus
preferred counterterrorism approach	- criminal justice model	- war model
attitude towards rule of law, human rights law, and international humanitarian law	- of central importance; must be respected	- luxury at best; hindrance at worst; can be circumvented or compromised in the interests of effective counterterrorism
attitude towards the use of torture in interrogation	- unacceptable; evidence based on torture not admissible in court	- acceptable under certain controlled circumstances; evidence based on torture admissible in court
place of military option in overall counterterrorism strategy	- last resort and only in aid of civil power	- central and primary role; civil power is secondary
kind of power preferred in dealing with state sponsors	- soft power; diplomacy and negotiation	- hard power; threats and sanctions; military strikes
preferred international strategy	- deterrence and containment	- preemption, including missile defence
attitude towards alliances and international cooperation	- international cooperation essential - multilateralism preferred	- international cooperation desired, but not essential - unilateralism if necessary

terrorism: Salafist–Jihadist terrorism of the Al Qaeda brand. Both approaches, taken alone, make sense in certain contexts and situations. Both exhibit serious limitations in other contexts or can trigger unintended consequences in particular situations.

The main aim of this book is to provide the reader with a clear understanding of the full variety of counterterrorism approaches that exist and the kinds of variables that underlie their differences. This will involve moving beyond the polarized discourse represented in table I.1, highlighting both the strengths and weaknesses of each side's favored approach, as well as considering other options that neither side emphasizes. The result will be a comprehensive survey that helps the reader to see through the ideological filters that often color people's understanding of counterterrorism and to grasp the complete picture that neither side permits. In keeping with the overall series of which this book is a part, the idea is to help the reader to understand the complexities and challenges related to countering terrorism in the contemporary world and to appreciate the full range of options available. The contrast between "September 10 thinking" and "September 12 thinking" can aid in understanding how conceptions of terrorism and its place in today's security environment can determine the particular approach taken to counterterrorism and the institutions that are marshaled to combat it.

Chapter 1 looks at the wider security environment within which terrorism exists today. This will provide the broader context for examining counterterrorism. It is an important first step, since it helps to understand the full range of security threats in today's world and how terrorism fits into the larger security framework. The following five chapters examine different types of counterterrorism.

Chapter 2 analyzes the two most commonly used models of counterterrorism: the criminal justice model and the war model.[24] Each model allows the state to exercise its monopoly on the use of violence, but each places strict limits on how this violence is to be used. The debate about whether the September 11 attacks by Al Qaeda constituted criminal acts or acts of war will be used to illustrate the tendency for these two models of counterterrorism to blur into each other.

Chapter 3 considers proactive approaches to counterterrorism that are concerned primarily with stopping the terrorist before s/he takes action. This is sometimes called preventive counterterrorism or simply anti-terrorism. It can include a wide variety of activities, ranging from risk and threat assessment and target hardening to preemption. However, the primary focus of the chapter will be on the intelligence function, blocking terrorist financing, and the particular challenges that countering secret activity poses for the police, the security services, and the military. More "defensive" preventive aspects will be examined in chapter 5 (see below).

Chapter 4 looks at the communicative dimension of counterterrorism. Propaganda, psychological warfare, hearts and minds campaigns, and the idea of providing incentives for terrorists to abandon violence and seek nonviolent paths instead all refer to this notion of counterterrorism as a form of communication. The chapter begins by examining two forms of "coercive persuasion" – deterrence and preemption – and then turns to the use of "soft power" or the propaganda dimension of counterterrorism. As such, it looks at political, social, cultural, and religious aspects of terrorism and counterterrorism and the importance of psychological operations (psyops).

Chapter 5 focuses on the kinds of preventive or protective measures that can be taken to minimize the risk of terrorist attack or to mitigate the impact of attacks that are carried out. Issues include target hardening, critical infrastructure protection, crisis management, emergency preparedness, consequence management, contingency planning and gaming, civil defense, and the promotion of citizen resilience in the face of terrorist threat and attack. Defensive models of counterterrorism treat terrorism, even of the mass-casualty variety, as one of many threats to public health or like any major disaster or catastrophe, whether man-made or not. Emphasis is placed not only on making it harder for terrorists to strike in the first place, but also on the social and psychological consequences of terrorist attack and how to minimize them.

Chapter 6 focuses on the kinds of counterterrorism initiatives that do not promise quick fixes, but play out in the long term. This includes the realm of "root causes" and the more structural factors that can create a suitable climate for the promotion and use of terrorism by ideologues and zealots. So much counterterrorism is focused on the short term, simply because the electoral horizon of most governments is so short, usually not exceeding five years. Structural factors usually play out over much longer periods than that – what the French historian Fernand Braudel calls *"la longue durée"* or the long term.[25] The chapter will focus on the kinds of long-term strategies that hold out promise for changing the environment in which terrorism thrives, as well as the difficulties and challenges that these strategies face.

The Conclusion brings everything together and evaluates the extent to which a comprehensive counterterrorism strategy can be achieved that would provide a framework for security in the twenty-first century while preserving the values that underlie democratic and global governance.

CHAPTER ONE

The context for counterterrorism: a complex security environment

During the Cold War, the world of terrorism and political violence was viewed through the bipolar lenses of East vs. West, Communism vs. Capitalism, Evil vs. Good. Definitional and typological complexities were papered over by Cold Warriors intent on forcing all conflicts into a Procrustean bed of a Soviet-sponsored, international terror network intent on destabilizing and subverting the West.[1] This resulted in several distinct trends in the terrorism literature, particularly during the 1970s and early 1980s:

- a tendency to focus exclusively on international and transnational terrorism and to ignore domestic terrorism or to cast it in a transnational light. This often involved stripping national conflicts of their social, political, and cultural contexts so as to more easily characterize the conflict as the result of Soviet influence;
- a tendency to ignore right-wing terrorism and to focus exclusively on left-wing terrorism. This was facilitated by the first trend, since many left-wing terrorist groups either cooperated internationally/transnationally or else used an internationalist rhetoric, claiming common goals with comrades and brethren throughout the world in their common fight against Western (US) imperialism and colonialism;[2]
- a tendency to focus primarily on insurgent terrorism and to ignore state terrorism, particularly of the variety used by Western- and particularly US-sponsored "authoritarian"

regimes. This may be why the state terrorism of the Shah of Iran, for example, was tolerated (and, it may be argued, facilitated, through technology transfer and police training) – until the Khomeini Revolution put an end to it in 1979 and replaced it with another form;[3]

• a willful blindness to any evidence of a US-sponsored terror network intent on destabilizing and subverting the Eastern bloc and creating market opportunities in the Third World.[4]

While the United States focused primarily on international terrorism, mainly because United States nationals were prime targets, the Soviet Union focused primarily on the danger of domestic terrorism. Much of the Cold-War-era terrorist literature took on a Manichaean flavor with titles such as *How the West Can Win*.[5] The enemy was clear and academic analysis often tended to cast itself in a cheering mode for increasingly militaristic policy solutions to the terrorist problem.[6] Academic studies of terrorism came chiefly from the disciplines of political science and psychology, though history and law, as well as other disciplines such as communications, also made contributions.[7]

With the end of the Cold War, the old enemy was gone, the war was won. When the bipolar lenses were removed, the world looked quite different. Domestic conflicts were more easily seen in their social, political, and cultural contexts; right-wing terrorism became more apparent; state terrorism was more easily seen to cross ideological divides and to have its own set of unique variables; and the idea of terror networks sponsored by superpowers was more easily seen to be a simplifying myth that conveniently obscured the complexity of the terrorism phenomenon.[8] In the post-Cold War era, terrorism at home became a prime focus of the Americans in the wake of the 1993 New York World Trade Center bombing and especially the 1995 Oklahoma City bombing, while the Soviet fears were proven to be justified by the Chechen use of terrorism in their ongoing insurgency against Russian rule.[9]

In short, the world suddenly became more complicated. As a result, the enemy became more diffuse. Phenomena such as drug trafficking, organized crime, and illegal immigration were included along with the more traditional objects of concern for those responsible for dealing with terrorism. In addition, new kinds of threats were formulated, ranging from infectious diseases[10] to information warfare.[11] The recognition of new/old threats was, in turn, translated into a broader operational mandate for agencies responsible for counterterrorism. The mandates of different control agencies that previously were quite distinct, such as customs agencies, border control, security intelligence, defense, and policing, began to blur into one another.[12] This tendency to place disparate phenomena into the same security basket was also reflected in various analyses of terrorism of that time. For example, one analyst[13] lumped drug trafficking, international crime, ethnic cleansing, religious fanaticism, rural guerrilla and urban terrorism all together as legitimate concerns for counterterrorism policymaking in the post-Cold-War world. In the mid- to late 1990s, the "new terrorism" thesis (see introduction) began to take hold as analysts recognized the threat of Islamist extremists and, in particular, demobilized Afghan fighters returning home after the defeat of the Soviets in Afghanistan. Islamist terrorism became the new post-Soviet enemy and began to attract increasing attention away from the wide range of other threats that emerged in the wake of the Cold War. This trend only became more acute after the September 11 attacks of 2001.

This chapter will examine this wider geopolitical context in which terrorism and counterterrorism interact. This will involve a description of the different kinds of actors who take part in international politics, the kinds of security threats which coexist with the terrorist threat, and the overall security architecture that has emerged under the influence of globalization, both technological and cultural.[14] In describing this wider context, the chapter will raise a series of questions concerning the nature of terrorism and the kinds of approaches needed to deal with it. This, in turn, will lead to a consideration of a detailed inventory of counterterrorism approaches that is suitable for countering terrorism in such a complex security environment.

A proliferation of new actors on the world stage

Today's world is one where people, goods, and services cross borders with increasing ease, and entities other than states interact and play an increasingly important role in international politics. With the rapidly expanding reach and speed of global communications technologies and jet travel, areas such as trade, finance, and migration have been transformed. Immigration, welfare, development, human rights, education, and tolerance of diversity and difference within societies and between states have all been greatly affected. All this has created severe challenges for state sovereignty and authority and increasing limits to state control over a wide variety of policy problems, including terrorism. Some have argued that the state is disappearing, weakening, or eroding as a result of these challenges and limits. While they probably go too far, it is fair to say that the state is transforming under the pressures of globalization.[15] State actors must now interact with a wide variety of nonstate actors and deal with a diverse array of transnational threats and vulnerabilities – not alone, but within a framework of international and regional cooperation and global governance. This is the wider geopolitical context in which terrorism and counterterrorism coevolve. And it is in this complex environment that security, in particular, needs to be addressed.

We live in a world of eroding boundaries and increasingly porous borders. The distinctions between foreign and domestic affairs, internal and external security, and public sector and private sector are blurring.[16] It is a world in which nonstate actors, many of whom are transnational, acting across borders via the internet or cellular phones, are becoming increasingly important and influential players in international affairs. In such a world, the traditional object of study for international relations – the nation-state and the international system of states – becomes problematic. This is because the number and variety of actors on the world stage has increased enormously, and focusing strictly on state actors and institutions misses out on these other actors and their increasing influence in world affairs.

Who are these nonstate actors with whom the traditional state actor must interact? They include:

- intergovernment organizations (IGOs) or supranational organizations and their international secretariats;
- multinational enterprises/corporations (MNEs/MNCs);
- banks and international financial institutions;
- non-governmental organizations (NGOs), both domestic and international, including charitable, humanitarian, and religious organizations, plus a wide array of transnational advocacy networks;
- media networks, particularly electronic media such as radio and television, the internet, and the World Wide Web (WWW), with its web blogs, alternative websites, and online communities, and all the mobile devices that facilitate the use of these networks anytime, anywhere;
- transnational migrants, including immigrants, refugees, asylum-seekers, guest and migrant workers, tourists, international students, international consultants and researchers, and business travelers;

- domestic, international, and transnational terrorist groups;
- drug traffickers, arms traffickers, smugglers, pirates, and other transnational criminal organizations;
- mercenaries, demobilized fighters, private security companies, private armies, and a whole conglomeration of privatized entities that perform what have traditionally been state-run security operations, including VIP protection, target-hardening, surveillance, policing, imprisonment, and war.

This vast array of nonstate actors has led one scholar to speak of a "multicentric world" which coexists alongside the more traditional state-centric world of international relations, interacting with it in a variety of ways.[17] In this world, there are many different kinds of collective identity other than the more traditional ways of identifying with a group, such as national, ethnic, religious, or ideological.[18] The range and diversity of coalitions and alliances that advocate or promote particular policy initiatives can be enormous.[19] The result is a huge increase in the complexity of communications, including more kinds of consultation, more diverse and heterogeneous partnerships, and a greater range of competing interests.

The inability of governments to come up with common solutions to some of the most pressing global problems, such as poverty reduction, debt reduction, global health, environmental protection, and even counterterrorism, has led nonstate actors such as individual entrepreneurs, non-governmental organizations, and private corporations to step into the breach. The continuing debate about UN reform, the slow and ponderous pace at which state bureaucracies and international organizations function, and the continuing tension between national interest and global policy harmonization all underscore how difficult it is for state actors to implement effective global strategies alone in today's complex world. This has led to an increasing reliance on nonstate actors to work together with state actors in the management of global problems. The tendency for national governments, particularly in the West, to offload responsibilities to civil society and to rely more and more on the private sector[20] has its counterpart at the international and global level. The UN Global Compact, launched at UN Headquarters in New York on July 26, 2000, is one example.[21] Spearheaded by the former UN Secretary-General Kofi Annan, the Global Compact is an international network of companies, labor, civil society, and six UN agencies.[22] Companies are asked, on a completely voluntary basis, to embrace, support, and enact, within their sphere of influence, a set of core values in the areas of human rights, labor, the environment, and anti-corruption. This initiative is not without critics, who argue that many companies with terrible records in human rights, working conditions, or environmental protection are merely using the UN association to improve their image.[23] What this example highlights, however, is the new kinds of partnerships between state and nonstate actors that are proliferating in today's world to meet the complex global challenges with which we are faced (see box on next page). Subsequent chapters of this book demonstrate how this trend is also occurring in the area of counterterrorism.

Many kinds of security

Where state actors coexist with nonstate ones, there are multiple referent objects when one asks the question: security for whom? While international security used to be about protecting states from attack, invasion, or conquest, it is no longer just the state that needs to be secured. In today's world, societies, markets, individuals, and the environment must also be protected. We now speak of a whole array of securities – societal security, economic security, human security, environmental security – all of which demand attention alongside, and often intertwined with, the demands of international security.

> At the moment, many businesses say "governments must do more." Yet, what we've seen over the last three decades is a retraction of governments' role in many respects through increased liberalization, privatization, bilateral investment agreements and the like. The view has been that government needed to get out of the way and let the market do its magic. But the market alone can't ensure social stability and equitable development. The state must have the capacity to ensure social welfare and manage the negative impacts of market forces. This again raises the notion of shared responsibilities – the idea that governments are key, but in an increasingly interconnected world other social actors must also be directly involved in addressing common challenges.
>
> Mary Robinson, President, Realizing Rights: The Ethical Global Initiative, in Q & A blog, "Managing Globalization," by Daniel Altman, *International Herald Tribune*, March 14, 2007, viewed at http://blogs.iht.com/tribtalk/business/globalization/?p=401(last accessed on August 7, 2008).

Since the attacks of September 11, a new term, "homeland security," has entered the lexicon, and its main tenet is that we must work on many fronts at once to ensure security of the state, its societies, its people, its resources, and its infrastructure.[24] One international relations scholar has argued that security involves not only military concerns, but also political, social, economic, and environmental ones. This broadened security agenda therefore includes five elements: political security, societal security, economic security, environmental security, and military security.[25]

In today's world, the traditional focus of realist theory in international relations – the prevention of war between states – is now complemented by issues of culture and identity, poverty, disease, environment, and resource utilization.[26] In the area of economic security, for example, states need access to resources, finances, and markets in order to wield power and to sustain acceptable levels of welfare for their citizens.[27] Companies and interest groups, too, must be able to work to sustain acceptable levels of welfare, if not state power. Corporate responsibility and ethical globalization have become the central elements in many state–nonstate partnerships.[28] In the area of societal security, states try and maintain traditional patterns of language, culture, identity, and custom so as to provide citizens with a continuing sense of belonging to a community.[29] A less state-centric conception that recognizes society and its citizens as referent objects for security would put greater emphasis on the role that citizens and social groups play in ensuring a sense of community. Such a conception of security is "societal" rather than "national," focusing on feelings of cultural and social insecurity engendered by problems such as maintaining cultural identity in the face of globalization, crime and crime control, and the preservation of "family values." Fear of immigrants and foreigners and concern about crime and job loss have fueled the rise of the extreme right in Europe, for example. Similar insecurity was triggered in American society by the attacks of September 11. Debates about homosexual marriage and women's right to abortion in the USA reflect larger concerns about the changing nature of the family.

The concept of human security, particularly in the area of foreign policy, reflects the view that international security cannot be achieved unless the peoples of the world are free from violent threats to their lives, their safety, or their rights. In this view, the referent object for security is the individual human being. Some key policy issues that have been addressed from within this framework include the international campaign to eliminate land mines, the banning of child soldiers, the creation of the International Criminal Court, and the impact of war and conflict on individuals and communities, particularly women and children.[30] Such an approach to security is compatible with the broadened security agenda mentioned above. Taken together, these different kinds of security suggest that threats can take many forms and can impact upon a wide array of policy areas not previously considered to be relevant to security studies. The same is true for terrorism and counterterrorism. This leads to a consideration of the range of security threats in today's world.

Security threats

We live in a world of de-territorialized threats which come from far away, not just from neighboring states. Pollution, sudden market swings, epidemics such as SARS and avian flu, and transnational terrorism are some examples. The coexistence of old and new threats is another feature of today's complex security environment. This was brought home to many observers when North Korea announced that it had successfully completed a nuclear test in October of 2006.[31] One observer put it this way:

> In the 19th century, Britain and Russia struggled for control of Central Asia in what was called "the Great Game." In the 21st century, the great game is far more complex, taking place across the globe between an expanding number of actors with a multiplicity of interests and a variety of weapons. Yet certain basic facts – war is an extension of politics, politics are often driven by a need for resources as well as collective feelings of pride or shame – remain much the same in the wake of Sept. 11. We are obliged to focus on Islamism and the terrorist threat it has produced, to study Arabic and the work of Sayyid Qutb, but we should not fail to consult Kennan, Clausewitz or Thucydides either.[32]

Traditional threats, such as nuclear proliferation, remain, as not only North Korea but also India and Pakistan remind us, but they are also transformed, as the threat of nuclear material falling into the hands of terrorists becomes an increasing concern. This concern intensified after the collapse of the Soviet Union, amidst fears about the security of nuclear installations within Russia and in former Soviet states and worries that discontented nuclear scientists would sell their expertise to the highest bidder. Since 9/11, however, it has become even more acute as it has become linked with the problem of rogue states and failed states. The 2003 invasion of Iraq was in large part justified by a supposed link between Saddam Hussein, his purported WMD program and Al Qaeda. While George W. Bush's "axis of evil" focused on North Korea, Iran and Iraq as prime candidates for rogue state, it was actually a top Pakistani nuclear scientist, Abdul Qadeer Khan, who spread nuclear technology and know-how to Libya, North Korea, and Iran.[33] And it was Libya who exposed the operation, renounced its nuclear program, and was rewarded with removal from the US list of state sponsors of terrorism.[34] As for failed states, several cases of uranium smuggling have been detected in Georgia, where separatist regions such as South Ossetia have become lawless zones that share porous borders with Russia.[35]

Failed or collapsed states, particularly in Africa, are potential breeding grounds for a host of possible security threats, including environmental degradation, economic collapse, pandemics, or mass migration. The continuing conflict in Somalia, where one party to the conflict wishes to impose a strict form of Islamic government, has triggered fears that terrorists of the Al Qaeda brand could operate there with impunity, much as Al Qaeda did in pre-9/11 Afghanistan.[36] In fact, there are growing concerns that Al Qaeda has reconstituted itself in the tribal areas in northwestern Pakistan.[37] The war in Iraq has created large flows of refugees to neighboring states such as Jordan, Syria, and Lebanon. By early 2007, according to the UN High Commissioner for Refugees, almost 2 million people had fled,

representing about 8 percent of the prewar population. A further 1.7 million had been displaced internally.[38] Many of those
who fled were the very people who could contribute most to the
country's reconstruction and recovery, such as doctors, engi-
neers, academics, and other professionals. This influx of
migrants creates problems for the host countries, including
placing a strain on basic services and increasing fears that
Iraq's sectarian violence will spill over the border along with the
migrants themselves. The transnational spread of threats does
not only occur between neighboring states. The outbreak of
SARS in certain Canadian cities in the mid-1990s was triggered by international travel between Canada and China by
Chinese-Canadian citizens and their relatives.

Global warming has increasingly come to be seen as a security issue, particularly as rising sea levels, flooding due to
severe storms, increasing drought, spread of disease, or
scarcity of arable land produce environmental refugees and
increase the risk of conflict and war over scarce resources.[39]
Two examples of chronic conflict areas – Darfur in the Sudan,
and the Middle East – are more and more recognized as
driven in large part by concerns about resources. In the
Sudan, the majority of Arabs in the north are nomadic
herders, while the majority of Black Africans in the south are
farmers. While the conflict can easily be depicted as ethnic,
based on the Arab/Black divide, at a more fundamental level it
is really a conflict over scarce resources such as land and
water.[40] Similarly in the Middle East, while the conflict is traditionally depicted as an Arab/Jewish one, issues of water,
aquifers, and the protection of water sources are increasingly
recognized as central to it.

In sum, security threats in today's world are increasingly
interrelated, transnational, and multifaceted in their impacts on
individuals, societies, and nations. From a policy perspective,
this creates particular challenges when it comes to deciding

which threats require immediate attention and how to deal with particular threats. Given that the typical electoral horizon is measured in years rather than decades, most emergency planning and crisis management is focused on the acute crisis that plays out rather quickly. The slow crisis, which develops over a long period of time and can take unexpected directions as it evolves, is much more difficult to handle. For example, the environmental and health impacts of the 9/11 attacks took a lot longer to be recognized than the immediate death and destruction,[41] though evidence exists that the deleterious effects of the Twin Towers' destruction were deliberately downplayed by the Environmental Protection Agency.[42] Some threats demand attention simply because they are so horrible to contemplate. Other threats can pale by comparison and, if their pernicious effects are only visible months or years later, they may not even be recognized as serious. This can lead to a disconnect between perception of threats and assessment of vulnerabilities.

Uncertain threats and certain vulnerabilities

A characteristic of the current security environment is that the many threats with which we are faced have different levels of impact and occur with different degrees of probability. The current fixation with WMD (weapons of mass destruction) and CBRN (chemical, biological, radiological, nuclear) terrorism is a perfect illustration of this. While the vulnerability to such attacks is certain, the threat itself is far from certain.[43] Bombing and assassination remain the favorite tactics of terrorist groups around the world. As such, the threat is more certain, but the vulnerability is less, especially as policies are developed to reduce their impact even further. Some threats, such as the effects of global warming, become more certain as science progresses and more and more stakeholders recognize that the threat is serious. A clearer picture is emerging of what areas in the world are most susceptible to deleterious consequences of climate change. In a 2007 report, International Alert, a London-based nongovernmental organization concerned with peacebuilding, identified 102 countries whose instability or experience with armed conflict will be aggravated by the impact of climate change.[44] Will this identification of certain vulnerabilities to global warming in particular regions of the world lead to concerted international efforts to protect these countries from the threat? Studies have shown that those countries that will suffer the least from global warming – Western industrialized countries – are preparing the most, while those countries that are most vulnerable – Third World developing countries – lack the resources and know-how to protect themselves.[45] The irony is that the consequences of climate change in the South may trigger mass migration of environmental refugees to the North. This means that vulnerabilities, like threats, can also change over time and space. This injects further complexity into the assessment of threats in today's world. How do governments and international organizations apportion scarce resources – money, time, personnel, political will – when faced with such uncertain threats at the same time that other, more certain threats, but with less devastating impact, continue to pose a serious problem? And how do they deal with certain threats that may take a long time to have a discernible effect? Do they delay action now at the risk of being unable to do something effective later on? Or do they act now, even if it means diverting resources from more immediate problems? Counterterrorism, particularly the "war on terror," is often criticized precisely for diverting attention and resources from other threats that are considered to be more serious, more pressing, or both.[46]

The dangers of securitization

Another characteristic of today's security environment relates to the ideological component of threat and vulnerability assessment: the global securitization of terrorism and WMD. The term "securitization" was coined by the Danish international relations scholar, Ole Waever.[47] When a social problem or a public policy issue is securitized, it is presented as an existential threat requiring special powers or emergency measures to deal with it. Characterizing a problem as an existential threat justifies adopting extraordinary measures that go beyond normal rules and procedures and lie outside the generally accepted framework of democratic governance. Issues as wide-ranging as migration, organized crime, and drug trafficking have all been securitized, having been absorbed into the mandate of security services seeking to find new enemies in the wake of the Cold War. After September 11, and particularly after the spread of anthrax in the US postal system, public health, local emergency preparedness, and environmental safety have all been securitized, becoming important elements in counterterrorism policy in the USA and the EU. But the most striking example of securitization has been the post-9/11, pre-Iraq War rhetoric conflating rogue or pariah states with the increasing risk of WMD terrorism. Part of this was driven by opportunism and a desire to demonize Saddam Hussein. But part of it was related to the need to justify a new doctrine of preemptive defense to replace the longstanding one of deterrence and containment. The ideological work underlying this securitization of terrorism and WMD is, again, related to the challenge of maintaining balance and perspective in the face of terrifying threats and vulnerabilities. The prospect of a rogue or failed state helping a terrorist group to acquire WMD is indeed a terrifying one, but does it justify a whole new approach to security that undermines existing strategic doctrines and international legal regimes?

A widening technology gap between the USA and the rest

The dilemma posed by the disjunction between threats and vulnerabilities over space and over time is compounded by the persistence of a technology gap between the world's only superpower and the rest of the world, including the European Union. In the United States, the Revolution in Military Affairs has led to increasing financial and research commitment to new technologies and new ways of conducting wars.[48] This has increased the possibility of an economic security dilemma, whereby states feel they must remain competitive in the global market while maintaining control over new technologies.[49] A generational shift in weapons systems has begun in the United States that will put it several generations ahead of other major powers. This change could very well trigger new security dilemmas and could greatly affect many states' economic and military policies as they seek to update their military technology and capabilities. China's increased military spending in recent years, as well as the confirmation that North Korea has succeeded in producing and testing a nuclear weapon both reflect this dimension of the current security environment. Every state is now faced with the challenge of updating military technology within budgetary limits. States experiencing rapid economic growth, such as China, can afford the expensive advanced technology of modern warfare more than others.[50] This injects further insecurity into those states that cannot. The American decision to deploy missile defense systems in two Eastern European states, Poland and the Czech Republic, has triggered insecurity in Russia, contributing to a more belligerent stance by Russian President (now Prime Minister) Vladimir Putin vis-à-vis the EU and the USA. In April 2007, Putin announced a suspension of the 1990 Treaty on Conventional Armed Forces in Europe (CFE), originally signed by members of NATO (North Atlantic Treaty

Organization) and the old Warsaw Pact, including Russia, and renegotiated in 1999.[51] Similar tensions surround the US drive to develop space-based intelligence and communications systems. In the wake of the Iraq War, other states targeted by the USA as members of an axis of evil undoubtedly feel these pressures and dilemmas all the more strongly. North Korea's successful development of a nuclear weapon demonstrates how certain declaratory policies can become self-fulfilling prophecies if coupled with military action. After the invasion of Iraq, a co-member of the axis of evil, it may have become imperative for North Korea to demonstrate that they had a nuclear deterrent to reduce the likelihood that they would be next.

Another technological challenge in today's security environment is that of dual-use technology. US concerns, especially post-9/11, over satellite imagery aiding terrorist planning is one example. This concern led to the removal of many satellite imaging maps from internet websites. Similar concerns have been raised by British army intelligence, who claim that Google Earth has been used to target British troops in Iraq.[52] The problem of dual-use technology has been a central part of American and European concerns over Iran's nuclear ambitions. While Iran insists that its nuclear program is strictly for peaceful purposes related to energy needs, the USA, EU, and many countries in the region fear the possibility of a nuclear-armed Iran. This problem is not a new one. In the 1950s and 1960s, Canada had a nuclear technology-transfer program with India, having been given assurances that the technology was for peaceful purposes only. India went on to develop nuclear weapons and is now a member of the nuclear club, followed by Pakistan, who felt obliged to pursue a similar path in response to India's nuclear build-up. One military analyst suggests that Iran's reactivation of its nuclear program in the late 1990s was primarily motivated by Pakistan's successful nuclear tests in 1998.[53] Add to all this the recognition that nuclear technology represents one possible solution to the dangers of fossil fuel consumption and it becomes clear that the problem of dual-use technology in the nuclear arena will only increase in the future. Some countries, such as Saudi Arabia, Libya, and Egypt, are looking at the nuclear option as a means of generating electricity for desalination plants, which are increasingly seen as the only option for dwindling fresh water supplies.[54] As more and more states opt to build nuclear plants as a clean alternative to current energy production methods, the security of these facilities will become an important policy issue.[55] For counterterrorism, these trends can only increase concerns about the likelihood of nuclear terrorism.

Liberalization, democratization, state-building, and humanitarian intervention

Another characteristic of the current security context relates to the kinds of states that coexist in today's world. One distinction is that between the trading state and the garrison state and involves the complex interrelationships among market liberalization, democratization, and state-building.[56] There is a common belief that trading states do not wage war, that democratization reduces the risk of violence and terrorism, and that state-building in post-conflict situations should prioritize the strengthening of state capacity in the judicial, policing, and security areas. These are all more problematic than they appear at first glance.[57] For one thing, democracy and violence are not necessarily mutually exclusive, as the prevalence of electoral violence in many countries demonstrates. Democratization can actually lead to violence as previously repressed groups exercise new-found power and influence and previously privileged groups fight to retain or regain power and influence. Post-war Iraq is a perfect example of this. Strengthening state capacity often means giving the monopoly on the use of state violence to those very people and institutions that were responsible for repression or gross human rights violations in the previous regime. In Iraq, the decision to de-Baathify the political elite and to disband the army may have been designed to avoid this problem. The result, however, was to create a power vacuum that led to disorder, chaos, and widespread violence. Many Eastern European countries faced a similar problem after the collapse of the Soviet Union. Attempts at "lustration," or the purification of state institutions of all Soviet influence, were often compromised by the need to preserve continuity in state functioning.[58]

Similar problems surround the practice of humanitarian intervention. The widely accepted doctrine of non-intervention in internal affairs of states provides a significant legal barrier to such interventions, while moral considerations often work the other way. One solution that has been proposed by some is to redefine sovereignty so as to switch the emphasis from authority to responsibility.[59] From this perspective, states have a responsibility to protect the rights of their citizens and residents and other states have the right to intervene if a government fails or refuses to exercise this responsibility. While some justify intervention in this case on moral grounds, others justify it on the grounds of preserving international peace and security, such as preventing spillover of conflict to neighboring states or mass refugee flows. Critics argue, however, that intervention is simply contrary to international law, regardless of moral considerations.[60] All these ambiguities highlight the difficulties that surround any attempt to establish good governance in a rapidly globalizing world. How do we reconcile interdependence with sovereignty, and national security with regional or international security? These questions have direct relevance for the "global war on terror" and international efforts to deal with transnational terrorism with a global reach.

The international system of states: an unevenly distributed structure

Related to the question of state type is the structure of the international system itself, particularly as it relates to international security.[61] The bipolar world of the Cold War, where two superpowers dominated international politics and security, has given rise to a more complex picture since the end of the Cold War. One international relations scholar refers to a 1 + 4 global structure – the USA, as the world's only superpower, plus the EU, China, Russia, and Japan.[62] Such a structure highlights the uneven distribution of power and influence – even of the most powerful states – in today's security environment. The issue of pivotal states, such as India, Brazil, South Africa, and Mexico, highlights the fact that other states are beginning to assert their own claims to power and influence within the international system.[63] Former UN Secretary-General Kofi Annan's proposal for Security Council reform and the continuing and contentious discussion over which states should become permanent members underscore this issue. After the September 11 attacks, other states became important as the USA attempted to establish and maintain a global coalition in its "war on terror." The Sudan, Colombia, the Philippines, Indonesia, Georgia, and Uzbekistan all received special attention.

The international system has been described as one involving the interleaving of two worlds, the core and the periphery.[64] The core is characterized by liberal thinking and interdependence, while the periphery is characterized by realist thinking and balance-of-power politics. This bifurcation is not only an international one, but also an intra-national one, since the poor and dispossessed within the core constitute a periphery within the core, while the elites in the periphery constitute a core within the periphery. This bifurcated, nested structure highlights the challenge of interdependence and the danger of creating regional "gated communities" instead of addressing the root causes of conflict and terrorism, namely the grievances that are used by charismatic leaders to mobilize resentment, hatred, prejudice, discrimination, and the adoption of terrorist violence. This marginalization of the periphery can occur in theory as well as practice. In the field of international relations and, particularly, security studies, the predominant theories and perspectives tend to privilege the core, while marginalizing the periphery.[65]

Rogue states and failed states revisited

One final aspect of the security architecture of today is the distinction between rogue states and failed states. Both terms are as much rhetorical devices as empirical phenomena, as is, for example, George W. Bush's "axis of evil." If a rogue state is one which ignores international law and rejects international cooperation, then the consistent rejection of international treaties by the US Administration under George W. Bush, including the refusal to apply the Geneva Conventions to prisoners captured in Afghanistan and Iraq, makes the United States look like a rogue superpower.[66] If a failed state is one that cannot provide security for peoples, groups, and cultures that live within its borders, then Russia can sometimes look like a failed state. This was particularly true in the decade or so following the end of the Cold War. With its newfound oil wealth and the widespread domestic popularity of Vladimir Putin's foreign policy when he was president, the lack of protection for certain peoples, groups, and cultures within Russia now receives less attention. In fact, Russia is beginning to look more and more like an authoritarian state, with little tolerance for dissent and considerable disregard for human rights. Post-war Iraq certainly fits the description of a failed state more and more, as violence continues to escalate and evolve in frightening ways. In many Western countries where neoliberal policies prevail, government services have become commodities that are marketed as products to be consumed not by citizens but by clients or customers. Coupled with downsizing state capacity and offloading government services to the private sector and civil society, the result has been that many states in the "core" have abdicated their responsibility for the welfare of their citizens, even in the area of security. Whether this is a new form of failed state – by refusing to act like a state – is an open question. One result has been the increasing importance of the private sector in conducting much of what used to be state business, including many functions related to security, such as policing, prisons, surveillance, peacekeeping, foreign aid, and even war.[67] China, for its part, has begun to look like a hybrid between a rogue state with little regard for environmental protection, food and drug regulation, or trade rules, and a failed state with little control over its burgeoning entrepreneurial class.[68] Government corruption and bribery abound and when toys, toothpaste, or other consumer products are recalled in the West because of dangerous defects or contamination, it is increasingly likely that they were made in China.

The phenomenon of rogue states is certainly real enough. Many states unfortunately adhere to international law only when it serves their national interest, as in the case of extradition and international conventions against skyjacking and piracy. As for failed or weak states, many governments lack the resources or power to provide security for their people or to develop their resources. One analyst calls such states "quasi-states," arguing that many post-colonial states from the periphery that were admitted into the international system rely on international recognition and a negative interpretation of sovereignty that focuses on territorial integrity, self-determination, and non-intervention.[69] As in the case of global warming, it is often these same countries that are most at risk from a wide variety of security threats. The African continent is a particularly troublesome region in this regard (see box on p. 40).[70]

How terrorism fits in

The place of terrorism in the volatile mix of threats that characterizes today's security architecture is a hotly debated issue. Some see terrorism as the central security threat of our time. Others argue that it is a minor irritant compared to the greater threat of global warming or pandemics. Still others argue that terrorist violence pales in comparison to other forms of criminal violence or even the daily carnage of traffic accidents in many industrialized states.[71] Terrorism is a gray-area phenomenon, something between crime and war, state violence and insurgent violence, conflict and violence, and propaganda and direct action.[72] It is often intermeshed with other phenomena, such as migration, competition for resources, social movements and social protest, political and religious ideology, mass media and electronic communication, ethnic conflict and identity or single-issue politics, subversion, insurgency and revolution, and self-determination of peoples and nations. All this introduces a high degree of complexity and even ambiguity into the contextual framework within which terrorism must be addressed.

Countering terrorism is intimately related to understanding the nature of the terrorist phenomenon and how it fits into the wider security environment. How we conceive of terrorism determines to a great extent how we go about countering it and what resources – money, manpower, institutional framework, time horizon – we devote to the effort. The following questions concerning the nature of terrorism highlight the kinds of conceptual problems that continue to plague our understanding of terrorism in today's complex world.

- *Change vs. continuity*: Is there truly a "new" form of terrorism, as some argue for today's religiously motivated terrorism, that is so different from what preceded it that it must be dealt with in a completely different way, or is terrorism

---

Failed states in sub-Saharan Africa

Sub-Saharan Africa is home to more failing states than any other region in the whole world. But even in more or less functioning states such as Kenya and Tanzania, the state is hardly capable of effectively maintaining a monopoly on violence and controlling the entire territory of the country. Border areas and the slums of the big cities are already de facto zones outside the state's control. The security forces' training and equipment are entirely insufficient and corruption and criminalization of the police is far advanced. The shadow economy of these crumbling states makes capital transactions and trafficking in weapons, raw materials, and consumer goods possible, without which terrorist networks would be unable to function. Thus, the incapacity of the majority of African security forces to protect targets threatened by terrorism is in stark contrast with the great variety of such potential targets including embassies, the numerous agencies and projects of international development organizations, subsidiaries of American and European companies, and international tourist hotels.

Moshe Terdman, "Factors Facilitating the Rise of Radical Islamism and Terrorism in Sub-Saharan Africa," African Occasional Papers (PRISM, GLORIA, Interdisciplinary Center, Herzliya, Israel), 1(1) (March 2007). PRISM website: www.e-prism.org.

---

simply evolving and adapting to a globalizing environment that is itself evolving? The policies required for countering truly "new" forms of terrorism may require new tools of analysis, new frameworks for thinking, and new forms of training and education of intelligence and policy analysts. If it is more a question of continuity, where terrorism emerges, evolves, and develops in a more complex environment rather than terrorism itself changing fundamentally, then it may be possible to adapt current tools, frameworks, and training to new contexts and situations while still maintaining the pool of knowledge and practices accumulated from past experience.

- *Agency vs. structure*: Can terrorists be considered to be free agents and rational actors who decide whether and when to adopt violence to achieve their goals or are they determined by structural variables that constrain their freedom of action and push them along predetermined paths? Does democratization, for example, necessarily reduce the likelihood of terrorism or can people choose a violent path despite the opportunity to participate in political life? Does extreme poverty necessarily mean that terrorism is not an option, unless middle-class intellectuals choose the terrorist path as a means to awaken the impoverished to their plight? What is the relationship between micro variables, such as individual choice and life history, and macro variables, such as social, economic, or political structure? To the degree that terrorists are indeed free agents and rational actors, then deterrence policies may work. Some argue, however, that today's terrorism is not amenable to deterrence or negotiation policies.[73]

- *Discourse vs. action*: Does what terrorists say in their public communiqués and on the internet always provide clues to what they intend to do or is there a propaganda dimension to terrorist discourse that has to be taken into account? For example, many experts fear that Islamic terrorists will ultimately resort to WMD terrorism, in part because they talk about it a lot and videos and training manuals that deal with WMD have been seized from terrorist training camps.[74] Yet researchers who have interviewed imprisoned terrorists in Israel found that, on the whole, their respondents were not interested in WMD.[75] While interview data have their limitations, particularly when the respondents are in prison, such findings suggest that knowledge about what terrorists think, say (in different contexts), and ultimately do is extremely important. In particular, it is vital to understand to what extent discourse serves propaganda and recruitment purposes (via impressing potential recruits with rhetorical flourishes and daring threats) and to what extent it conveys plans of action. In each case, different sets of policies may be called for.

- *Values vs. capabilities*: Do certain groups end up adopting or rejecting the terrorist option because of limits in capabilities or because of preferences or values? Terrorism is the weapon of the weak in the sense that they cannot muster sufficient manpower or weaponry to mount an insurrection or revolution. This is a limit in capabilities. Yet some groups are discriminate in their targeting, while others are not. While this may reflect limits in capabilities, it could also reflect values. For example, terrorist groups wanting to take over territory tend to limit their tactics in order to maintain the support of local constituencies, but if a group wants to break up the state, they have fewer restrictions or limits and can therefore use more violence. This is a deliberate choice based on goals. Knowledge about value systems and belief systems of terrorist groups and particularly their constituencies is an important part of understanding terrorist strategy and tactics, targeting patterns, and choice of weaponry or level of violence. Different counterterrorism policies may be more appropriate when it is a question merely of capabilities, such as target hardening or preemptive strikes, while other policies may be more appropriate when it is a question of values, such as negotiation, psychological operations, or education.
- *Political vs. religious goals*: Terrorism experts disagree over whether Islamic terrorist groups have primarily religious or political goals. One scholar argues that religious terrorism that has political objectives and roots is probably susceptible to political solutions, just like any other form of terrorism.[76]

This suggests that counterterrorism policies for religious terrorist groups need not be divorced from policies that have been developed for other kinds of groups. On the other hand, some scholars suggest that religious terrorism is fundamentally different from other kinds of terrorism[77] and argue, for example, that negotiation with religious or messianic terrorists is impossible. The problem with this argument is that it conflates different kinds of people, with different levels of belief and different life experience, into the same basket, "religious terrorist." Granted, it may be hard to talk reason to a dedicated suicide bomber, though even this may be possible. But what about his or her family, recruiters, or peers? The role of religion in motivating the move towards – or away from – terrorism and indiscriminate violence is complex. For some Islamic extremists, there really is no distinction between political and religious goals. Signs of God are everywhere and their worldview is pre-Westphalian and pre-Enlightenment. The modern state is irrelevant; only the *ummah* is important. Other religiously motivated terrorists, however, are much more pragmatic. Much of Al Qaeda's terrorism, for example, is aimed at overthrowing Muslim governments in countries such as Egypt, Jordan, and Pakistan, who are seen to be Western puppets.[78] Is it possible that these more politically oriented goals could be susceptible to some form of compromise, adaptation, or accommodation to changing conditions? Or are these political goals merely stepping stones to imposing a new religious order? Again, different policy approaches may be required depending on how these questions are answered.

- *Certain vulnerabilities vs. uncertain threats*: Do we focus on those vulnerabilities that we know without question would lead to catastrophic consequences were we to ignore them? Here, we are talking primarily about the threat of WMD

terrorism and, in particular, CBRN threats. As we have
seen, the problem here is that the probability of terrorists
carrying out such attacks is extremely low, the persistence of
supposedly well-informed doomsday predictions notwith-
standing. As the Bali bombings, the Moscow theatre siege,
the Madrid train bombings, or the London suicide attacks
demonstrate, terrorists can wreak havoc using the traditional
tactics of bombing and hostage-taking which have long been
the favored weapons of the weak. The key is that these tactics
can be used in new contexts (Bali, London) or in frighteningly
new variants (Moscow, Madrid, London). In the Chechens'
theatre take-over in Moscow, the number of hostages and
hostage-takers was large and explosives strapped to some of
the hostage-takers' bodies increased the potential for high
casualties.[79] In Madrid, multiple bombs triggered by cellphones increased the impact of the attack. In London, multiple suicide attacks were the first such attacks in Europe,
and the July 21 failed attempts indicate that serial, multiple,
copycat attacks are now possibly a new variant. Such attacks
constitute uncertain threats as opposed to certain vulnerabilities. Should policy be focused on the former – a task fraught
with difficulties relating to understanding terrorist recruitment, motivation, and target selection – or the latter – a task
that usually requires worst-case thinking that often ignores
what we know about terrorist motivation, and is more focused
on emergency preparedness and damage limitation – both
infrastructural and sociopolitical?

An inventory of counterterrorism approaches

Distorted or truncated conceptions of terrorism can lead to
wrongheaded approaches to counterterrorism. Rather than
base our policies on one conception or another, it is therefore
essential to consider a full range of options and examine their

particular strengths and weaknesses in light of particular kinds of terrorism. There are several basic dimensions that can help to identify the variety of approaches that are available for countering terrorism in different contexts. These dimensions are time, space, type of power, and type of intervention. The approaches can be categorized as a series of opposites: short-term/long-term (tactical/strategic); coercive/persuasive; offensive/defensive; reactive/proactive; local/global (domestic/ international).

- *Short-term vs. long-term*: Do counterterrorism efforts focus on the short term, which means primarily looking at current groups, their motivations, preferred targets and tactics, and their organizational structure, or do they focus on the long term, which necessitates not only a consideration of the larger picture – the social, religious, political, and economic context in which known groups operate – but also a consideration of how such groups might transform themselves in response to counterterrorist measures and of which new issues might trigger new (or old) groups to consider terrorism or nonviolent alternatives? It took years for the IRA to finally end their terrorist campaign, at the end of July 2005, and several more months to finally decommission their weapons, at the end of September of that year. The Tamil Tigers in Sri Lanka began talking peace after years of insurgency, but the talks have continually been punctuated by renewed violence and new ceasefires until, more recently, they were supplanted by a return to violence. What will be the next issue that triggers terrorism? Will it be water shortages, or perhaps global warming? It is hard to think outside the box when everyone, for good reason, is focused on Islamist terrorism.
- *Hard power vs. soft power*: What kind of knowledge is necessary for supporting and rendering more effective those

counterterrorist measures that rely on the state's monopoly on the use of violence, namely police, courts, and military, and what kind of knowledge is necessary for supporting more persuasive forms of control, such as economic sanctions, public education, and diplomatic initiatives? If a criminal justice or military model of counterterrorism prevails, then certain kinds of knowledge about terrorist constituencies or terrorist financing may not be necessary. But if the exercise of soft as opposed to hard power is to be seriously entertained as an essential component of a comprehensive counterterrorism strategy, then other kinds of knowledge become important.

- *Unilateralism vs. multilateralism*: Similarly, a unilateralist approach to counterterrorism may have policy requirements that differ significantly from those of a mulilateralist one – the latter requiring a detailed knowledge of different policy approaches, different political cultures, and different levels of training and competency for those charged with counterterrorism that the former may not need to consider.

- *Tactical vs. strategic*: The distinctions outlined above boil down to the difference between tactical and strategic analysis, whereby the former tends to be more short-term, more oriented towards supporting the exercise of hard power, more easily done unilaterally, and more generally reactive in that the primary concern is to protect certain vulnerabilities exposed by a small sample of past attacks and the worst-case scenario projections that derive from them. Strategic analysis, on the other hand, tends to be longer-term, lends itself more easily to supporting the exercise of soft power, which must consider a much broader range of issues than tactical analysis, and is better done on a multilateral basis since it can allow for the kinds of research and study, such as comparative and historical analysis, that take longer to do. As such, strategic analysis is better suited to dealing with uncertain threats – who will do what, when, and how – in a complex environment of ever-evolving threats and vulnerabilities.

• *Local vs. global*: Is terrorism always ultimately locally driven or is there a truly global variant that can strike anywhere and anytime? Some argue that Al Qaeda approaches the latter, especially pre-September 11, though since the launch of the "war on terror," many now feel that such an Al Qaeda no longer exists, if it ever did, and that the spate of attacks since that fateful day represent local initiatives that are inspired, more than instigated, by the Al Qaeda example. Can terrorism in one region spread to other regions? Does terrorism in the periphery of the international system of states necessarily increase the likelihood of terrorism in the core? Is international or transnational terrorism more a threat to international security than domestic terrorism, or vice versa? These questions highlight the complexity of the geography of terrorism and that knowledge about the interaction between local and global phenomena – what some call "glocalization"[80] – might be an important element of a comprehensive counterterrorism strategy.

Each of the next five chapters highlights a particular kind of counterterrorism and surveys the particular tasks and challenges of that approach, as well as its strengths and weaknesses and the particular problems and limitations that arise. Each chapter will examine both domestic and international aspects of the particular approach that is being dealt with. Since there is some overlap among the types of approach, only some of them will be the focus of individual chapters, and there will be some overlap among chapters. The entire spectrum of approaches will be addressed in the concluding chapter.

CHAPTER TWO

Coercive counterterrorism

This chapter examines the traditional counterterrorism tool-box that relies on the coercive capacity of the State. It analyzes the two most commonly used models of counterterrorism: the criminal justice model and the war model. Both these models rely heavily on the State's monopoly on the use of violence, i.e., the exercise of hard power. In the criminal justice model, it is the police who carry the primary responsibility, although other elements of the criminal justice system, such as the courts and the prisons, are also involved. In the war model, it is the military who carry the primary responsibility. The rules of engagement in the criminal justice model involve the use of *minimal* force, which usually requires an exercise of judgment on the part of the officials involved, particularly in the areas of arrest and pre-trial detention. Military rules of engagement, on the other hand, require the *maximal* use of force, designed to overpower the enemy, however defined.

In both models, however, there are strict limits on who can be subjected to state violence. In the criminal justice model, it is only those suspected and found guilty of committing a crime. In the war model, it is only combatants and those directly providing military support to those combatants. These restrictions on the exercise of violence in both models form the basis of the legitimacy bestowed upon the State by the rule of law, whether national or international. In the case of the criminal justice model, these rules include the prerogatives of due process, which must be followed at all stages of arrest, indictment, trial, and punishment. These include: the right to be informed of charges; to be tried without undue delay; to prepare and present a defense; to be assisted by counsel; not to be forced to confess; and to be presumed innocent until proven guilty. For the war model, it is the rules of war as embodied in international humanitarian law and human rights law that legitimize the actions of the State. For example, Common Article 3 of the 1949 Geneva Conventions, which applies to non-international armed conflict, in paragraph 1(d), forbids "the passing of sentences and the carrying out of executions without previous judgment pronounced by a regularly constituted court, affording all the judicial guarantees which are recognized as indispensable by civilized peoples."[1] These judicial guarantees are generally assumed to include the prerogatives of due process listed above, although this assumption has become problematic in the context of the US "war on terror" and the treatment of those considered to be enemy combatants by the US Administration.[2]

Without these legally mandated restrictions on the use of state violence, the exercise of violence by state agents such as the police or the military would itself be criminal – violating either domestic criminal law or international law, such as the laws of war. Table 2.1 demonstrates this by listing two sets of labels: one describing actions that are legitimized by adherence to the rule of law and one describing actions that are not. On the left-hand side of table 2.1, we find six terms commonly used for the different procedures of criminal justice, as well as two for the conduct of war. In the case of criminal justice, we tend not to think of these procedures as violence, even in the case of capital punishment, simply because it is generally accepted by everyone that they are legitimate. That is what legitimation is all about.[3] It removes any kind of stigma from the actions that the labels signify. In the case of war, terms like "neutralizing" or "collateral damage" also serve to reduce or even eliminate any aura of stigma from the violence inflicted

Table 2.1 The power of words: legitimate and illegitimate forms of state violence	
Legitimate exercise of state violence	Illegitimate exercise of state violence
arrest	abduction
bail	extortion
interrogation	torture
trial	kangaroo court
imprisonment	forcible confinement / hostage-taking
execution / capital punishment	murder
killing / neutralizing the enemy	murder / mass murder / genocide / war crime
collateral damage	crime against humanity
counterterrorism	state terrorism

by state actors.[4] On the right-hand side of table 2.1, we find terms that would be used to describe the same actions committed by nonstate actors or by state agents acting outside the rule of law, such as in reigns of terror where people are picked up in the middle of the night and detained and tortured without any regard for due process or human rights.

Liberal democracies are distinguished from authoritarian or totalitarian regimes by their adherence to the rule of law and other democratic principles, such as openness and transparency of procedures, accountability of government agents and institutions when things go wrong, and the maintenance of a bond of trust and confidence between citizen and government that results from a citizenry that is informed about public affairs. Inherent to these principles are many of the human rights that are entrenched in a number of international conventions since the Second World War, most notably the Universal Declaration of Human Rights (UDHR) and the International Covenant on Civil and Political Rights (ICCPR). These rights include, among others:

- freedom of opinion and expression (UDHR, Article 19; ICCPR, Article 19);
- freedom of thought, conscience, and religion (UDHR, Article 18; ICCPR, Article 18);
- freedom of assembly and association (UDHR, Article 20; ICCPR, Articles 21 and 22);
- equality before the law (UDHR, Article 7; ICCPR, Article 26);
- the right to privacy (UDHR, Article 12; ICCPR, Article 17); and
- the right to take part in the government of the country (UDHR, Article 21) and to take part in the conduct of public affairs (ICCPR, Article 25).

When citizens exercise these rights by promoting or using violence or at the expense of other people's rights, such as in the case of hate propaganda (freedom of opinion and expression) or rioting and vandalism (freedom of assembly and association), they can be held accountable before the law. Similarly, when state agents exercise their duties in a way that contravenes the rule of law or democratic principles, they too can be held legally accountable. This is the essence of social control and the exercise of power in democratic societies, and it is equally applicable to counterterrorism. When state agents acting in the name of counterterrorism consistently contravene the rule of law or the laws of war with impunity, using their coercive powers in ways that create a reign of terror that is sanctioned by the State, then they have become state terrorists, mirroring the behavior of the terrorists they are fighting. This point is highlighted in the last row of table 2.1.

The following sections of this chapter will examine each coercive model of counterterrorism in greater detail, highlighting their strengths and weaknesses as well as the particular problems that they pose for countering terrorism effectively. In examining the limits and problems associated with each model, at both the national and international levels, we shall see that the two models are transforming and, in a sense, blurring in response to the complex challenges of the broader security environment described in chapter 1.

The criminal justice model

A criminal justice approach to counterterrorism treats terrorism as crime. This makes perfect sense, since most terrorist acts constitute crimes defined in criminal codes. If one considers the most common terrorist tactics, such as kidnapping, assassination, bombing, and armed attacks, the end result is usually the infliction of injury or loss of life on persons or the destruction of property, all of which are universally proscribed in the criminal law of all nations. When terrorism first became a high-profile object of attention for policymakers in the 1960s and 1970s, terrorism as a crime in and of itself did not exist in most criminal codes. Terrorist acts were usually prosecuted under articles that pertained to specific criminal acts. While the creation of special terrorist offences was sometimes considered, particularly in the wake of serious incidents of terrorism, it was generally agreed that this was not a good idea. This stemmed from a desire to treat terrorism as ordinary crime so as not to glorify the terrorist in any way.[5] Treating terrorism as ordinary crime, not as a special offense requiring special procedures or punishments, performs a delegitimation function. By criminalizing the acts that terrorists commit, emphasis is placed on their criminal nature and not on their political or ideological motive. In this way, the terrorist's claim to be acting in the name of a higher purpose is undermined and the means by which s/he attempts to achieve these supposed higher goals is stigmatized.

All this changed after the 9/11 attacks and, in the case of countries where the level of terrorist violence was particularly high, even before that. The United Kingdom, for example, has long relied on special terrorist offenses and procedures to deal with "The Troubles" related to the conflict in Northern Ireland. The Northern Ireland (Emergency Provisions) Act (NIEPA) and the Prevention of Terrorism (Temporary Provisions) Act (TPA) both predate 2001, as does the Terrorism Act 2000, which replaced those "temporary" measures with one permanent statute – after more than 30 years.[6] France has had quite draconian anti-terrorist measures in place since the mid-1990s, when it suffered a series of attacks from Islamic terrorists.[7] A decade earlier, a special section of the Paris Court was created to deal with terrorism cases. Israel, too, had strong anti-terrorism legislation and procedures in place long before September 11, reflecting that country's long and turbulent experience with Palestinian terrorism.

Many Western countries that did not have special anti-terrorism legislation before 2001 created special terrorist offenses after the 9/11 attacks: the USA and Canada in 2001; Australia and Norway in 2002; Sweden in 2003.[8] Offenses have included committing terrorist acts as variously defined or committing acts for terrorist purposes as variously defined, as well as membership in a terrorist organization and contributing to the financing of such organizations. The UK and France, among others, also strengthened or expanded their pre-9/11 anti-terrorism legislation after the 9/11 attacks. Germany's *Anti-Terror-Paket* (Anti-Terror Package), which came into force at the beginning of 2002, was an omnibus package of legal amendments to preexisting statutes. The Madrid bombings of 2004 and the London suicide attacks of 2005 also triggered enhanced legislation and police powers in several European countries. Glorification of terrorism has become an offense in several countries, such as the UK and Spain. In the UK, this has triggered controversy and criticism because of the limits such an offense places on free speech (see box on next page).

Some countries, such as Germany, still do not have a legal definition of terrorism, while others, such as Spain, have no special anti-terrorist laws, treating terrorism as a form of serious crime.[9] Such countries have at various times, however, created special procedures to deal with terrorist acts and actors.

Creating a new offense – public provocation to commit a terrorist offense

We wish in our conclusion to emphasise our view that the combination of the breadth of the definition of "terrorism", the vagueness of "glorification", and the lack of a requirement that there be at least a danger that an act of terrorism will result, makes the encouragement of terrorism offence in section 1 of the Terrorism Act 2006 incompatible with the requirement in Article 12 of the Convention[1] that the establishment of any new offence of public provocation to commit a terrorist offence be compatible with the right to freedom of expression, and proportionate to the legitimate aim pursued. In our view the offence as defined in section 1 is likely to have a disproportionate impact on freedom of expression, contrary to the express requirement in Article 12.

UK Parliament, Joint Committee on Human Rights, *First Report* (2007).

1. The 2005 Council of Europe Convention on the Prevention of Terrorism (CECPT).

At the international level, there are currently 13 international conventions that deal with some aspect of terrorism.[10] They compel all signatory states to adopt national legislation proscribing a variety of terrorist activities or prohibiting states from supporting or financing terrorist activity in any way. The 13 conventions deal with the following subjects, presented in chronological order according to where and when they came into force:

1. acts committed on-board aircraft (Tokyo 1963);
2. unlawful seizure of aircraft (The Hague 1970);
3. acts against the safety of civil aviation (Montreal 1971);
4. crimes against internationally protected persons (New York 1973);
5. taking of hostages (New York 1979);
6. nuclear materials (Vienna 1980);
7. acts against the safety of fixed platforms on the continental shelf (Rome 1988);
8. maritime navigation (Rome 1988);
9. violence at airports (Montreal 1988);
10. plastic explosives identification (Montreal 1991);
11. terrorist bombings (New York 1997);
12. terrorist financing (New York 1999);
13. nuclear terrorism (New York 2005).

Taken together, these terrorism conventions can be considered a kind of legal regime that attempts to create an international consensus on combating terrorism throughout the international system of states. There are also regional conventions and accords, such as the Organization of American States (OAS) Convention to Prevent and Punish Acts of Terrorism (Washington 1971), the European Convention on the Prevention of Terrorism (Strasbourg 1977), the Arab Convention on the Suppression of Terrorism (Cairo 1998), and the Organization of African Unity (OAU) Convention on the Prevention and Combating of Terrorism (Algiers 1999).[11] Post-9/11 accords include the Inter-American Convention Against Terrorism (Bridgetown, Barbados 2002), the Council of Europe Convention on the Prevention of Terrorism (Warsaw 2005), and the Association of Southeast Asian Nations (ASEAN) Convention on Counter Terrorism (Cebu, The Philippines 2007). There are two international disarmament treaties that could also be conceivably linked to fighting terrorism, in particular WMD terrorism. These are the 1972 Biological Weapons Convention and the 1994 Chemical Weapons Convention. Most discussion of international conventions related to countering terrorism does not include these two, but they can be important in that reducing the stockpiling and use of biological and chemical weapons by states can prevent or diminish the possibility that terrorists could obtain such weapons themselves.

Supposed benefits of the criminal justice approach
The criminal justice approach to counterterrorism is assumed to carry additional potential benefits other than the delegitimation function mentioned above. As with all criminal law, criminalization also performs a general educative function: the use of threat and violence in the pursuit of political, social, religious, or ideological goals is not acceptable. This can be particularly important with respect to terrorists' constituencies – their supporters or sympathizers. Often, people may be in favor of a terrorist group's goals, but not necessarily the means they use to achieve them. Criminalization of terrorist actions can reinforce public repugnance with terrorist violence. Related to this general educative function is the concept of deterrence, both general and special. General deterrence aims at a wide audience, the general public, threatening sanctions if anyone dares to engage in acts proscribed in the criminal code. Special deterrence aims at the criminal offender, threatening further sanctions if the offender repeats the offense. Because deterrence is basically a communicative function, further discussion will be reserved for chapter 4, which deals with persuasive counterterrorism.

There are other functions of criminal justice that are pertinent to terrorist acts as well as other criminal acts. Treating terrorists as ordinary criminals reinforces the retributive function of criminal law. Those who are prosecuted, convicted, and punished for contravening the criminal law are required to pay for their transgression through fines, deprivation of liberty, or, in the case of capital punishment, their lives. For many victims and their families, punishment of offenders can provide a measure of relief for their suffering, since the application of criminal sanctions to the terrorist serves as a public confirmation that what they did was wrong.

The criminal justice model can also perform a rehabilitative function, helping the convicted terrorist rethink the error of his or her ways and reintegrate into society. In Italy, for example, repentance laws which required convicted terrorists to renounce the use of violence in exchange for more lenient treatment helped to convince many terrorists to take the path away from terrorist violence and towards more socially acceptable means of protest and dissent.[12] Article 2 of Law 155/2005 permits the discretionary granting of one-year renewable (and also rescindable) residence permits, or full residence permits, to illegal foreigners who collaborate with the authorities. This is another example of the way in which the law can be used to induce or promote cooperation with authorities. For this more rehabilitative approach to work, of course, the operations of criminal justice must respect the rule of law and the rights of the criminal – something that is difficult to promote or to implement in time of crisis and fear.

Finally, the criminal justice model can perform an incapacitation function. This simply means that imprisoned terrorists cannot continue their actions while behind bars. For many violent offenders, lengthy prison sentences mean that they will be too old to continue their violent ways once released from prison. Violent crime in most instances is the province of young men. It is generally easier, for example, to recruit young men into a terrorist group than it is an older person, with more of a stake in society, though some Islamist terrorists, including some of the 9/11 and London 2005 perpetrators, are exceptions to this rule.

In sum, then, the potential *benefits* of a criminal justice approach to counterterrorism are as follows:

1. a delegitimation function, whereby the use of terrorism is stigmatized via a process of criminalization;
2. a general educative function, whereby the unacceptability of terrorism is publicly confirmed via the application of a criminal justice process to apprehended terrorists;
3. a deterrent function, whereby terrorist acts are prevented through the threat of criminal sanctions;
4. a retributive function, whereby those who use terrorism are punished according to due process;
5. a rehabilitative function, whereby convicted terrorists are given the chance to renounce the use of violence and to reconsider their role in society;
6. an incapacitation function, whereby imprisoned terrorists are isolated from the environment where they wish to carry out their terrorist activities.

A possible further benefit of a criminal justice approach to counterterrorism is the salutary effect that convicting and punishing terrorists can have on victims of terrorism and their families.

The efficacy of many of these functions is highly dependent on the manner in which the criminal law is enforced. If it is arbitrary, discriminatory, or disproportionate to the severity of the offense or the threat posed by the offender, then it can be counterproductive (see chapter 4). If enforcement is inconsistent, poorly executed, or hampered by bureaucratic delays, insufficient funding, or institutional turf wars, any or all of the above functions can be undermined as well. This leads us to a consideration of the limits to the criminal justice model and the problems that such an approach faces in combating both domestic and international forms of terrorism.

Limits and problems of the criminal justice model

1. *Nullum crimen, nulla poena sine lege*: A fundamental principle of criminal law is that there is no crime or punishment without law. This means that in a society where the rule of law prevails, no-one can be said to have committed a crime if what they have done has not been proscribed in a specific law. If this is the case, then they cannot be punished for it either. In a criminal justice model of counterterrorism, then, no-one can be prosecuted, tried, or convicted for an offense that has not been defined in a criminal code or law. Because of this principle, Canada was unable to demand the extradition of Quebec separatists who hijacked a plane to Cuba in the 1960s and sought refuge and asylum in that country. The offense of skyjacking (unlawful seizure of aircraft) was only created in 1970 and translated into Canadian law in 1976. This means that states must always keep up with new forms of criminality in their legislation for a criminal justice model to be practical or useful. Similar problems exist in the area of computer crime, where criminals continually update their methods as the technology develops, leaving gaps in criminal legislation which make arrest and prosecution technically impossible.

2. *Evidence*: Because terrorist acts are planned in secret and usually executed without warning, gathering evidence in a criminal investigation can be particularly problematic. Terrorists generally do not act alone, and they belong to groups with strong ties of identity, conviction, or loyalty. Witnesses can easily be intimidated to remain silent or refuse to cooperate with authorities because they sympathize with the terrorist cause or even support the group in some way. Captured terrorists often remain silent in order to protect colleagues or to allow them time to escape

capture. The pressure to get suspects to confess or to reveal group secrets and plans can lead to the use of questionable or illegal methods of interrogation, including torture. Evidence extracted in such ways is usually inadmissible in court. Sometimes, suspects have to be released due to insufficient evidence, even though it is likely they are guilty. In some cases, they can go on to commit new acts. In June 2007, for example, a failed attempt to detonate two car bombs in central London was linked to a suspect who had been released due to insufficient evidence in a previous bomb plot.[13]

In some countries, a suspect's right to remain silent has been compromised by allowing juries to consider their refusal to answer questions in deciding on a verdict. After the 9/11 attacks, some countries, such as Australia and the USA, permitted suspects to be detained incommunicado without trial, access to a lawyer, or the right to remain silent. These restrictions of longstanding prerogatives of due process have all been justified by the need to compel terrorist suspects to provide information to police, prosecutors, or intelligence agents. The Bush Administration's decision to hold certain suspects as enemy combatants rather than charge them with a specific crime was ostensibly to avoid granting them certain rights, such as the right to remain silent. The case of dirty bomber suspect and US citizen Jose Padilla highlights the issues very well (see box on pp. 61–3).

3. *Trials* The question of whether to charge a suspect or a detainee with criminal offenses and bring them to trial is a complex one in terrorist cases. One US Justice Department official provided a list of considerations: "national security interests, the need to gather intelligence and the best and

The Padilla case: highlighting problems of the criminal justice model in terrorism cases

Jose Padilla, a US citizen and former gang member who converted to Islam, was arrested at Chicago's O'Hare International Airport on May 8, 2002, and held as a material witness on a warrant issued in New York State.[1] Then Attorney General John Ashcroft claimed, in a dramatic news conference from Moscow, that authorities had just foiled a plot by Mr. Padilla and other Al-Qaeda operatives to detonate a radioactive or "dirty" bomb in the USA.[2] The linking of Padilla's arrest with WMD terrorism ensured that it would be a high-profile case from the beginning. On June 9, 2002, instead of charging him with any crime, the Bush Administration decided to designate Padilla an illegal enemy combatant and hold him indefinitely in a military prison, a navy brig in Charleston, SC.[3] This decision to detain a US citizen without trial reflected a desire to thwart an extremely dangerous kind of terrorist plot rather than continue to gather evidence that might help convict the suspect in court at a later date. Padilla was considered a continuing threat since he was associated with Al Qaeda and had engaged in preparations for committing acts of international terrorism. Authorities also believed that he possessed intelligence that could help thwart future attacks. The question of when to arrest is a difficult one in dealing with terrorism and underscores the difference between criminal and security intelligence (see chapter 3).

A series of judicial decisions concerning the government's right to hold Padilla without charge culminated in a decision by the US Court of Appeals for the Fourth Circuit in Richmond, Virginia, supporting the government. This was on September 9, 2005. Padilla appealed to the US Supreme Court, which agreed to hear the case, increasing the possibility that Padilla's incommunicado detention might be declared unconstitutional. The deadline for filing arguments before the Court was November 28, 2005. On November 22, the Bush Administration announced criminal charges against Padilla and, on January 3, 2006, Padilla was transferred to a jail in Miami, Florida. The timing of the criminal indictment triggered suspicion that the move was primarily motivated by a desire to avoid the Supreme Court ruling on the detention without trial, thereby allowing the Fourth Circuit decision supporting the government to stand. Padilla was charged with three offenses: conspiracy to "murder, kidnap, and maim"; conspiracy to materially aid terrorists, under 18 USC § 371; and providing material support to terrorists (18 USC § 2339A). The indictment stated in part that "It was a purpose and object of the conspiracy to advance violent jihad, including supporting, and participating in, armed confrontations in specific locations outside the United States, and committing acts of murder, kidnapping and maiming for the purpose of opposing existing governments and civilian factions and establishing Islamic states under Sharia." No mention was made of Padilla's alleged association with Al Qaeda, his supposed plans to launch attacks within the USA, or, in particular, the alleged dirty bomb plot. The first, most serious charge of conspiracy to murder was dismissed by the Federal Court in Miami on August 16, 2006, but was reinstated by the US Court of Appeals on January 30, 2007. The trial began on May 15, 2007.

These legal maneuvers all revolve around questions of evidence and testimony: compelling information from suspects while detained without trial or, if a trial is permitted, protecting valued sources from testifying in court, preventing the revealing of intelligence in court or having prosecution witnesses cross-examined by the defense. In the Padilla case, a further concern that lay behind dropping certain charges was the difficulty of using in court any intelligence obtained from Padilla or other terror suspects when they were in military custody without lawyers.[4] This is because such evidence may not be admissible if it was extracted using torture or inhumane treatment. Evidence concerning the dirty bomb plot, for example, was apparently revealed during interrogation of Khalid Sheikh Mohammed, alleged mastermind of the September 11 attacks, who was held incommunicado in a secret CIA prison from his arrest in Pakistan in March 2003 until he was transferred to

Guantánamo Bay in September 2006, along with 13 other "high-profile" suspects. If the dirty bomb plot charge was retained, Padilla's defense could ask questions about where the evidence came from and how it was obtained. If torture was used to extract the information from Mohammed, then it would be inadmissible. Padilla himself has accused the government of torturing him by solitary confinement and sensory deprivation, sleep deprivation, forced standing, and stress positions. His defense tried to get him declared incompetent to stand trial due to post-traumatic stress disorder induced by his detention and interrogation. However, on February 28, 2007, after several days of hearings, the Federal judge declared him competent to stand trial. On August 16, 2007, he was found guilty on all counts. On January 22, 2008, he was sentenced to 17 years, 4 months in prison – a sentence that was considerably less than the life sentence demanded by prosecutors. The judge also took into account the 3.5 years spent in the navy brig before he was charged with specific offenses. In the end, Padilla was tried, convicted, and punished not for any concrete act of violence, but for intentions and plans to commit violence at some future date, as well as providing material support for terrorism.[5]

1. Jodi Wilgoren with Jo Thomas, "Traces of Terror: The Bomb Suspect; From Chicago Gang to Possible Al Qaeda Ties," *New York Times*, June 11, 2002.
2. James Risen and Philip Shenon, "Traces of Terror: The Investigation; U.S. Says It Halted Qaeda Plot to Use Radioactive Bomb," *New York Times*, June 11, 2002; Benjamin Weiser with Dana Canedy, "Traces of Terror: The Bomb Plot; Lawyer Plans Challenge to Detention of Suspect," *New York Times*, June 12, 2002.
3. Deborah Sontag, "Secret Justice: Terror Suspect's Path From Streets to Brig," *New York Times*, April 25, 2004.
4. Eric Lichtblau, "In Legal Shift, U.S. Charges Detainee in Terrorism Case," *New York Times*, November 23, 2005.
5. Adam Liptak, "Padilla Case Offers New Model of Terrorism Trial," *New York Times*, August 18, 2007.

quickest way to obtain it, the concern about protecting intelligence sources and methods and ongoing information gathering, the ability to use information as evidence in a criminal proceeding, the circumstances of the manner in which the individual was detained, the applicable criminal charges, and classified-evidence issues."[14] In Denmark, for example, even though a jury found four suspects guilty of plotting terrorist attacks somewhere in Europe, a panel of judges overturned the guilty verdicts for three of the four accused because of insufficient evidence, which consisted primarily of character witnesses.[15] There is always a tension between a desire to arrest suspects before they advance too far in a suspected terrorist plot and the need to take more time to gather sufficient evidence to stand up in court (see chapter 3).

The due process requirements inherent in the criminal justice model, particularly the right to counsel, the right to cross-examine witnesses, and the right to know the charges of which one is accused, all provide an advantage to the defendant, while limiting what the prosecution can do. All these protections have become problematic in the "war on terror" and the solutions to these problems have been controversial. The military tribunals created for trying suspects detained in Guantánamo Bay, Cuba, for example, allow evidence obtained by coercive interrogation and hearsay and deny suspects and their lawyers the right to see classified evidence used against them. These provisions are not consistent with the rule of law as generally conceived, and highlight the Bush Administration's determination to legalize and legitimize special rules concerning interrogation and the admission of evidence that contradict international law, particularly Common Article 3 of the Geneva Conventions.

In Europe, where Al Qaeda suspects were brought to trial in regular criminal courts that respect the rule of law, without resort to special rules and limitations, convictions were undermined by US refusals to provide access to witnesses and statements that may have assisted in a conviction. For example, in the trial of Mounir al-Motassadeq, the first person convicted of offenses directly related to the 9/11 attacks, in Germany in 2003, problems arose concerning the availability and acceptability of evidence from Al Qaeda operatives held in US custody, particularly Ramzi bin al-Shibh, one of the 14 high-profile detainees who were later transferred from their secret CIA-run prisons to Guantánamo Bay.[16] Though al-Motassadeq was convicted and sentenced to 15 years, the inability of the German court to obtain either bin al-Shibh himself, as a witness, or a direct transcript of his interrogation, where he allegedly mentioned al-Motassadeq, led to a successful appeal and the latter's release the following year, pending a retrial. In 2005, al-Motassadeq was convicted for being a member of a terrorist organization and imprisoned for 7 years. In this retrial, the US Justice Department released summaries of interrogations of several Al Qaeda suspects, including bin al-Shibh. Al-Motassadeq's sentence was later increased to 15 years by adding a second conviction for 246 counts of abetting murder.[17]

When suspected terrorists are brought to trial, there is also a danger that the trial can become a political platform for the accused. This happened in the Zacarias Moussaoui trial, for example, where the accused often launched into emotional tirades against the judge, his lawyers, and the US Administration.[18] Political criminals have always posed special problems for the criminal justice system,[19] and ideologically motivated terrorists are no exception.

4. *Detention and imprisonment*: Special regimes of imprisonment for political criminals have two opposing traditions.
One tradition offers special privileges for the political
prisoner and less harsh conditions, while the other treats
political prisoners more severely. An example of the former
would be allowing political prisoners to maintain their
organization within the prison or not to wear prison uniforms, while the latter is exemplified by solitary confinement or, in the extreme, the *oubliette* of the French *ancien
régime*. The "dirty protest" by imprisoned Provisional Irish
Republican Army (PIRA) members during Margaret
Thatcher's tenure as British prime minister revolved precisely around the first issue. Similarly, a campaign of hunger
strikes by prisoners and their supporters in Turkey was
related to the introduction of new prisons, with cells hous-
ing one to three inmates rather than the former ward
system, where up to 100 inmates were housed together in
large communal areas which facilitated the maintenance of
group cohesion and solidarity.[20] Prisons can become breeding grounds for recruitment and radicalization, and training
grounds for best terrorist practices.[21] The Irish Republican
Army (IRA) maintained military discipline in prison and
used hunger strikes and "dirty protests" as effective political
tools for mobilizing support outside the prison and maintaining morale within. During the 1981 hunger strike at the
Maze Prison in Northern Ireland, Bobby Sands, a convicted
member of the PIRA, was elected as a British member of
parliament just three weeks before his death from starvation
at the age of 27. His death triggered widespread protests
both in Northern Ireland and around the world.[22] Detainees
in Guantánamo Bay have engaged in hunger strikes, riots,
and other protests, and authorities could never be sure if
they were interested merely in improving their living conditions or in continuing the fight within prison by other

means.[23] The whole issue of political prisoners is a complex one. Imprisoned terrorists often claim to be political prisoners, while authorities who imprison them claim they are common criminals. In the UK, the status of Irish Republican prisoners became a major political issue during Margaret Thatcher's tenure. In Canada, during a hostage crisis in 1970, then Prime Minster Pierre Elliott Trudeau chastised the media for referring to imprisoned Quebec terrorists as "political prisoners," calling them "bandits" instead.[24] Similar controversy surrounds the Bush Administration's designation of captured fighters as illegal enemy combatants rather than prisoners of war (see below).

5. *Extradition, expulsion, and deportation*: The area of extradition has long been fraught with difficulties in the area of counterterrorism. National interests and international cooperation can come into conflict despite a commonly perceived threat. It has long been recognized that states refusing to extradite terrorist suspects to requesting states because they do not feel that the suspects will receive a fair trial in that country (the political offense exception[25]) are obligated to prosecute these suspects themselves. This is the principle of *aut dedere aut iudicare* – either extradite or prosecute. Many international and regional counterterrorism conventions, such as the 1977 European Convention for the Suppression of Terrorism (Article 1) or the 2007 ASEAN Convention on Counter Terrorism (Article XIV), even except terrorist offenses from the political offense exception that allows states to refuse extradition in the first place (the exception to the exception). This principle has, however, been honored more often in the breach than in the observance. For example, in 1977, Palestinian terrorist Abu Daoud was arrested in France. Widely believed to have masterminded the 1972 Munich Olympics attack on

Israeli athletes, Daoud entered France on January 7, 1977, from Beirut, using a false name and a false Iraqi passport, to attend the funeral of a PLO representative who had been murdered. Tipped off by Israel, the French police arrested him. Both Israel and (the then) West Germany applied for his extradition. The French government refused both requests on flimsy technical grounds and, within four days, he was flown to Algiers.[26] It was widely believed that France acted in its own national interest, not wishing to antagonize Arab states with which it wanted to maintain good relations.[27] Twenty-two years later, when Abdullah Öcalan, leader of the Kurdish Workers' Party (PKK), was apprehended in Italy in 1999, Italy refused an extradition request from Turkey, while Germany, which had an international arrest warrant out for the Kurdish leader, rescinded the warrant and did not even request extradition. Italy eventually refused to grant Öcalan refugee status in Italy but allowed him to leave the country. When the Turks finally seized him in Nairobi, Kenya, Öcalan was carrying a fake Greek Cypriot passport with a false name and had been a "guest" of the Greek government which had secretly flown him to its embassy there. Again, national interest prevailed in both Italy and Germany and the principle of extradite or prosecute was not followed in either case. Germany, in particular, did not want to antagonize the many Kurdish refugees living in the country, while a longstanding enmity towards Turkey and the principle of "the enemy of my enemy is my friend" explained Greece's behavior.[28] In the current "war on terror," several EU countries have said that they would refuse extradition requests from the USA because that country allows capital punishment.

An increasing number of countries have struggled with the problem of refugees, permanent residents, or even naturalized citizens who are suspected, accused, or convicted of planning terrorist attacks within their host countries or elsewhere. What does a government do with suspected terrorists who cannot be deported to their country of origin because of fears that they might be tortured there? In some countries, such as Canada and the UK, courts have declared that deportation in such cases is not permissible.[29] The European Court of Human Rights in Strasbourg has ruled unanimously that deportation to countries where torture is practiced is not permitted, despite assurances by the recipient country that deportees will not be tortured. Though the particular case that the Court was ruling on involved Italy, the judgment is binding for all countries of the Council of Europe, including the UK.[30] These court rulings have forced governments to find ways to detain such people indefinitely, often without providing recourse to the courts or the chance to review or challenge the evidence held against them. In the case of captured terrorists deemed so dangerous that they cannot be released at all, such as the high-profile detainees in Guantánamo Bay, solutions that respect the rule of law and can withstand scrutiny by the courts seem difficult to come by. The very fact that detainees are held in Cuba and not in the USA is to prevent them from having access to judicial review in US courts.

In Canada, under the Immigration and Refugee Protection Act, security certificates allow the government to detain foreign nationals considered too dangerous to release or too problematic to prosecute, primarily because of the sensitive nature of the evidence against them, and who refuse to leave the country of their own free will, usually because of fears of torture or persecution in their home countries. Named individuals and their lawyers are usually not permitted to know the nature of the charges against them and are not able to challenge this evidence in court. A Federal judge decides whether the evidence is sufficient to detain the person and can give a summary of evidence to the named individual or their lawyer. In February 2007, the Supreme Court of Canada declared the security certificate procedure unconstitutional and gave the government one year in which to change the legislation so as to provide persons named in such certificates more rights to see the evidence against them and to challenge it. The idea of a Federal judge acting as advocate for the named individual was suggested as a possible solution.[31]

In the UK, where courts have ordered the release of people held incommunicado, without access to the courts, the government has issued control orders amounting to house arrest and electronic monitoring, curtailing their movements, tagging them and restricting who they can meet. Obligations can include curfews, prohibition of arranged meetings with non-approved persons and of use of the internet or mobile phones, and a requirement to live at a specified address.[32] Introduced in 2005, the use of control orders quickly became a hotly contested subject.[33] Several individual control orders were quashed by High Court judges and, in August 2006, the whole process was declared illegal and in contravention of Article 5 of the European Convention on Human Rights, which prohibits indefinite detention without trial, and from which the UK has not derogated.[34] Despite this, suspects continued to be subjected to control orders.[35] Control orders were also established in Australia by the Australian Anti-Terrorism Act 2005. In the Philippines, a new Human Security Act of 2007 has been criticized by the UN Special Rapporteur for Human Rights for similar problems concerning the competence and independence of bodies authorized to review detention of individuals and the legal basis for restricting movements of suspects.[36]

6. *Addressing root causes*: Most terrorism is not the act of lone individuals, though there are exceptions, such as Ted Kaczynski, the US Unabomber, who sent bombs through the mail to various universities and airlines. The vast majority of terrorism is group-based and embedded in social, political, cultural, religious, or historical contexts. As such, the criminal justice system, which focuses on individual acts (crimes) and individuals (suspects, accused, convicted, punished) cannot address these wider contexts. Imprisoning or executing a convicted terrorist who acts alone will obviously stop that person's terrorism, though it could conceivably trigger copycat terrorism or mobilize others to take action in his or her place. For group-based terrorism, however, capturing, convicting, and punishing individual terrorists will not necessarily bring an end to terrorism. When leaders of the Basque group, ETA, are arrested, for example, new people take their place. The criminal justice approach can dissuade potential recruits from taking the terrorist path or convince supporters of terrorism to withhold or withdraw support. It can deter convicted terrorists from continuing their terrorism once released, especially if repentance is a prerequisite for amnesty or early release. But in many cases, even these limited goals are hard to achieve. In cases where terrorism is driven by firmly held ideological beliefs, conviction and punishment may simply be way stations along the path towards continued struggle. In nationalist struggles, such as in Northern Ireland and the Basque region of Spain, terrorism can even become a way of life that is passed on from generation to generation. When the criminal justice system is badly used, in an unfair or unjust manner, or when

criminal justice procedures become politicized, such as in political prosecutions or show trials, or are compromised, such as when amnesties and early release are given to people convicted of murder, then it can inflame grievances, trigger counter-grievances, or create the impression that violence is the only way to achieve anything. In such cases, a criminal justice approach to counterterrorism can prove counterproductive. In short, other approaches are necessary to address the grievances that charismatic leaders and ideologues use to mobilize recruits, supporters, and sympathizers.

In sum, the criminal justice model relies on a complex bureaucracy with strict rules of governance and many interacting institutions, with their own traditions, culture, and language. It can be slow and ponderous, with appeals stretching the process out for years. For some, it seems to favor the terrorist, especially over the victim. This is true of all criminal justice, where it has taken a long time to recognize the needs of victims throughout the criminal justice process. While the criminal justice model can achieve some important goals in terms of deterrence, retribution, education, incapacitation, and rehabilitation (see above), these benefits are largely dependent upon how the system is used, how fairly it is seen to be used by others, and how committed individuals are to terrorist violence either as a means to other goals or as an end in itself.

The war model

The war model of counterterrorism treats terrorism as if it were an act of war or insurgency. Because wars are usually fought between states, countering terrorism within a war model implies that the terrorist group represents the equivalent of a state. Treating terrorism as war therefore tends to credit the terrorist with the status of equal partner in a zero-sum conflict. This is why many terrorist groups use the word "army" in their names, such as the IRA, the German Red Army Faction (RAF), and the Armenian Secret Army for the Liberation of Armenia (ASALA). Since the attacks of September 11, the US Administration, in particular, has argued that we are "at war" with global Islamist terrorism. Al Qaeda readily accepts this framing of the struggle, having already declared "war" itself, and gains credibility and even legitimacy as the only group willing to stand up to the imperialist West.

Although the central element of the war model is the use of maximal force, designed to overpower the enemy, this does not mean that the conduct of war occurs in a legal vacuum. The laws of war lay down rules for how wars should be fought and, in particular, how noncombatants – whether captured enemy soldiers or citizens of enemy states – should be treated. The 1949 Geneva Conventions represent a kind of trade-off that legitimizes killing or detention without trial in time of war, as long as it is directed at overpowering an enemy combatant. The trade-off is that, once a combatant is captured and disarmed, or gives up and abandons the fight, he must be accorded humane treatment, protection, and care.[37] The term "illegal enemy combatant" attempts to create an exception to this rule for combatants who use stealth and do not wear uniforms or insignia identifying them as enemy combatants, namely terrorists, guerrillas, or insurgents. Much of terrorism, in fact, takes place in what is generally considered peacetime, further complicating the issue. The current "war on terror" is not a conflict between states; no formal declaration of war exists between any states, although Osama bin Laden has attempted to act like a state in issuing fatwahs declaring war on Americans and Jews. His first "declaration of war" was issued on August 23, 1996, entitled "Declaration of *Jihad* against the Americans Occupying the Land of the Two Holy Sanctuaries,"

and initially published in the Arabic-language London news-
paper *Al-Quds Al-Arabi*. The second, published on February
23, 1998, also in *Al-Quds Al-Arabi*, and entitled "Declaration
of the World Islamic Front for Jihad Against Jews and
Crusaders," called for the killing of Americans, both civilian
and military. It was signed by bin Laden; Ayman al-Zawahiri,
then head of Egyptian Islamic Jihad; and three others.[38]

Traditionally, the war model has always been seen as a
method of last resort. For example, the military has been used
"in aid of civil power," to guard buildings or VIPs or to mount
a rescue operation in the case of hostage-taking or skyjacking.
In October 1970, when Quebec terrorists kidnapped a British
diplomat and a Quebec cabinet minister, the Canadian government called in the army to guard government buildings and
members of parliament and diplomats in Ottawa. As the
hostage crisis continued, with public protests escalating in
support of the demands of the kidnappers, the Canadian government invoked special emergency legislation under the War
Measures Act – since repealed and replaced with less draconian legislation – which gave the police special powers of arrest
and detention.[39] In 1976, the Israeli government used military
special forces to launch a rescue operation at Entebbe airport
in Uganda, where an Air France plane that had been hijacked
by Palestinian and German terrorists was being held. Before it
was determined that such a risky operation was feasible, the
Israeli government had decided to try negotiations, despite a
firmly established no-negotiations policy. When the president
of Uganda at the time, Idi Amin, visited the hijackers and
seemed to be supporting them, a military operation became
almost imperative. The raid cost the lives of only 3 out of 103
hostages, while 1 Israeli, all 7 terrorists and 20 Ugandans were
killed.[40]

The emphasis has sometimes shifted from using the military option as a last resort to using it as a primary means to

punish terrorists and their state sponsors. Following the 1972
Munich Olympics massacre of Israeli athletes, the Israeli
government embarked on a covert operation of targeted assassination of those implicated in the massacre, called "Wrath of
God." The operation was only aborted after an innocent
person was killed.[41] Targeted assassinations have also been
used more recently in Lebanon and in Gaza.[42] The first clear
example of this approach being used for state sponsors was
the Reagan Administration's April 1986 bombing of Libya
(Operation El Dorado Canyon) in which Colonel Muammar
Qadaffi's home and headquarters in Tripoli and Benghazi, as
well as several other sites, were bombed by US warplanes.
Colonel Qadaffi escaped unharmed, though his adoptive
daughter was killed, as well as several civilians. The French
Embassy was also hit by mistake. France and Spain both
denied the US planes overflight rights, necessitating multiple
aerial refuelings en route to the attack sites. The airstrike was
ordered ostensibly in retaliation for the bombing of a dis-
cotheque in West Berlin, where intelligence suggested that
Libyans were responsible. Many felt that Colonel Qadaffi himself was the real target.[43] The next time that a US government
explicitly retaliated for an act of terrorism was when President
Bill Clinton ordered cruise missile strikes against targets in
the Sudan and Afghanistan (Operation Infinite Reach) in a
direct response to the simultaneous US embassy bombings
in Nairobi, Kenya and Dar-es-Salaam, Tanzania in August
1998.[44]

In a war model of counterterrorism, success tends to be
defined in terms of victory or defeat.[45] As such, a "war on
terror" only ends when the terrorist enemy is defeated. If the
struggle is a protracted one, even spanning generations, then
counterterrorism efforts must be maintained as long as a state
of war exists. This has led some to argue that we are engaged in
a "long war" or even a "never-ending" war with Islamist

terrorism.[46] This infinite vision of the war on terror has important policy implications, including constitutional ones.[47]

Supposed benefits of the military approach

Proponents of the war model of counterterrorism usually emphasize retaliation and retribution as major benefits of the war model. When President Ronald Reagan promised "swift and effective retribution" for all future acts of terrorism, it was 1981 and the occasion was the return of US hostages from Teheran. When he said "swift," Reagan underscored what many feel to be a prime virtue of the war model: speed and timeliness. Strike quickly and you will send a strong message to all future terrorists that they will not be able to get away with it: in Reagan's words again, "You can run, but you can't hide."[48] When Reagan said "effective," he underscored the prevalent belief that military action is more effective than criminal justice action. Stemming from these two primary benefits are the following:

1. *Boosting morale at home*: Striking hard at terrorists abroad makes the domestic constituency feel good and gives the impression that the government is serious about doing something.

2. *Unilateral action is possible without having to cooperate with other nations*: Military action can be implemented without having to negotiate with other nations. Interoperability with other militaries, for example, is not an issue if one's military acts alone. There is also the added benefit of not having to ask for suspected terrorists through extradition treaties or other kinds of negotiations, such as with countries where no extradition treaty exists in the first place. In the extreme case of targeted assassination, such as the Israeli policy following the 1972 Munich massacre and, more recently, in

Lebanon and Gaza, covert action has been carried out in allied or neutral countries without the knowledge of their governments.

3. *Maintaining a tough image/posture in the international arena*: Military action signals a nation's resolve to tackle the problem of terrorism. It gives the impression that the nation using military force cannot be intimidated or pushed around.

4. *Making use of science and technology*: Proponents of the war model value the remarkable things that science and technology can achieve. Examples include remote sensing, satellite imagery and spy drones, missile technology, smart bombs and other sophisticated weaponry, and facial recognition and other biometrics. More recently, discussion has centred on "the need for 'birth to death' tracking and identification of critical targets, whether they are people or things, anywhere in the world."[49] Among the kinds of capabilities being considered is an automatic translation system that can translate foreign languages into English as people speak. The idea that a nation's military can watch, listen, record, and track anyone or anything anywhere in the world and strike at will with guided, pilotless attack planes or space-based weaponry is the ultimate individualized war model, designed to fight an atomized, dispersed enemy rather than the traditional hostile state or terrorist group.

In sum, the war model is considered quick, effective, and ideally suited to the new kinds of threat posed by decentralized, ideologically driven terrorist networks whose adherents are not deterred by traditional criminal justice or contained by traditional military power.

Limits and problems of the war model

1. *Playing into the terrorist's hands*: A primary goal of terrorism
    is to provoke a repressive response in the hope that such a
    response will evoke sympathy for the terrorist cause and
    promote recruitment or other kinds of support. This is what
    the 9/11 plot was designed in part to achieve: triggering a
    massive US military response that would infuriate Muslims
    throughout the Middle East and Asia, leading to uprisings
    against their governments. The initial military strike in
    Afghanistan, under a United Nations mandate, avoided this
    trap. The invasion of Iraq in 2003 played directly into the
    terrorists' hands, providing them with a grievance that
    could be exploited and legitimacy as an important actor in a
    war of equals. The increase in terrorism around the world
    and the ease with which homegrown terrorists are spawned
    by the now-pervasive Al Qaeda, Salafist–jihadist "brand,"
    attest to this.[50]

2. *Escalating violence and triggering revenge attacks*: While pro-
    ponents of the war model emphasize the deterrent function
    of the military option, military strikes often simply trigger
    further attacks, often in the name of revenge. The 1988
    downing of PanAm flight 103 over Lockerbie, Scotland, was
    an act of revenge for the 1986 bombing of Libya. Even
    before that, several hostages were executed and attempts
    were made by Libyan agents to attack US interests. Targeted
    assassinations against Hizbollah leaders usually result in
    the replacement of those leaders and increased resentment
    that facilitates recruitment and mobilization. Military inter-
    ventions breed similar results. When the Indian military
    attacked the headquarters of Sikh militants in the Golden
    Temple, Amritsar, in June 1984, the result was a revenge
    assassination of Indian Prime Minister Indira Gandhi by

two Sikh bodyguards several months later. This act of revenge, in turn, triggered widespread anti-Sikh violence by Hindu mobs out for their own revenge. Iraq and Afghanistan show how committed ideologues can simply innovate in the face of superior military might and develop devastating techniques of destruction, such as sophisticated roadside bombs. The propaganda benefits of posting videos of such attacks on the internet only magnify their impact over the longer term. Collateral damage, where civilians or allied soldiers are killed or wounded during military counterterrorism operations, can also fuel resentment and mobilize terrorist recruitment, as well as strain international cooperation and coordination of counterterrorism efforts with allies.

3. *Facilitating a slide towards anti-democratic governance*: Reliance on the war model opens the door to a slippery slope leading towards more and more anti-democratic means of social control. Security nets widen as surveillance targets more and more people. Intelligence requirements are relaxed as more and more people are considered to be enemies. National security becomes a justification for all types of shortcuts and excesses. It is no coincidence that human rights and the rule of law have often been abrogated or suspended in the name of fighting terrorism. Authoritarian regimes in Argentina, Brazil, Chile, El Salvador, Guatemala, and Uruguay all justified their repression by the need to counter terrorism.[51] Countering terrorism continues to be an excuse for harsh repression, for example in Chechnya or in Uzbekistan. Israel and the United Kingdom have both moved significantly away from the rule of law in their prolonged fight with terrorism in the Occupied Territories and Northern Ireland, respectively.[52] The same is happening in many countries involved in the current "war on terror."

4. *Questionable effectiveness*: Despite its vaunted effectiveness, the war model has certain inbuilt problems that undermine any effect it may have on future terrorism. Because terrorists generally lack addresses to which bombs or troops can be sent, the importance of intelligence is central to the war model (see chapter 3). Unfortunately, intelligence is not always reliable or, if it is reliable, it is not always followed for political reasons. The LaBelle disco bombing in West Berlin that served as the trigger for the US bombing of Libya in 1986, for example, was more likely Iran's responsibility, and intelligence supported this. However, Libya was seen to be the easier target and so Libya was attacked instead. The intelligence that was used to justify the 2003 Iraq invasion was subject to distortion and opportunistic selection of data that supported a preconceived notion and a predetermined military plan. The invasion triggered widespread terrorism both inside and outside Iraq itself. The Israeli reliance on the military option to resolve hostage-barricade incidents usually results in the death of the hostages along with their captors. Studies have shown that hostages are more likely to die during a rescue attempt than at the hands of their captors.[53] The Moscow theatre siege of 2002, where many hostages were killed or gassed by security forces, and the botched rescue attempt in Beslan, North Ossetia, in 2004, where 40 percent of the hostages were killed and another 40 percent injured, are two recent examples of this trend.[54] Not only do more hostages die when the military option is pursued, but military strikes can escalate the violence or trigger revenge attacks, as noted above. Even a full-scale military intervention designed to crush the infrastructure of a terrorist group or regime can have unintended consequences. The Vietnamese intervention in Cambodia in 1978, the Israeli invasion of Lebanon in 1982, and the Indian intervention in Sri Lanka in 1987 all led to unexpected consequences that

included increased violence. The Israeli and Vietnamese armies both became embroiled in protracted conflict from which it was difficult to extricate themselves.[55] When the Israelis finally withdrew, the Palestinians simply returned, and Hizbollah persisted and grew stronger despite sporadic Israeli military incursions. The latest Israeli incursion, in summer 2006, also failed to destroy Hizbollah, which only emerged stronger and more enmeshed in domestic Lebanese politics. In Cambodia, the continuing Vietnamese presence contributed to the persistence of the Khmer Rouge as a viable partner in the country's reconstruction, despite its genocidal past. In Sri Lanka, the Indian army also became caught in the crossfire between Tamils and Sinhalese. In 1991, Rajiv Gandhi, who as prime minister had sent Indian troops into Sri Lanka, was killed in a revenge suicide bomb attack by a female Tamil Tiger operative.[56]

In sum, the war model of counterterrorism carries a high risk of unintended consequences that can escalate violence, undermine the legitimacy of governments that use it, or pull governments along a dangerous path to anti-democratic governance.[57] Military strikes or interventions do not tend to reduce terrorism over the medium or long term (see box on p. 82). On the contrary, they tend to exacerbate violence and to create an environment where resentment and anger can be manipulated by terrorist ideologues to radicalize and mobilize new recruits. This does not mean, however, that the war model cannot be a useful and valuable tool in an overall counterterrorism strategy. As in just war theory, the use of force can be justified under certain strict conditions.[58] It must be discriminate, proportionate, declared by a proper authority, used for a justifiable cause, with just intentions that outweigh the evil of the means used by the good of the ends sought, have a high probability of success, enjoy public support, and be used only as a last resort, when all other means have been pursued. In these limited circumstances, the war model can be a legitimate tool and can be considered just and appropriate.

> It does not appear that troop strength or military activity, in itself, reduces terrorism immediately, and in fact military activity and terrorism are usually positively and significantly correlated. These results could be interpreted in two ways; either that military activity provokes terrorism or, more plausibly, that military activity is frequently a response to terrorism. The statistics do not suggest that military activity reduces terrorism in subsequent months. In only two cases do we find a negative lagged correlation, and in neither case is the correlation significant.
>
> Christopher Hewitt, *The Effectiveness of Anti-Terrorist Policies* (New York: University Press of America, 1984), p. 86.

The blurring of criminal justice and war approaches and the emergence of a hybrid model of coercion

Countering terrorism by coercive means poses special problems and difficulties for liberal democracies, where respect for the rule of law, the safeguarding of individual rights and freedoms, and the maintenance of openness and accountability in government are central features. If counterterrorism deviates too far from these democratic principles, then it risks becoming state terrorism. At that point, the terrorists have won at least a moral victory in that their avowed enemy can no longer claim the moral high ground. We have seen that neither the criminal justice model nor the war model is a perfect tool for combating terrorism. Each offers some advantages, while each poses special problems. What is more, the two models have evolved over time, as the pressures of real-life crises have led governments to adapt to new threats and challenges. The debate about whether the September 11 attacks by Al Qaeda constituted criminal acts or acts of war highlights the tendency for these two models of counterterrorism to blur into each other when faced with a complex crisis. The US proposal to use military courts to try foreign nationals suspected of terrorist crimes in the wake of September 11 has been so controversial precisely because no formal state of war exists, and neither has martial law been invoked. Instead, the proposal was part of a Presidential Executive Order,[59] thereby bypassing debate by legislators in the House and Senate completely – something which would not normally be expected in time of peace. Of course, the US Administration did declare "war" on terrorism even while insisting that the primary aim of this war, including the military campaign in Afghanistan, was to apprehend those responsible for planning and helping in the implementation of the September 11 attacks and "bringing them to justice." In his televised address to the nation on the day of the attacks, President Bush spoke of both justice and war: "I've directed the full resources of our intelligence and law enforcement communities to find those responsible and to bring them to justice. . . . we stand together to win the war against terrorism."[60] The blurring and even merging of criminal justice and war goals here is unmistakable.

Two complementary trends that began in the 1970s and continued throughout the 1980s and 1990s helped to bring the two models closer together. The first was the militarization of the police (see box on p. 84). This usually involved the creation of special weapons and tactics (SWAT) teams to deal with hostage incidents, riots, and violent demonstrations. Sometimes called "third forces,"[61] they were usually based with the police, but were given the right to use maximal force in certain circumstances. Sometimes, they were even based with the military, such as the Special Air Service (SAS) in the

> **Militarization of the police**
>
> In the name of fighting terrorism, more and more firepower and weaponry is given to the ordinary police, special weapons and tactics which permit greater use of force are allowed, less judicial control is placed on police operations, especially when targeting specifically identified classes of individuals, and less redress is provided targeted individuals when things go wrong.
> Ronald Crelinsten, "Analysing Terrorism and Counterterrorism: A Communication Model," *Terrorism and Political Violence* 14(2) (2002): 77–122, at p. 87.

UK. In the case of alleged "shoot-to-kill" policies, where such forces kill suspected terrorists rather than arresting them, the police involved clearly are closer to the war model than to the criminal justice one. The fatal shooting of the Brazilian electrician, Jean Charles de Menezes, by London police in the wake of the attempted bombings of July 21, 2005, is a tragic example of how shoot-to-kill policies can go awry.[62] Such incidents can only be expected to increase in an era where the tactic of suicide bombings has migrated from the battlefields of Iraq and Afghanistan to the urban centers of the West and police can never be sure if the decision to arrest a suspect will end up in a deadly explosion.[63]

The second trend was the increasing use of the military in peacetime or the "policification" of the military.[64] At the domestic level, this involved aid to civil power during terrorist crises such as in Canada in 1970. At the international level, this involved using the military for peacekeeping duties in zones of conflict. In severe cases, where no peace was yet established, peacemaking duties required military forces to separate warring parties, disarm them, and arrest suspected war criminals. Examples include the conflicts in Bosnia, Kosovo, Sierra Leone, Lebanon, and Sri Lanka. In peacekeeping and peacemaking missions, the military essentially play a police role; some have called this the criminalization of war.[65] As such, soldiers are held accountable for their actions in a way not usually done for military action. As a result of this, British soldiers in Iraq, for example, have reported that the most stressful aspect of their mission was not the prospect of combat, but the accountability procedures that had to be followed whenever their weapons were fired. In short, they feared prosecution more than combat.[66]

There are other ways in which the criminal justice and the war models are blurring to create a kind of hybrid model of coercive control. Many of these precede the post-9/11 surge in special anti-terrorist legislation, police procedures, and militarized court processes. Special courts have been used in France and Spain. Special detention regimes have been adopted, such as internment without trial in Northern Ireland. Limiting the rights of the defense, such as in Germany, and allowing certain witnesses to testify on videotape, thereby making it impossible for the defense to cross-examine, have undermined traditional due process. Post-9/11, there have been similar trends, such as the use of special rules of evidence in military tribunals and the regimes of imprisonment in Guantánamo Bay. The use of questionable interrogation techniques that amount to torture in secret prisons scattered around the world, and the abduction and rendition of terrorist suspects to countries where human rights or due process are not respected, have created a Bermuda Triangle-like gray zone where people disappear. Sometimes they reappear, shell-shocked and disoriented, like the Syrian–Canadian, Maher Arar, who was picked up in the USA, en route home to Canada, and shipped off to Syria, where he was tortured.[67] Other times, faint echoes of their existence surface in trials of other suspects who made it to the criminal justice system, their voices heard in highly censored or condensed versions of their interrogations or confessions while in secret detention. This hybrid model is sometimes applied selectively, in certain territories, such as by the British in Northern Ireland or the Israelis in the Occupied Territories. Usually, however, the special procedures seep into the State itself: for these two cases, the British mainland and Israel proper.[68] Sometimes, the special regime is reserved for foreign nationals, not citizens. Again, however, this can change as first naturalized citizens and then native-born citizens are included as well.

Whether this hybrid model of coercive control amounts to a form of state terrorism depends to a great extent on degree. There are two complementary paths towards an erosion of legitimacy and a descent into full-blown state terrorism. The militarization of the police can lead, via systematic police deviance and the creation of a secret police, to the establishment of a terrorist state. Increasing the length of time that a suspect can be detained without access to a lawyer or without laying specific charges is the most common feature of anti-terrorism legislation, both pre- and post-9/11. It is during incommunicado detention that the temptation to stray from due process, human rights law, and humanitarian law is greatest. Coupled with a tendency to target certain classes of people as prime suspects for terrorism (see chapter 3), it is this area of pre-trial detention (or post-combat captivity) that poses the greatest danger of sliding into state terrorism. In complementary fashion, the policification of the military can evolve into the use of out-of-uniform, paramilitary forces working in the stealth of night to enforce a reign of terror through abductions, assassinations, or rendition to jurisdictions where the rule of law is weak or absent. While the former route strays from the rule of law and the imperatives of due process, creating a system of political justice, the latter strays from the rules of war and the restriction of operations to combatants and combat zones. The net widens and the distinctions between combatant and noncombatant and combat zone and safe zone begin to disappear. This reflects the difficulty in counterterrorism of determining who actually is a combatant. Because of terrorism's clandestinity, it is often very difficult to determine who is in fact a combatant, who is lending logistical support, and who is a mere sympathizer or simply caught in the wrong place at the wrong time, as are many villagers in guerrilla and counterinsurgency campaigns. Many of the worst human rights violations in the context of counterinsurgency have revolved around this question, the 1968 My Lai massacre in Viet Nam being a classic example.[69] And when a combatant is declared illegal and shipped off to a secret prison or a country where torture is common, then international humanitarian and human rights laws are undermined.

In the area of *proactive* counterterrorism, which aims at preventing terrorism *before* it happens, the emergence of a hybrid model of coercive counterterrorism has been particularly striking, even before 9/11. Through the merging of internal and external security, the mandates of domestic police, security intelligence agencies, and border and customs officials have all coalesced around the problem of tracking the movement of people, goods, and money. Through intrusive techniques involving surveillance, wiretapping, eavesdropping, and other means of spycraft, agents of all stripes have devoted their energies more and more to stopping terrorists before they act and thwarting terrorist plots before they develop too far. The war model embodies these more proactive elements in that the targets of such intrusive techniques are increasingly treated as enemies, whether abroad or "within." This is most evident in the notion of preemption. But the criminal justice model also has proactive elements, particularly in the area of policing. In some countries, such as France, such "political policing" has a long tradition. In operational terms, proactive policing and security intelligence are very similar, both in goals and in methods, and, increasingly, in whom they target. Good intelligence is a central and crucial element in all forms of proactive counterterrorism, whether legal, military, or otherwise. This is the primary focus of the next chapter.

CHAPTER THREE

Proactive counterterrorism

Our examination of the coercive models of counterterrorism in the previous chapter focused primarily on the reactive aspects of these models, which deal with terrorist actions already committed. This chapter considers those approaches to counterterrorism that are concerned primarily with preventing terrorists from taking action in the first place or their plots from coming to fruition. This is sometimes called preventive counterterrorism or simply anti-terrorism and can include both coercive and non-coercive measures. The latter kind of measures, such as target-hardening and other purely "defensive" measures, will be discussed in chapter 5. Deterrence and preemption, which are both examples of coercive persuasion, will be examined in chapter 4. The primary focus of this chapter will be the intelligence function[1] and the particular challenges that countering secret plots, conspiracies, and activities poses for the police, the security services, and the military. The chapter will also examine the problem of terrorist financing and how to block it, since good intelligence is important here as well.

It is almost a truism to say that the intelligence function is a central element in any counterterrorist effort. Terrorism is generally planned and carried out in secret and terrorist groups try and ensure that their plans are not revealed until it is too late to stop them. Many groups carry out both overt and covert activity. Legal organizations and enterprises serve as fronts that mask or distract attention away from illegal activity.

Terrorist groups involve organizational structures that include a clandestine, hence invisible, core that is connected in a variety of ways to other more overt entities. Membership in the core often requires oaths of secrecy or the commission of criminal acts by new recruits to ensure fidelity to the organization's norms and values rather than mainstream ones and to make it more difficult to exit from the group. In the more networked organizations, the links between different cells or particular individuals can become even more tenuous, to the point of "leaderless resistance," in which individuals or small groups embark on projects without any direct orders or clear direction from any leader.[2] From a counterterrorism perspective, all this poses particular kinds of problems and challenges related to goals, methods, and targets.

Goals

There are two kinds of policing that can be used in counterterrorism. The more traditional model of policing, central to the criminal justice model, is *reactive* policing. This involves the arrest of someone suspected of having committed an act proscribed in criminal law. It is reactive because control agents only respond once a criminal act is committed and then reported to them. The ensuing police investigation focuses on gathering evidence that can be used in a court of law and this process of data collection is regulated by due process, as described in chapter 2. In *proactive policing*, information gathering is not directed at building a criminal case against a person accused of committing a crime. It is directed at determining whether individuals targeted by the investigation are planning to commit a crime or are involved in a criminal organization. Reactive policing is related to crime *solving*, while proactive policing is related to crime *detection*. In this sense, then, proactive policing is very similar to *security intelligence*.[3] Security intelligence is directed at determining whether individuals or the groups to which they belong are engaged in activities that pose a threat to national security. In both cases, the kinds of concerns related to the determination of the guilt or innocence of a target/suspect are less important than the gathering of information, per se.

In proactive policing and also in security intelligence, information is not gathered for evidentiary purposes but for intelligence purposes. The ultimate goal is not necessarily criminal prosecution, though it can be, especially in the case of proactive policing. Instead, the goal of intelligence operations, whether criminal, security, or military intelligence, is to learn more about what the targets are up to. If enough evidence to support a criminal prosecution *is* gathered during such operations, it is not a foregone conclusion that an arrest will be made. In many cases, potential suspects are allowed to bargain away arrest and criminal charges for continued cooperation as informers. Sometimes, particularly in the area of security intelligence, individuals are even protected from prosecution for ordinary crimes, including violent ones, that are unrelated to the sphere of activity for which they are providing intelligence. As such, the demands of information gathering often conflict with those of criminal investigation and due process.

The most common example of this conflict between intelligence and prosecution goals is the dropping of criminal charges rather than revealing sources or intelligence during a trial. The necessity to allow the defense the right to cross-examine witnesses clashes here with the need to protect intelligence sources and information, as discussed in chapter 2. The dropping of charges undermines the chances of a successful prosecution while allowing intelligence gathering to continue. The alternative would be to have a successful prosecution but to lose the opportunity of gathering any more intelligence.

In the current "war on terror," the USA tends to break up plots early, arresting suspects and trying them on lesser charges that may or may not stick in court. In 2006, for example, suspects in Miami and in Brooklyn and Trinidad were arrested long before their alleged plots came close to fruition – blowing up the Sears Tower in Chicago in the first case and blowing up a tunnel between New York and New Jersey in the second.[4] This trend has led some lawyers to question whether arrested suspects actually intended to commit a terrorist act or merely talked about the possibility in internet chat rooms that were monitored by the authorities.[5] The intent to commit a crime, known as *mens rea* or criminal intent, is a central element of any criminal prosecution. It is one thing to talk openly about how the US government should be attacked and quite another to take concrete steps towards planning and executing such an attack. American officials argue that action must be taken to preempt such plots before they go operational and the suspects disappear. In the UK, by contrast, police wait much longer before arresting, in the hope that enough evidence will be gathered to reveal all details of the plot and lead to the wider network behind it. This would enable them to make more serious charges stick and to capture more people.[6]

This difference in approach reflects a variety of factors, including differing police cultures and legal traditions. The UK police, for example, can hold a suspect for up to 28 days under new anti-terrorism legislation introduced in 2005, while American police usually must charge a suspect after 48 hours. With a shorter time period in which to interrogate any suspect, the American police have little room to maneuver once an arrest has been made. It may therefore be more practical to use arrest as a means of disrupting suspected terror networks rather than to try and tease out the details of a plot and who else is involved by interrogating those who can be caught. The length of time that police can hold a suspect before charges must be laid varies considerably across different countries. In some cases, legislative attempts to increase this period of post-arrest detention have been blocked or even reversed. In Britain, the 28-day period was a compromise. The Blair government had asked for 90 days. Blair's successor as prime minister, Gordon Brown, first sought to double this period to 56 days, but later reduced it to 42 days. Resistance both domestically and internationally was fierce, including a threat by the government's human rights watchdog to launch a legal challenge if it ever became law.[7] In Canada, the 2001 Anti-Terrorism Act allowed preventive arrest, where a terrorist suspect can be held without trial, as well as investigative hearings in which a person was compelled to testify, even though his testimony might be self-incriminating. Both these provisions were, however, given a five-year sunset clause and in February 2007, the Canadian parliament defeated a government motion to extend them another three years.[8]

These different approaches to arrest reflect deeper underlying philosophies concerning counterterrorism itself. The USA frames its counterterrorism policy in military terms, using a war model approach that prioritizes preemption and the thwarting of terrorist plots long before they become operational. Arrests and prosecutions – whether or not they lead to convictions – can be used as a means to disrupt terrorist plots and tie up the time and resources of conspirators with defending themselves in court. These kinds of political prosecutions are more typical of authoritarian regimes and dictatorships, which use their criminal justice systems as political tools to disrupt and ultimately eliminate effective opposition.[9] American efforts to bring suspected terrorists to trial may be an incipient form of preemptive disruption or simply a response to stringent legal conditions on when to arrest and when to lay charges. However, many widely publicized arrests ultimately fail to lead to terrorism-related convictions, such as the Lackawanna Six from New York State, who never plotted anything, but pleaded guilty to attending a terrorist training camp.[10] There can definitely be a public relations aspect to announcing high-profile arrests or the break-up of serious plots, even if they do not lead to equally high-profile convictions. Such arrests can demonstrate to the public that the terrorist threat is real and ongoing and that the government is achieving concrete results in their battle with the terrorists. As such, they can serve political ends as much as counterterrorism ones.

The British approach, which prioritizes successful prosecution even if some plots are allowed to develop quite far, does take the risk that an attack might happen before preventive action can be taken. When in August 2006 British police arrested 24 men accused of conspiring to blow up planes flying from the UK to the USA, the plot was well advanced and the authorities had been aware of it for several months.[11] Here, the gains of catching the wider network of conspirators and successfully prosecuting them[12] take precedence over the benefits of disrupting potential threats before they move beyond the idea stage to take concrete form in specific plans of action. The tension between these two approaches underscores the double-edged nature of proactive counterterrorism. It can nip a burgeoning threat in the bud or destabilize a terrorist network enough so that its operatives cannot move from the planning stage and go operational. On the other hand, it can permanently erase any chance of learning more about the enemy and his plans or of identifying and apprehending those who have not yet appeared on the radar screen. Proactive, preemptive arrests can also yield political and public relations benefits that can become addictive in the short term and detrimental in the long term, ultimately undermining counterterrorism efforts. This is why political interference in intelligence work can be so damaging to long-term counterterrorist strategy.[13] The US intervention in Iraq is a case in point, where politically motivated "cherry-picking" and outright distortion of intelligence was used to justify invading Iraq on counterterrorism grounds. The mismanagement of the post-invasion period and the chaos and sectarian violence that ensued created an environment in which terrorism thrived. Iraq has joined other lingering conflicts as ideological fuel for further radicalization and recruitment. In 2004, a US media report on the arrest of a key Al Qaeda operative in Pakistan, Mohammed Naeem Noor Khan, who was cooperating with the CIA and Pakistani police, triggered the premature arrest by British police of 13 Al Qaeda suspects who had been under surveillance in the UK. Khan's arrest was revealed in a White House briefing designed to dispel concerns that the US Administration was raising its terror alert based on faulty or old intelligence. British and Pakistani police were infuriated by the media leak and felt that it had curtailed a golden opportunity to round up the top Al Qaeda leadership. The fact that all this occurred shortly after the Democratic National Convention also aroused suspicions that the briefing had been politically motivated.[14]

The need to protect secret information and intelligence sources can lead to additional problems when arrests are made and prosecutions launched. Some defendants and their lawyers try to take advantage of this dilemma by demanding secret information or classified documents from the prosecution, hoping that they will decide to drop charges rather than reveal the information or that the judge will rule that they cannot receive a fair trial without this information. This practice is called "graymail" – a lighter shade of blackmail.[15] Sometimes, a plea bargain in which the suspect pleads guilty to lesser charges in exchange for more serious charges being dropped obviates the need for a trial at all. The prosecution often initiates such deals to avoid having to present evidence in trial to support the more serious charges. In the case of the "American Taliban," John Walker Lindh, for example, there were concerns that the suspect's confession might be declared inadmissible because it was extracted under duress, and so the plea bargain was offered instead.[16] This stark choice between prosecution goals and intelligence goals has led to the kinds of compromises described in the previous chapter, such as allowing a trial to proceed, but not providing the defense with access to evidence related to intelligence sources or methods of data collection, or videotaping intelligence sources' testimony, which protects the identity of the source but also deprives the defense of the opportunity for cross-examination. This has contributed to a growing trend to circumvent the controls built into the criminal justice system by the classical (deterrent) approach to punishment and to rely more and more on certain kinds of expertise that are tailored to the identification of dangerous "enemies" (see below on targeting). In the worst cases, those identified as extremely dangerous have been killed rather than brought to trial, as in targeted assassinations. This is the ultimate manifestation of a preemptive, proactive strategy. Israel, for example, has relied on this approach in killing leaders and top operatives of Hamas in the Occupied Territories and Hizbollah in Lebanon (see chapter 2).

The question of whether or when to arrest someone raises special problems that have all been exacerbated in the fight against terrorism. Intelligence obviously plays an important role in determining when and whom to arrest. Issues such as racial profiling, mistaken identity, inadequate or erroneous information, or abuse and ill treatment post-arrest – often in the name of further intelligence gathering – will always pose serious challenges to those charged with preventing or countering terrorist attacks. In the USA, post-9/11, and the UK, post-7/7, these issues have become particularly important. The fatal shooting by police of Jean Charles de Menezes in London in July 2005 is an example of how mistaken identity can lead to tragic consequences. In this case, it also appears that a

surveillance officer failed to communicate important information to those directing the response operation.[17]

Another trend in the area of proactive counterterrorism with
important implications for goals is the increasing privatization
of police functions, particularly in the areas of guarding at
public events and in private prisons, surveillance, and even
investigation: "It is generally agreed that private security personnel outnumber public police by a factor of 3:1 with some
international variability. The ratio in South Africa is 4:1; in the
United Kingdom, Canada and Australia 2:1; and the United
States 3:1."[18] This "gray policing" has created an increased
ambiguity between private and public policing and a resulting
lack of accountability.[19] Efficiency supplants legality, partly
because the profit motive prevails in the private sector. This, in
turn, has led to abuses of power which are rarely pursued by
the public police in the name of protecting their private
colleagues' sources from retaliation by the targets of their
investigations. The distinction between public and private
becomes even grayer in cases of "sunlighting" (the opposite of
"moonlighting").[20] Here, public police do private work during
working hours. Many police leave the public sector to join the
private sector, a trend known as the "blue drain." Private security companies often employ ex-police officers, as well as
former intelligence agents or military officers. When public
and private police collaborate, it is the private sector that tends
to dominate, gaining access to information held by the public
police in return for favors granted in the past. An inherent conflict of interest between sectors and the primacy of professional secrets shared by a common subculture can lead in
some cases to corruption. This trend decreases accountability
and increases the possibility that the rights of those who are
the object of such policing will be compromised. One area
where this has been particularly evident, since well before
September 11, is the policing of immigrants and ethnic

minorities. Gray policing has also seeped into the "war on terror." In Iraq, where the abuses of Abu Ghraib led to some degree of accountability within the armed forces who were, in effect, engaged in policing and prison duties, private contractors involved in similar abuses were never brought to account. For example, in September 2007, Blackwater USA, a private security company that guards American diplomatic convoys, was banned from operating in Iraq after a shooting incident in which at least eight Iraqis were killed. The company had a reputation for aggressiveness, excessive weaponry, and inadequate training.[21] Private security companies have immunity from Iraqi law under a US order created before Iraqis took over governing the country. Despite an ongoing FBI investigation into the shooting incident, the State Department renewed Blackwater's contract for one year in April 2008.[22]

Methods

Because of their special characteristics, terrorist organizations are resistant to traditional methods of policing or intelligence gathering. More intrusive techniques, such as electronic surveillance, mail-opening, or secret searches of premises, are usually required. By their very nature, these techniques infringe on the personal liberties of those under investigation or surveillance. Such intrusive techniques are admissible within the rule of law, but there are strict legal procedures that must be followed before they are allowed, usually involving the obtaining of judicial warrants. The judge granting these warrants generally requires evidence to support the suspicion that a crime or an act of terrorism is being planned before the warrant is granted. In cases where time is of the essence, it is sometimes possible to go ahead without a warrant and get it later on.

The most common techniques involve special kinds of surveillance or information gathering. Electronic technology has greatly enhanced the capabilities of intelligence agencies to collect data on their targets and to track their activities and conversations. This is known as signals intelligence or SIGINT. With the advent of the internet and electronic telecommunications, such as cellphones, the ability to monitor people's communications has increased exponentially. The Kurdish leader Abdullah Öcalan was captured in 1999 (see chapter 2) because he used his cellphone, allowing a foreign intelligence agency to locate his whereabouts in Kenya. It is believed that it was either the Israelis or the Americans (or the Israelis via the Americans) who provided Öcalan's location to the Turks.[23] After 9/11, the most controversial surveillance program in the "war on terror" has been the US National Security Agency's (NSA's) eavesdropping program that was authorized by President Bush in the wake of the September attacks.[24] In this program, the international phone conversations and email messages of people suspected of links to Al Qaeda were monitored without obtaining judicial warrants. In addition to listening into specific phone conversations or reading specific email messages, the NSA program also included what is known as "data mining." Here, large volumes of phone and internet traffic are collected and analyzed for particular words or word patterns that indicate a link to terrorist planning. In this way, new suspects can be discovered without monitoring their specific communications directly.[25] In August 2007, the US Congress passed new legislation making this warrantless surveillance legal, though a sunset clause was included that required the legislation to be revisited in six months.[26]

The use of closed circuit television cameras (CCTV) in public places, such as downtown cores of major urban centers or subway systems, or private places such as shopping malls, is another source of data for intelligence gathering. Casinos use such cameras, equipped with face recognition software, to watch patrons and to spot and track people before they commit crimes. Images taken in real time are constantly compared with databases of known criminals and, when a match occurs, security guards move in. In the area of public security and counterterrorism, the United Kingdom has led the way in greatly expanding the use of CCTV in public spaces to aid in terrorist investigations. France's president, Nicolas Sarkozy, is considering the same thing for French urban centers.[27] In July 2007, New York police announced a plan to install over 100 security cameras in Lower Manhattan to monitor car license plates.[28] China, too, has plans to install thousands of surveillance cameras with face recognition capabilities in major cities. The Chinese government also wants to distribute residency cards with computer chips containing detailed information on the bearer, including educational background, work history, religion, and ethnicity.[29] Biometric identity cards have been discussed in many countries as a valuable means of distinguishing law-abiding citizens from potential terrorists. Biometric screening at airports and border entry points is also a means of identifying potential threats before they enter the country.[30] The reliance on sophisticated surveillance technology to prevent terrorists from gaining access to places where they might launch attacks, or to track them in pursuit of further intelligence about their networks and activities, has its critics. From a human rights and privacy perspective, critics argue that we suffer from an overreliance on surveillance technology that has led to what amounts to a surveillance society.[31] From an efficacy perspective, it is often argued that good intelligence needs people with linguistic skills and knowledge of the mindset, culture and worldview of terrorist groups. Known as human intelligence or HUMINT, the use of trained agents or the exploitation of people involved in terrorist networks is often considered as the most valuable kind of intelligence.[32]

Surveillance, SIGINT, and other intrusive techniques are indeed not always sufficient to determine whether terrorist attacks are being planned. Because members of clandestine organizations do not usually divulge information about what they are up to, control agencies sometimes have to rely on providing incentives to informers to break their oaths of secrecy and to betray the trust of their colleagues. The use of informers is fraught with difficulties and dangers, some of which have direct bearing on the protection of individual rights.[33] Informers sometimes provide false or misleading information that incriminates innocent people. Reasons vary from personal vendettas to trying to prove to the agencies that employ them that they have valuable information. Sometimes the reason is purely economic, since informers are sometimes paid for their information. Sometimes, the information is part of a plea bargain, where the informer gets more lenient treatment or more serious charges are dropped if s/he cooperates. In some cases, informers become *agents provocateurs*, encouraging or convincing those in the groups they inform upon to engage in activities that they might not otherwise have considered. In the Sears Tower plot mentioned above, defense lawyers of the accused claimed that their clients were actually entrapped by FBI informers into committing to the plot and that they would never have considered such a thing on their own.[34]

Control agencies can also make use of their own agents to penetrate these secret organizations and to collect information from the inside. This often leads to ethical dilemmas, whereby the agent must commit criminal acts, sometimes even murder, to gain entry into the organization. Sometimes they, too, act like *agents provocateurs*, providing the means necessary for the terrorist group to launch an attack or an operation or to engage in some other form of activity, such as giving support to a terrorist operation. This is known as "covert facilitation" in the intelligence world or "entrapment" in the police world. Once inside the organization, undercover agents encounter a variety of difficulties and challenges related to maintaining a double identity.[35] In some cases, especially when agents remain undercover for a lengthy period, they can even begin to act as double agents, serving both those for whom they are supposed to be working and those whom they are supposed to be watching. Some become corrupt and seek monetary gain by engaging in criminal activities, such as drug dealing or gunrunning. All these methods of intelligence gathering involve ethical dilemmas of varying degrees, whether used by the police, the military, or private agencies.

Targets

In liberal democracies, there are two primary justifications for singling out an individual for attention and subjecting them to the violence inherent in criminal justice, whether it be surveillance, arrest, detention, or punishment. The first derives from a classical tradition of punishment originating from the Enlightenment and such thinkers as Cesare Beccaria and Montesquieu. The idea is that the State has the right to protect its citizens from dangerous *acts*, i.e., those acts that contravene the criminal law. This leads to the following principles:

- proportionality of punishment, where the punishment must fit the crime;
- non-retroactivity of the law, where one cannot punish someone for doing something which was not proscribed at the time; and
- general deterrence, where punishment performs a moral educative function: by punishing an offender, others are taught what is right and what is wrong and, in the process, are deterred from committing a similar offense.

What differentiates the State's use of violence from that of the ordinary citizen is the rule of law and the requirements of due process. The rights of the accused are protected and the powers of the police are limited by such concepts as reasonable suspicion. Redress is supposed to be available to those wrongly accused or imprisoned. Because of these safeguards, the State's use of violence in the exercise of criminal justice is legitimized.

The second idea derives from a positivist tradition of punishment that tailors its goals to a classification of criminal types. The central idea of this school of thought is that the State has the right to protect its citizens from dangerous *people*, i.e., those identified as incorrigible or inherently criminal. This leads to the following two principles:

- rehabilitation as a valid goal of punishment for those who are redeemable; and
- neutralization (exile, deportation, death, or life imprisonment) for those who are not.

It is up to science to identify those variables that will help law enforcement and criminal justice agents to determine who is who. Central to this approach is the idea that criminals differ in some fundamental way, be it biological, psychological, social, or cultural, from the law-abiding citizen. It is this splitting off of the criminal from the noncriminal that is the progenitor of the notion that the criminal is an "outsider," a stranger, an alien, different from the rest of us, especially in the case of those determined to be unredeemable, incorrigible, or untreatable. Many theories of criminal behavior within this tradition have had racist overtones and have singled out immigrants or racial and ethnic minorities as the source of crime and disorder in societies undergoing rapid change.[36]

In the film, *Majority Report*, a futuristic society detects criminals before they take action by tracking their thoughts and intentions. When someone thinks of committing a crime, they are arrested. The hero, played by Tom Cruise, is one of these investigators and the drama begins when he is accused himself and he must struggle to clear his name. This is the ultimate dream of those who wish to harness technology to the needs of proactive counterterrorism: the equivalent of George Orwell's thought police.[37] Many of the techniques used in proactive policing and intelligence gathering (see above) are attempts to achieve the same goal in different ways. The practice of entrapment comes closest to criminalizing a person's intentions and thoughts, before they have a chance to put them into action. A classic sting operation will involve control agents or a police-directed informer enticing a target with an idea or an opportunity to commit a crime, and when the target acts on this opportunity, police close in and arrest him/her.

In societies where the gap between social, ethnic, cultural, or economic groups widens or the politics of fear and loathing selects certain groups for vilification and scapegoating, a counterterrorism policy that is based on selective targeting of dangerous classes of people can too easily become fertile ground for enemy construction and the kinds of simplifying myths of good vs. evil that were so prevalent during the Cold War. A central element of a war model or counterinsurgency model is the importance of intelligence about the enemy. More than a decade before the September 11 attacks, the end of the Cold War necessitated the identification of a new enemy. During the 1990s, this led to a proliferation and intermingling of a variety of threats, including organized crime, illegal immigration, and transnational terrorism (see chapter 1). Another aspect of this post-Cold-War trend, particularly in post-Schengen Europe, where internal borders disappeared, was a tendency to focus increasingly on "outsiders" as the enemy to be tracked and controlled. This usually meant immigrants, refugees, and asylum-seekers, or inner-city dwellers and the underclass of industrial society, among whom many of these people took up residence. After the 9/11 attacks, this trend intensified and spread across the Atlantic to the USA, where other targets were incorporated into the list of possible enemies. One prime category became foreign students, particularly from Muslim countries.

After the 2005 suicide bombings in London, and the discovery that the perpetrators included British citizens, the enemy broadened to include "the enemy within." Naturalized citizens and native-born citizens, particularly converts to Islam, have become legitimate targets of surveillance programs, despite official denials of racial, ethnic, or cultural profiling. As the boundary between external security and internal security increasingly blurs, so too does the notion of national security begin to fuse with that of societal security, where society itself rather than the State, per se, is perceived to be threatened. Instead of the classic external enemy or subversive agent acting within society to overthrow the State, one finds an internal enemy who threatens the identity and, by inference, the cohesion of that society. In the criminal justice model, this has led to official attempts to criminalize speech, such as glorification of violence,[38] and membership in specific organizations. For example, UN Security Council resolution 1624 (2005) calls for Member States to take steps aimed at prohibiting by law and preventing incitement to commit terrorist acts, and to report to the Counter-Terrorism Committee on the steps they have taken to implement the resolution. In the war model, this has led to massive surveillance of a wide category of individuals and detention without trial of citizens as well as resident aliens. The operational consequence of a counterterrorism policy based on enemy creation is a widening of the surveillance net to include more and more potential enemies. The result of this is increasingly large numbers of people being processed by control agents and ending up under surveillance or in detention. Much of the debate post-September 11 surrounding counterterrorist efforts in the area of intelligence and surveillance relates to how wide the net should be cast and whether profiling of specific target groups is justified or acceptable.

Targeting decisions can play an important part in determining who becomes labeled as an enemy and who does not. Consider the case of secondary or tertiary targets. When a person is being watched, or his communications are being monitored, there are usually reasonable grounds for targeting this particular individual. In most cases, a judicial warrant has been issued, based on such grounds. When this targeted individual meets someone else, or communicates electronically with someone else, it is not a foregone conclusion that this second person will also be monitored after the exchange is over. Two of the London suicide bombers, Mohammed Siddique Khan and Shehzad Tanweer, were under police surveillance because they had met with members of a different terrorist plot that was under heavy surveillance. When they separated from the primary targets and went in a different direction, they were not followed, since they were not considered targets worthy of separate surveillance. The fact that they had been known to have committed criminal offenses such as credit card fraud was not sufficient to declare them reasonable surveillance targets in their own right. The fact that local police were not notified, however, highlights the perennial problem of intelligence sharing between criminal and security forces.[39]

A failure to share intelligence is not the only problem. Sometimes erroneous information is shared. This was the case when Maher Arar, a Syrian-Canadian engineer, was arrested by US authorities on his way home to Canada from a vacation abroad. The Canadian federal police, the Royal Canadian Mounted Police (RCMP), had erroneously made him a secondary target for surveillance because he had met several times with someone deemed by them to be a security threat and who was already under surveillance for this reason. They shared their information with the FBI, and the American authorities placed Arar on their terrorism watch list. When he entered American territory, Arar was arrested and sent to Syria, his country of birth. There, he was tortured into confessing a relationship with Al Qaeda.[40] After his return to Canada, and a lengthy Commission of Inquiry that cleared his name and recommended financial compensation of millions of dollars, the USA still retains Arar's name on its terrorism watch list.[41] This highlights how the shelf life of data collected in the name of fighting terrorism can last well after it has been discredited.

Targeting decisions face particular analytical problems and ethical dilemmas when dealing with social groups and organizations. Is a social movement or a cultural association a legitimate organization involved in social or cultural activity or is it a front for criminal, subversive, or terrorist activity? In a surveillance society that values security over privacy, many troubling questions arise concerning individual rights and freedoms and how they balance with the duties and responsibilities of a public citizen. Prevention is particularly problematic, especially when selective targeting of particular segments of society deemed to be potential security threats, however defined, can infringe on individual rights and create social divisions that can, in turn, constitute security threats themselves. If intelligence experts or other official voices characterize security threats in particular ways, and the media reproduce and amplify this discourse, the result can be the creation of moral panics about some exaggerated or distorted threat, scapegoating of particular groups or communities, or disingenuous claims-making that merely benefits those who might profit in some way from a particular approach.[42] For example, it may be true that the threat of WMD terrorism is on the rise. It might also be true that those who make this claim are merely catching the ear of the media with their dire warnings and thereby capturing tax dollars and political support for expanding their own professional activities.[43] Similar dynamics are at work in the USA concerning whether or not to attack Iran. Declaring that country's Revolutionary Guards a terrorist group is a significant step in preparing the way for justifying a military strike on Iran as a means of countering terrorism in Iraq.[44]

Selective targeting and doomsday claims-making pose several dangers for democratic governance. These include:

- the undermining of public trust in government through misinformation about the nature of security threats or by deliberate disinformation campaigns;
- the promotion of public anger and outrage at scapegoat targets, which, in turn, create social divisions;
- the fostering of public fear and moral panics as a means of garnering consent for certain control programs;
- the undermining of minority rights;
- the creation of a surveillance society that by its very nature infringes on freedom of expression, assembly, and movement;
- the criminalization of certain kinds of dissent and protest activity that in a less security-conscious society would be considered tolerable and could be controlled by less coercive means; and
- the stampeding of domestic and international support for military interventions that have a strong likelihood of exacerbating regional instability and escalating tension and conflict.

The ascendancy of a war model of counterterrorism since 9/11, with its blurring of police and military functions, has important implications for liberal democracies. As the police become more militarized and the military assume more policing functions, the problems that proactive policing and security intelligence pose for due process and the rule of law have become more acute. These problems include:

- a lack of adequate judicial control of surveillance techniques;
- the undermining of openness and accountability of government control agencies by the need for secrecy;
- the entrenchment of selective targeting as a prime means of intelligence gathering; and
- the reliance on informers or coerced information from detainees, particularly in deciding who to watch or arrest.

In the area of arrest and detention based on intelligence gathering, problems include:

- the determination of reasonable grounds for arrest;
- discrimination, racism, and anti-immigrant/foreigner violence by control agents; and
- selective enforcement based on the identification of dangerous classes of people.

These problems, in turn, pose clear dangers for democracy. They include:

- a lack of openness and accountability that are a direct result of the nature of proactive policing and security intelligence;
- infringement of individual rights and freedoms by discrimination due to selective targeting and the identification of dangerous classes of people;
- a widening of the net of surveillance to include legitimate organizations or "secondary targets," i.e., those who communicate with those who are already targeted;
- the possibility of law-breaking by control agents or crime creation through covert facilitation, entrapment, or infiltration, resulting in the undermining of public trust and confidence in government;

- the inherent conflict between security intelligence and criminal prosecution (the problem of when to arrest and when to admit evidence in court) and its impact on cooperation between security intelligence agencies and police agencies, again undermining public trust and confidence, but this time because of ineffectiveness.

Some of these dangers have been addressed in liberal democracies by the creation of security oversight committees and the requirement of judicial warrants for intrusive techniques of surveillance. In some cases, sunset clauses are placed on emergency anti-terrorism legislation, requiring that the legislation be re-examined after a set period of time, with a view to correcting problems or even abolishing the legislation because it is no longer needed, ineffective, or proven in practice to be seriously flawed. In August 2007, for example, a six-month sunset clause was placed on legislation that legalized the surveillance of phone and internet traffic passing through the USA without recourse to judicial warrants (warrantless surveillance).[45] Another principle that tries to alleviate some of the inevitable problems surrounding proactive policing and security intelligence is that agencies must use the least intrusive techniques that are still effective, resorting to more intrusive ones only when the lesser ones are ineffective. Two opposing concerns underlie these attempts to address both security concerns and concerns about democratic acceptability. On one hand, a fear of false negatives (failure to detect a security threat) leads to widening the surveillance net as much as possible, thereby running the risk of infringing upon civil liberties of those targeted and, ultimately, facilitating the commission of human rights violations by control agents. On the other hand, a fear of false positives (targeting innocent individuals, organizations, or communities) leads to the imposition of judicial restrictions upon intelligence gathering and the creation of oversight committees and the imposition of sunset clauses on anti-terrorism legislation, thereby running the risk of attenuating the effectiveness of intelligence gathering operations. Clearly, both fears can be socially constructed by organizations with a stake in the outcome. This is why the media can play such an important role in tipping the balance one way or the other (see chapter 4). A good example of the inherent tensions and unexpected consequences of a proactive counterterrorism strategy based on enemy creation and the identification of a select class of targets is the area of terrorist financing.

Blocking terrorist financing

If one is interested in stopping terrorists in their tracks before they can plan an operation or launch an attack, one of the best ways to do this would be to dry up the source of their funding. In this way, one can make it difficult, if not impossible, for the terrorist group to obtain the weaponry and other logistical material necessary for planning, preparing for, and implementing an attack. Terrorist funding has often been a neglected aspect of counterterrorism strategy, although it has been recognized as an important issue by some, even before September II. The finances of the Palestine Liberation Organization (PLO), in particular, have been the object of detailed study.[46] In 1999, the International Convention for the Suppression of the Financing of Terrorism was adopted by the UN General Assembly, on December 9. The Convention

- requires parties to take steps to prevent and counteract the financing of terrorists, whether direct or indirect, through groups claiming to have charitable, social, or cultural goals or which also engage in such illicit activities as drug trafficking or gun-running;
- commits states to hold those who finance terrorism criminally, civilly, or administratively liable for such acts;

- provides for the identification, freezing, and seizure of funds allocated for terrorist activities, as well as for the sharing of the forfeited funds with other states on a case-by-case basis. The Convention explicitly states that bank secrecy will no longer be a justification for refusing to cooperate.[47]

Since September 11, terrorist financing has become a central concern for counterterrorism analysts.[48] Two areas in particular have received considerable attention:

1. the tracking, freezing, and seizure of funds directed towards terrorist activity; and
2. the role of charitable organizations in raising funds for groups that engage in terrorism.

The result has been increasing interaction between intelligence agencies, financial institutions, and charitable organizations.[49]

Freezing terrorist assets or requiring greater transparency from banks in an attempt to prevent money laundering are examples of counterterrorist activity in the first area. The secret monitoring of international financial systems to detect and verify suspicious transactions was one measure that President Bush instituted shortly after the 9/11 attacks. It only became public several years later, when the *New York Times* and other news publications, such as the *Wall Street Journal* and the *Los Angeles Times*, published details about the secret program.[50] The electronic messaging system, operated by Swift, the Society for Worldwide Interbank Financial Telecommunication, which is based in Brussels, Belgium, routes roughly $6 trillion a day in transfers among thousands of financial institutions, including banks, brokerages, fund managers, and stock exchanges. The records that have been monitored and searched by the CIA, under the direction of the US Treasury Department, consist primarily of wire transfers between the USA and other countries, not within the USA itself, though some purely domestic transactions have also been included. Instead of obtaining judicial warrants to examine specific transactions by specific individuals, businesses, or charities, treasury officials relied on broad subpoenas issued to Swift for millions of records. As such, it was more like a data mining operation than a judicially guided security investigation, although one control put in after Swift executives expressed uneasiness about the operation involved an outside auditing firm verifying that the data searches were based on specific intelligence leads about suspected terrorists. Nevertheless, Privacy International, a London-based human rights group, filed complaints in 40 countries alleging that Swift had violated European and Asian privacy laws by giving the United States access to its data.[51] The USA also has more limited agreements with specific companies to provide records of ATM transactions, credit card purchases, and Western Union wire payments.[52]

In the second area, some charitable and religious organizations, particularly those with links to countries where it is known that Al Qaeda operates, have become suspect and are considered either as fronts for terrorist planning and organization or as engaged in illegal activity as well as more legitimate charitable work. It is well known, for example, that Hamas engages not only in suicide bombings, but also in important charity and social work. In December 2001, the US government seized the assets of the Holy Land Foundation for Relief and Development, the largest Muslim charity organization working in the United States, accusing it of funneling money to Islamic charity (*zakat*) committees in the West Bank and Gaza that were controlled by Hamas. These Hamas agencies, in turn, used the money to support the families of suicide bombers, as well as for broader social services.[53] Five of the organization's leaders were charged with supporting terrorism. In October 2007, however, the judge declared a mistrial.

The main prosecution evidence came from Israeli intelligence agents using false names, but the jury acquitted some defendants on most charges and could not reach a verdict on others.[54]

A few months after the 9/11 attacks, President Bush ordered that the accounts of al-Barakaat be frozen.[55] Al-Barakaat, which began in Somalia in the early 1990s to replace that country's failed banking system, is an international financial network of "hawalas." Hawalas are an informal system of remittances that many people use to transfer money from one country to another or within a country. Because they do not use banks, these transfers leave no paper trail and cannot be tracked by computers. A person simply goes to the hawala office in his place of residence, pays a sum of money to the person there, and an identical sum of money is paid to the designated beneficiary by the hawala office in the recipient's place of residence. In the case of transfers between different countries, there is literally no transnational movement of funds.

Many immigrants and guest workers rely on such paperless systems to send money to families back home. In Somalia itself, a large majority of the population relies on money transfers from abroad as their main source of income. This amounts to some $500 million annually, compared with just $60 million in international humanitarian aid to Somalia for the year 2000.[56] Because al-Barakaat was the main banking, telecommunications, and construction group in Somalia at the time, the US move to freeze its assets seriously aggravated that country's already critical economic situation.

The massive effort to block terrorist funding since 9/11 has run into obstacles related to infighting between agencies, most notably the US Treasury Department and the FBI. Another problem has been skepticism on the part of allies in the "war on terror" about the credibility of the evidence used to justify an organization's assets being frozen. In other cases, such as those of Saudi Arabia, Pakistan, and the United Arab Emirates, allies are reluctant to cooperate in tracking and freezing financial assets of charitable and religious organizations for fear of a domestic backlash.[57] From an intelligence point of view, differentiating between legitimate charitable organizations and fronts for terrorist financing is made all the more difficult by the fact that many organizations perform multiple functions that can range from legal to illegal. For a long time, many countries in Europe and the Middle East refused to consider the political wings of Hizbollah and Hamas to be terrorist organizations, despite continuing pressure from the USA. Some still do not. In some cases, those who give money to such organizations do so in good faith, unaware of any duplicity about where the donated funds go, yet they can be charged for supporting terrorist activity, have their assets seized, or become targets for continuing surveillance. This is even more problematic in the case of Muslim charities, since practicing Muslims are required by their religion to make charitable donations on a regular basis if they are able to do so. Known as *zakah* or alms-giving, this religious obligation is one of the Five Pillars of Islam. In other cases, such as that of the Syracuse Muslim charitable organization, Help the Needy, which sent money to Iraq in violation of sanctions, it is even doubtful that terrorist links existed, though prosecutors and politicians commenting on the case continually alluded to terrorism.[58]

Clearly, intelligence can be deficient, faulty, or based on definitional assumptions about the nature of terrorism that not all governments share. For example, the Consolidated List maintained by the Al Qaeda Sanctions Monitoring Group, established under UN Security Council Resolution 1390, which mandates freezing financial and economic assets, a travel ban, and an arms embargo for designated individuals and entities, has failed to keep up to date with the rapidly growing ranks of

Al Qaeda-related entities.[59] In 2003, the Saudi government failed to report in-country Al Qaeda activity to the Monitoring Group, which it was obligated to do under Resolution 1390, because it did not want to admit that Al Qaeda was active within the country.[60] In other cases, enforcement is difficult for technical, cultural, political, or ideological reasons. Some countries, like Afghanistan or Somalia, lack an effective banking system. Others lack the technical and technological expertise necessary for sophisticated tracking. Some refuse to antagonize local populations, while others do not believe that certain groups are financing terrorism, since they view the violence of groups like Hamas or Hizbollah as legitimate opposition to Israeli repression. By 2003, however, according to the US Treasury Department, 173 states had frozen some assets, more than 100 had introduced legislation to fight terrorist financing, and 84 had established financial intelligence units to investigate suspicious financial activity and to share information with other states.[61] Yet even as the international system gets better at cooperating and tracking terrorist financing, the terrorists alter their methods of transporting funds, relying more on couriers who carry gold, gems, and cash, none of which is traceable at all.

At the international level, economic sanctions have often been used to try and stop state sponsorship of terrorism or to prevent the transnational flow of arms and supplies to terrorist groups. The main problems here are twofold:

1. economic sanctions often hurt the citizens of a targeted country rather than the government or authorities involved in supporting or supplying terrorist organizations;
2. national interests regarding trade, production, diplomacy, and influence often lead to breaking or ignoring sanctions or blocking international consensus on imposing them in the first place.

International cooperation on countering terrorism is difficult at the best of times.[62] When financial gain, trade opportunities, or international influence are at stake, the will to cooperate on a shared threat or problem often becomes compromised or evaporates completely. There can also be double standards that stem from differences over the definition of terrorism or the application of the terrorist label to groups being supported. While the USA accuses Iran of aiding terrorist groups in Iraq in the first decade of the twenty-first century, a previous US administration in the 1980s supported a Nicaraguan group, the Contras, who used terrorism against the Sandinista government of the time.[63]

Intelligence, oversight, and accountability

The operational secrecy required to investigate terrorism poses special challenges for open societies that value accountability on the part of those who protect them. There are intrinsic contradictions between criminal prosecution and intelligence functions in counterterrorism and a balance has to be struck between preventive and reactive aspects. The balance that is struck depends to a great extent on how one perceives the threat. The greater the threat assessment, the greater the tendency to take proactive measures, to claim the need for secrecy, and to circumvent due process and judicial review or oversight.

The primary analytical problems faced by intelligence services involved in counterterrorism usually revolve around the need to distinguish between different levels of threat or illegality. These include how to distinguish between:

1. legitimate opposition movements and fronts for criminal, subversive, or terrorist activity;
2. legitimate charitable and financial institutions and those that serve as vehicles for money laundering and terrorist financing;

3. violent protest of a less serious nature and violence that clearly threatens national security;
4. sympathizers or fellow travelers and active supporters or members of criminal, subversive, or terrorist groups; and
5. those who loudly advocate violence but never intend to take action and those who secretly plan to commit violence and will do so if they can.

How these problems are operationalized and – one hopes – solved has clear implications for the protection of privacy rights and other civil and political rights in an increasingly pervasive surveillance society.

The case of Yassin M. Aref, an imam of a mosque in Albany, NY, highlights the kinds of problems that can arise. Aref became a target of warrantless surveillance because his name appeared in a notebook that was seized after a raid by US soldiers in Iraq in June 2003. The surveillance revealed a series of calls to Syria and so the FBI began a sting operation to involve Aref in a money laundering scheme. A fictional plot to assassinate the Pakistani ambassador to the UN using a shoulder-launched missile was created and a Pakistani immigrant, Shahed Hossain, was used as an informer to entice a colleague of Aref into agreeing to launder $50,000 needed to obtain a missile for the planned assassination. Aref himself became involved when his colleague, Mohammed M. Hossain, asked him to serve as a witness, as is customary in Islamic law. Both Aref and Hossain were eventually convicted and sentenced to 15 years in prison. Aref's lawyers are appealing, claiming that evidence against him was obtained illegally, through the warrantless surveillance program. His lawyers claim that the camp that was raided in Iraq was full of refugees, and the discovery of his name did not mean that he was linked with insurgents or terrorists. In fact, Aref was himself a refugee, having fled Kurdish Iraq with his family after the first Gulf War, arriving in the USA, via Syria, in 1999.[64] Here we have another case where proactive counterterrorism makes use of special evidence and procedures not usually allowed under traditional rule of law. The argument is that the convicted men would sooner or later have taken action on their own, and the sting operation merely revealed their criminal intentions, much as in the film *Minority Report*.

The tension between prosecution and intelligence goals, and the emergence of special procedures to deal with this, reflect once again the contrast between "September 10 thinking" and "September 12 thinking" about counterterrorism. In "September 10 thought," the criminal justice and war models are primarily reactive models, and because terrorism occurs for the most part in time of peace, it is civilian authority that predominates, even when the military is used. In "September 12 thought," military options predominate and the executive takes precedence over the legislature and the judiciary.[65] "September 10 thinking" argues that security can only be achieved in the long run by preserving the rights and freedoms of citizens. In the short run, if rights are to be suspended and freedoms curtailed, then oversight over the forces exercising the State's monopoly on violence and sunset clauses on emergency powers must be an integral part of the security package. "September 12 thinking" argues that many rights and freedoms that we take for granted impede the establishment of better security because terrorists can take advantage of them to secretly plan attacks and to avoid detection. We all must sacrifice our freedoms to ensure security and only the guilty have anything to fear from this.

So can these positions be reconciled? Is there a place for watching the watchers in an effective counterterrorism strategy? In the area of proactive counterterrorism, the answer lies in a commitment to good intelligence that is reliable and accountable. This is the only way to resolve the concerns on both sides of the ideological divide. The answer to the insistence of "September 10 thinkers" on the primacy of rule of law is this. If increased powers or emergency measures are deemed essential, then they should be given a chance. But along with these new powers or measures, there is a parallel need for expanded oversight and sunset clauses. When the sunset deadline arrives, it will be intelligence successes, failures, or cover-ups that will determine whether to implement the sunset or extend the powers. The answer to the insistence of "September 12 thinkers" on the primacy of proactive measures such as preventive arrest and detention or preemption is this. If you need to take out "bad guys" or punish state sponsors militarily (or even economically), then you need reliable intelligence which should be made available to responsible oversight authorities to justify action and provide accountability. It should not be cherry-picked or distorted or politicized for ideological reasons or to cover up ineptitude or dishonesty.

The insistence on reliable and accountable intelligence does not, of course, solve everything. Problems of interagency cooperation, turf battles over the control and dissemination of intelligence, compartmentalization of information, and bureaucratic rules or classification procedures that slow down responses to time-sensitive intelligence continue to undermine effective intelligence sharing and analysis, in both the civilian and the military sectors.[66]

The unintended consequences of coercive counterterrorism outlined in chapter 2 are clearly exacerbated when counterterrorism is proactive. Because the measures are taken against people who have not yet committed terrorist acts or related criminal offenses, the burden of proof lies on the intelligence analyst to prove that the measures are justified. When proactive counterterrorist measures are seen to be arbitrary, disproportionate, or aimed at innocent bystanders, then the consequences can be disastrous. Legitimacy can be seriously undermined, credibility of intelligence agencies damaged, and distrust of future government claims or actions triggered. Counterterrorism does not take place in a vacuum. People of all stripes and persuasions are watching – and reacting. It is therefore important to look beyond purely coercive measures, whether reactive or proactive, and consider these wider audiences that watch and listen as the struggle between terrorist and counterterrorist plays out and evolves. This is the subject matter of the next chapter, which looks at persuasive counterterrorism and the communicative dimension of that struggle.

CHAPTER FOUR

Persuasive counterterrorism

Counterterrorism involves understanding and dealing with the ideas that underpin the use of terrorism in social and political life. This has ideological, political, social, cultural, and religious aspects. Terrorists have constituencies which include followers, sympathizers, and active or passive supporters. Counterterrorism must deal with these wider audiences. This is the propaganda or "hearts and minds" aspect of counterterrorism, which must complement the more coercive forms of communication embodied in the criminal justice and war models. This chapter examines the communication strategies that can be applied to countering and preventing terrorist recruitment, planning, and action, as well as state support of terrorism. It addresses the importance of multiple audiences and the need to coordinate different messages for each one.

The communicative nature of terrorism and counterterrorism

Terrorism, whether of the state, the insurgent, or the transnational, global variety, is a communicative strategy designed to propagate specific messages to a variety of different audiences using a combination of coercion (threat, violence, and terror) and persuasion (explicit or implicit demands). The definition of terrorism presented in the Introduction can be broken down into its constituent elements as follows:

- the combined use and threat of violence,
- planned in secret,
- usually executed without warning,
- directed against one set of targets (the direct victims),
- in order to coerce compliance or to compel allegiance,
- from a second set of targets (targets of demands), and
- to intimidate or to impress a wider audience (target of terror or target of attention).[1]

At least four different types or classes of audience can then be distinguished:

1. the *direct victims*, which includes surviving victims, and families and friends of victims;
2. *targets of terror*, which includes people who identify with the victims, for example members of the same ethnic group, class, nation, or profession, as well as the mass public in the case of highly indiscriminate or mass-casualty attacks;
3. *targets of attention*, which includes national and global elites, the mass public, and the media, as well as sympathizers, followers, and supporters of the terrorists, including, most importantly, potential recruits;
4. *targets of demands* (whether explicit or not), such as government officials, law enforcement, military, peace-keepers, humanitarian agencies, and other agents of social control.

The "terror" in terrorism refers to the impact of this particular mode of violence on a particular audience, those who view themselves as possible future victims. These are the targets of terror ([2] above). The direct victims of terrorism ([1] above) are simply a vehicle for generating this message of terror and delivering it to that audience, often via the media, though word of mouth, gossip, and rumor should not be underestimated either. But there are other possible messages, implicit or explicit, that the terrorist may wish to convey, depending on which type of audience the terrorist wants to address:

- if the audience is *the enemy*, the message could be one of *impunity and power*;
- if *the enemy's supporters*, the message could be *demoralization*;
- if *the terrorist's own supporters*, the message could be *pride or glory*;
- if *potential recruits*, it could be *glamor, excitement, or redemption*.

A terrorist group that has suffered severe setbacks may simply want to prove to the authorities and perhaps to its supporters that it is still a significant player. In short, the primary purpose underlying most terrorist events is to send messages to different audiences that are designed to alter or reinforce individual perceptions and attitudes. Who those individuals are – which audiences they belong to – certainly complicates the communication process. But it is communication nonetheless.[2]

Counterterrorism, like terrorism, is inherently communicative. It also contains both coercive and persuasive elements. The criminal justice model uses the threat of punishment as a means to deter potential terrorists from engaging in the violence that they threaten. The war model uses the threat of preemptive military strikes to deter presumed state supporters of terrorism, and the threat of targeted assassinations or preventive detention to deter individuals from taking the terrorist path. Whether the threat of military strikes can be effectively applied to terrorist groups themselves, since they tend to lack territory or physical infrastructure that can easily be located and targeted, is an increasingly debated question in the current "war on terror."[3] Like nuclear deterrence and its central principle of mutual assured destruction (MAD), the doctrine of preemption promises terrorist groups and any state that supports them what US President Ronald Reagan once called "swift and effective retribution" (see chapter 2). As such, the doctrine of preemptive defense can be viewed in communicative terms rather than purely military ones. Diplomatic and economic sanctions, too, involve the communication of threats and their linking to specific conditions. Propaganda, psychological warfare, "hearts and minds" campaigns, and the idea of providing incentives for terrorists to abandon violence and seek nonviolent paths instead all refer to this notion of counterterrorism as a form of communication, even political persuasion, where different messages are conveyed to different audiences.

The traditional counterterrorism toolbox emphasizes the coercive powers of the State and the exercise of hard power. These are exemplified by the approaches examined in chapters 2 and 3. Just as terrorism is a combination of coercion and persuasion, so is counterterrorism. Deterrence is the primary form of persuasion in a hard power sense. In the war model, it is the declaratory policy of preemption. These two forms of "coercive persuasion" will be examined first, before turning to the use of "soft power" or the propaganda dimension of counterterrorism.

Deterrence and the criminal justice model

The communicative nature of the criminal justice model is clearest when we consider the nature of deterrence. Stated in its simplest form, deterrence theory sees the sole aim of punishment as the prevention of future acts of a similar nature to the one punished. Modern terminology distinguishes between "special deterrence," which is directed at the offender, and "general deterrence," which is directed towards others. Deterrence can be defined as prevention by means of the imposition of a legal threat: "Deterrence . . . is principally a matter of the declaration of some harm, loss, or pain that will follow noncompliance; in short, the central concept is that of threat."[4] This recognition of the central role of threat in the notion of deterrence highlights the communicative nature of criminal law. Criminal codes are announcements. They proscribe specific acts and prescribe specific sanctions for noncompliance. The prescription of sanctions is the declaration of a legal threat; law enforcement (including police, court, and penal functions) constitutes making good the threat.

The same applies in the criminal justice model of counterterrorism. Both domestic and international law proscribe the use of threat and violence against persons, as well as violent attacks on property. Some legal codes go further and proscribe terrorism, per se, usually defined as the use of violence to intimidate or to further specifically political goals. Creating specific terrorist offenses is actually redundant, however, given that all legal codes proscribe the very activities that terrorists engage in. It was the amplitude and severity of the September 11 attacks that pushed many countries to create special offenses, including in some cases proscribing membership in a terrorist organization or creating speech offenses, such as the glorification of violence. Before September 11, only countries with persistent and severe terrorist campaigns had gone down that route, such as the United Kingdom, Israel, and Turkey.

How does legal deterrence actually work? What are its effects? Five have been identified by researchers:

1. simple deterrence;
2. moral education;
3. habit-building;
4. instilling respect for the law; and
5. providing a rationale for obedience.[5]

In the first, they include both "a mere frightening effect" or "intimidation" and a cost-benefit analysis effect, whereby the individual weighs the pros and cons and opts for the law-abiding course. Many consider this to be the direct effect of the threat of punishment. The other four are more indirect effects. "Moral education" refers to the moralizing or educative function of punishment whereby the attachment of sanctions to a proscribed act can change people's attitudes towards the act itself, making it appear wrong. "Habit-building" refers to how the threat of punishment can stimulate habitual law-abiding conduct. The other two are self-evident. If an individual learns something about the nature of social norms, the sanctity of the law, the value of obedient behavior, or the power of obedience as an excuse to fend off criminogenic peer pressure, these are additional effects over and above the purely deterrent one of intimidation. The implication, however, is that threat and the fear of punishment are not the only things involved in deterrence, though they are central. There are other lessons that can be learned, regarding norms, values, and obedience to them.

There are a number of assumptions about human nature that underlie the deterrent model of punishment. Humans are assumed to be rational and hedonistic (attracted by pleasure and repelled by pain), to possess free will, to always know what is harmful to them, to possess self control, to be able to learn from their own experience and from the experience of others, to be deterred by fear, and to be knowledgeable of laws and sanctions. Taken together, a particular image of the human being emerges: a rational, aware, calculating (in the sense of decision-making) individual who bases his or her actions on a careful analysis of the consequences of their acts, the analysis of which is, in turn, based upon experience, both direct and vicarious, and a knowledge of the law. This rational, controlled image of the human being stems, in turn, from a particular view of the origins of the human condition: the social contract and its role in preventing Hobbes' war of all against all.

This rational image of humans is the basis of the classical system of criminal justice, with its procedural constraints – the rule of law – on the exercise of state power. The law functions as a semiotic system of signs that conveys messages to specific and general audiences. One of them, as noted above, is threat and intimidation, but others concern acceptable norms of behavior, the value of obedience to certain codes, and justification of obedience to and respect for the law.

The main problem with this picture is that human beings are not always rational, nor is their behavior always driven by careful cost-benefit analysis. What it ignores of course is the broader social and political context of human existence. Human beings are embedded in social, cultural, political, and religious networks and this affects any individual's calculus of action and reaction. The job of the terrorist recruiter or propagandist is to use these wider contexts to convince people that the values, norms, and laws of the designated enemy are not worth respecting or obeying and, in fact, are detrimental or dangerous to the well-being of the recruit or supporter. They also erect a different, separate set of values to counter the mainstream ones of the "enemy." Many have argued that suicide bombers are "undeterrable"[6] because they are committed to dying for a cause underpinned by values completely foreign to secular, Western society: values such as a desire to enter Paradise and enjoy the virgins who await them there; reclaiming the honor of their family that has been shamed by some transgression of the suicide recruit; or bringing prestige and material gain to their family by becoming a martyr (*shaheed*).[7]

Because the central message of terrorism, like that of deterrence, is also threat and intimidation, the only things that separate the deterrent model of punishment from state terrorism are the rule of law and the prerogatives of due process. It is these "rules" that confer legitimacy upon the exercise of threat and violence by state actors. When states begin to arrest anyone they don't like, and use trumped-up charges or show trials to intimidate the population, then the deterrent model of punishment slides into a reign of terror. The mantle of legitimacy conferred by due process and the rule of law is lost and the exercise of power is simply a function of brute force, much like that of the terrorist.[8] This is the great danger of using special laws, special powers of arrest and detention, interrogative techniques contrary to legal norms, and special regimes of imprisonment. It is also why terrorist propagandists try to paint counterterrorism efforts in their darkest form and why counterterrorism excesses play directly into their hands.

Another way in which deterrence and terrorism are similar is that the communicative process underlying deterrence can also be complicated by a multiplicity of audiences and constituencies. Special deterrence aims at the offender and discourages repeat offenses. But general deterrence aims at a wider audience, using the convicted offender as a means by which to convey what is permitted and not permitted, and how those who transgress the law will be dealt with. Just as terrorism has direct victims and targets of terror, attention, and demands, so does the deterrent approach in counterterrorism. This is true at the individual, group, and state level. In the case of the suicide bomber, for example, there are also the family and friends, the recruiter, the trainer, the financier, as well as possible state sponsors of the group that uses the suicide bomber as a weapon. Each one may share the same values and goals, but not necessarily. Deterrence can be directed at different parts of the suicide bomber's social and political network, depending on whom one is addressing. Some, such as the family, the recruiter, or the state sponsor, may be open to influence.[9]

In multicultural societies such as Canada and, increasingly, much of the Western world, there can be a multiplicity of laws and codes to which individuals pay allegiance. One analyst speaks of "legal pluralism,"[10] whereby conflicting codes, values, and even laws can compete for the loyalty of the same people. Terrorist groups, too, have to deal with this problem. Many recruits share loyalties not only to the group, but also to family, tribe, or mainstream society. Part of inculcating a new recruit into the values of the terrorist group can involve cutting off these competing ties of loyalty and affection. Immigrants to new countries have to learn to conform to the laws of that land and this sometimes means contradicting other laws or codes from the home country. The custom of female genital mutilation is a good example: it is commonly practiced in sub-Saharan Africa, as well as in Egypt and in Yemen, but is banned in most Western countries. In Egypt, the practice has been banned since 1996, but a 2005 survey found that 96 percent of respondents had been circumcised,[11] demonstrating how difficult it is to change entrenched traditions. Shariah law has become a major source of tension in Western societies, where Muslim minorities wishing to follow that system come into conflict with the dominant legal system. The practice of women wearing the veil or other face-covering has also become a point of contention, particularly in the UK, while the headscarf has been a continuing source of tension in France and Turkey.[12]

The communicative complex within which both terrorists and counterterrorists interact and co-evolve is a crucial variable in understanding how individuals and groups choose to resort to terrorism, to abandon it, or to refrain from using it in the first place in favor of other means of protest, advocacy, and dissent. It also helps to understand how states choose to use coercive means to control terrorism, such as criminal justice or counterinsurgency, to abandon their use, or to refrain from using these means in the first place in favor of other methods of control. The communicative similarity between terrorism and the criminal justice model of counterterrorism is one element of this. What about the war model?

Deterrence, preemption, and the war model

The war model of counterterrorism, the use of counterforce to incapacitate a perceived enemy, is less obviously communicative in nature, at least at first glance. However, if we consider the nature of deterrence in the nuclear arena, the concept of mutual assured destruction is essentially a communicative process. One side promises swift and massive retaliation (second strike) in the event of a first strike, and the credibility of this threat is what deters the other party from striking in the first place.[13] In this sense, then, an announced policy of "swift and effective retribution" can be seen to be another form of deterrence, based upon the exercise of military power, rather than the application of the law. During the 1980s and 1990s, the emphasis on preemption was in the context of retaliatory strikes on state sponsors of terrorism or terrorist training camps and safe havens (see chapter 2). By contrast, the second Bush Administration's doctrine of preemption is primarily promoted as an alternative to containment and deterrence in the areas of state support of terrorism and WMD proliferation, particularly by so-called "rogue states" (see box on p. 132). One of the doctrine's main proponents, former US Vice-President Dick Cheney, stated in 2003: "Weakness and drift and vacillation in the face of danger invite attacks. Strength and resolve and decisive action defeat attacks before they can arrive on our soil."[14] Here is the Manichaean argument for preemption: doing nothing versus doing something before it is too late. It suggests that the only effective form of prevention is a unilateral, military one and implies that legal deterrence is impossible, particularly if it depends on international cooperation: "The United States is committed to multilateral action wherever possible, yet this commitment does not require us to stop everything and neglect our own defense merely on the say-so of a single foreign government. Ultimately, America must be

> Given the goals of rogue states and terrorists, the United States can no longer solely rely on a reactive posture as we have in the past. The inability to deter a potential attacker, the immediacy of today's threats, and the magnitude of potential harm that could be caused by our adversaries' choice of weapons, do not permit that option. We cannot let our enemies strike first.
>
> We must be prepared to stop rogue states and their terrorist clients before they are able to threaten or use weapons of mass destruction against the United States and our allies and friends. Traditional concepts of deterrence will not work against a terrorist enemy whose avowed tactics are wanton destruction and the targeting of innocents; whose so-called soldiers seek martyrdom in death and whose most potent protection is statelessness.
>
> Extract from George W. Bush, "National Security Strategy Statement," issued on September 17, 2002.

in charge of her own national security."[15] The implication here is that international cooperation is hostage to the veto of any permanent Security Council Member and that the threat of disagreement in the international community is equivalent to doing nothing. Just as "[s]trength and resolve and decisive action" are the antidotes to "[w]eakness and drift and vacillation," so preemption and unilateral (decisive) action are the antidotes to the insurmountable obstacles facing the more traditional deterrent strategy embedded in international law and international cooperation.

Yet does such a black-and-white depiction of policy choices actually reflect reality? Is the alternative to military preemption necessarily weakness and drift and vacillation or stopping everything and neglecting to defend ourselves? Such a polarized, either-or, zero-sum view of things is both misleading and dangerous. Misleading because it suggests that military preemption is the only option available. In fact, research has shown that deterrence can work, especially in preventing terrorist groups from cooperating with one another. In the Philippines, for example, the Moro Islamic Liberation Front (MILF) was prevented from cooperating with other groups by "accommodating some of the group's political goals and then holding that accommodation at risk to prevent the MILF from cooperating with al-Qaida and Jemaah Islamiah."[16] Many groups have local concerns and do not necessarily gain by associating with more globally oriented groups, particularly if governments and their allies nuance their approach to tip the balance in favor of these local groups cooperating with them instead. In its 2006 National Strategy for Combating Terrorism, the US government has now recognized this, particularly in deterring terrorists from using WMD. One of six objectives to deal with WMD terrorism now deals explicitly with deterrence:

> A new deterrence calculus combines the need to deter terrorists and supporters from contemplating a WMD attack and, failing that, to dissuade them from actually conducting an attack. Traditional threats may not work because terrorists show a wanton disregard for the lives of innocents and in some cases for their own lives. We require a range of deterrence strategies that are tailored to the situation and the adversary. We will make clear that terrorists and those who aid or sponsor a WMD attack would face the prospect of an overwhelming response to any use of such weapons. We will seek to dissuade attacks by improving our ability to mitigate the effects of a terrorist attack involving WMD – to limit or prevent large-scale casualties, economic disruption, or panic. Finally, we will ensure that our capacity to determine the source of any attack is well-known, and that our determination to respond overwhelmingly to any attack is never in doubt.[17]

Either-or rhetoric about policy options is dangerous because it blinds us to possibly more fruitful ways of combating

terrorism that might have a better chance of avoiding the spi-
raling violence that military approaches engender. Just as
terrorist discourse and propaganda can blind followers and
recruits to alternative pathways and options, so counterterrorism discourse and propaganda can blind citizenries and
publics, as well as policy elites and the media, to alternative
means of countering the terrorist threat. Consider the case of
Israel, which has been faced with a serious terrorist problem
since before its inception as a nation-state. As a result of this
history, Israel has become a world leader in counterterrorism.[18] Its military and security forces have developed both the
technological expertise and the resolve to use coercion in a
wide variety of ways. One Israeli analyst describes some of the
techniques: "covert and overt gathering of intelligence, setting
up permanent and temporary roadblocks, surrounding cities
and imposing curfews, conducting house-to-house searches
for arms and suspects, and capturing and killing terrorists."[19]

In responding to the first Intifada, Israel used these methods,
as well as raiding Palestinian targets abroad, including PLO
headquarters in Tunis; the assessment: "Some of the raids were
decidedly brilliant, technically speaking. Still, overall, none of
them made much of a difference."[20] In summing up 85 years of
counterterrorism experience, this well-respected analyst concludes that the two most effective countermeasures were building security fences along the Lebanese border with Israel and
around the Gaza Strip, and measures by Jordan and Egypt to
stop terrorists from crossing into Israel. In other words, the
actions of neighboring states and physical target hardening
along one's perimeters were more effective than the use of force
and coercion. Israel's experience suggests that counterterrorism has to be linked not only with the exercise of violence, legitimate or otherwise, but also with the exercise of power across a
wide range of policy domains that include not only "hard
power" – intelligence, policing, and military power – but also

"soft power" – political, social, and economic control. Terrorism and counterterrorism are obviously closely related and are best studied and analyzed together, not in isolation from each other. One way to do this is to move beyond the legal and military variants of counterterrorism, whether coercive or persuasive, to look more broadly at how it can deal with the multiplicity of audiences and messages that are central to terrorist communication. This means a closer look at the propaganda dimension of counterterrorism.

The propaganda dimension of counterterrorism: winning hearts and minds

For democratic societies, terms such as "propaganda," "psychological warfare," "political warfare," "information warfare," or "perception management" tend, for very good reasons, to have a pejorative connotation, conjuring up images of Big Brother and the thought police of George Orwell's novel, *Nineteen Eighty-Four*. Terrorism conceived as "propaganda by the deed" highlights the communicative nature of the phenomenon, whereby the medium of violence and threat of violence allows the propagation of messages to specific audiences. Countering terrorism, then, must involve countering not only the violence and the threat, but also the messages that are communicated. Terrorists are not interested in their direct victims as much as they are in the effect of their victimization on various audiences. In this sense, terrorists are not fighting for physical territory but for the more ephemeral territory of emotions, ideas, beliefs, and perceptions – the hearts and minds of those watching and listening. If terrorism is a form of psychological warfare, then the propaganda dimension becomes an important element in counterterrorism as well. The goal is to effect attitudinal and behavioral change in particular target groups or audiences.

The typology that divides terrorists' audiences into direct victims, targets of terror, targets of attention, and targets of demands is one way of conceiving who these audiences are. However, some of these audiences contain vastly different kinds of people: for example, targets of attention include both terrorist and government constituencies. A better way to divide the audiences up is according to reference group: one's own and that of one's opponent. One's own reference group can be called "internal," while one's opponent's reference group can be called "external." For the terrorist, the internal reference group would include supporters, sympathizers, and potential recruits – all part of the targets of attention mentioned above. The external reference group would include targets of demands, targets of terror, and larger mass audiences who are also among the targets of attention. For the counterterrorist, the reference groups would be reversed. The external reference group would include terrorist groups and their supporters, sympathizers, potential recruits, and state sponsors. The internal reference group would include governments and bureaucracies, including those of allies, victims' groups, citizens and mass publics, both domestic and international, and the media.

Attitudinal and behavioral change can be conceived in two ways: the strengthening or the modification of existing beliefs, attitudes, and habits. Modifying undesirable beliefs, attitudes, and habits is the goal of offensive operations, since the goal is to change what people believe, think, or do. Strengthening desirable beliefs, attitudes, or habits is the goal of defensive operations, since the idea is to buttress existing belief systems and the attitudes and behaviors that stem from them against unwanted or undesirable beliefs and the attitudes and behaviors that derive in turn from them.

Combining the two variables of target or reference group and attitudinal or behavioral results, four different kinds of psychological operations (psyops) emerge (see figure 4.1):

	directed at terrorist's constituency	directed at counterterrorist's constituency
promote desired beliefs, attitudes, habits	offensive external psyops	offensive internal psyops
prevent undesired beliefs, attitudes, habits	defensive external psyops	defensive internal psyops

Figure 4.1   Four varieties of psychological operations (psyops), depending upon targeted constituencies and effect on beliefs, attitudes, habits

1. *offensive external psyops* aim to *promote* desired perceptions, images, opinions, attitudes, or habits among the members of the *terrorist's* organization or base of support;
2. *defensive external psyops* aim to *prevent* undesired perceptions, images, opinions, attitudes, or habits among the members of the *terrorist's* organization or base of support;
3. *offensive internal psyops* aim to *promote* desired perceptions, images, opinions, attitudes, or habits among members of the *counterterrorist's* organization or base of support;
4. *defensive internal psyops* aim to *prevent* undesired perceptions, images, opinions, attitudes, or habits among the members of the *counterterrorist's* organization or base of support.

When thinking of psychological operations, targeting one's opponents most often comes to mind and is typically what the literature focuses on. Addressing one's own constituencies is equally important, if often ignored. A discussion of these four categories of psyops will show how the more coercive forms of counterterrorism embodied in the criminal justice and war models can be complemented and perhaps even replaced by strategies and tactics that rely less on the State's monopoly on violence. All response options convey information of some sort to different audiences; they are expressive and symbolic as well as instrumental. Of course the particular messages that are actually received by a particular audience may not be what the sender intended to convey. This is part of the complexity inherent in countering terrorism and can lead to unintended consequences. That is why it is important to understand the different kinds of messages, audiences, and communicative pathways involved in the complex web of terrorist–counterterrorist interaction.

Offensive external psyops

Democratic governments can try to promote desired perceptions among individual members of terrorist organizations, their sympathizers, and their foreign supporters. One of the most important perceptions is the futility of terrorism. Terrorists expect a strong response from the governments they attack and a panic reaction from their constituencies. One game-theoretic analysis concludes that credible declarations by governments that they will immediately reconstruct any cultural monument or icon destroyed by terrorists will effectively discourage such attacks by altering terrorists' expectations.[21] Public demonstrations of resolve and solidarity, as occurred following the 2004 Madrid bombings, or a determination to carry on with daily life despite terrorism, as the British did following the 2005 London bombings or the Israelis do after every suicide attack, send the message that the terrorist strategy is not working.[22] Media coverage often plays up the violence and victimization of terrorist attacks, ignoring or downplaying their message.[23] This, too, undermines the terrorist strategy, which expects the media to give them a platform for their grievances. Similarly, if law enforcement successes, such as the arrest, conviction, and punishment of terrorists, are widely publicized, then the message that goes out to other terrorists and their supporters can be that the terrorist path is not worth pursuing. These messages can lead to demoralization and a decision to pursue other means to achieve their goals. For convicted terrorists, the same can be true. Once released, they may choose to seek other avenues for achieving their goals or abandon the struggle altogether. They can also serve as examples to their former comrades, showing that the path of violence is unproductive. In Indonesia, for example, a former member of Jemaah Islamiya, who trained the Bali bombers, is now cooperating in a deradicalization program in Indonesian prisons, which have become breeding grounds for Islamic militants. Working with the police, Nasir Abas visits imprisoned Islamist militants and talks to them about the futility of violence and choosing a better path to pursue their goals.[24]

One problem with this approach is that terrorist constituencies may not see the criminal justice process as fair or legitimate (see chapter 2). In this case, the criminal justice approach can exacerbate the perception of grievance and lead to greater acceptance of terrorism as the only recourse available, unless efforts are made to ensure fairness and to address wider grievances. The granting of amnesties to imprisoned terrorists who renounce violence and promise to pursue legal activities upon release has proved a useful way to bring extremists back into conventional politics. This worked very well in Italy, with its repentance laws, and helped to disband the Red Brigades.[25] In France, such an approach appeared to backfire in the case of the members of Action Directe, who were granted an amnesty by the government of François Mitterrand in 1981. In that case, the terrorist violence came back much stronger than before 1979, with a move from bombing to assassination. For the majority of prisoners, however, the strategy did work and they refrained from any more violence. The smaller core that persisted and escalated the violence made the government look bad, but their smaller numbers made them more vulnerable and they were all rearrested.[26]

Reform-minded governments can try to meet at least some of the grievances professed by terrorists and their constituencies, thereby conveying the message that terrorism is unnecessary to achieve certain goals. This can create internal dissension within or between terrorist groups over the proper course to take. In Spain, for example, certain government reforms in the past have led some separatist groups to abandon terrorism and to pursue a dialog with the government. The problem is that others may decide to continue the fight anyway, despite the accommodation. This happened in Northern Ireland in 1998, when the Real IRA launched a terrible bomb attack in Omagh, killing 29 people. In this case, it only increased efforts to find a peaceful solution to the conflict. Known divisions among terrorist groups or leaders can and should be exploited. The dispute between the late Abu Musab al-Zarqawi and Ayman al-Zawahiri over the former's targeting of Shiites in Iraq is an example.[27] Here, the key is to team up with respected Islamic leaders within one's own constituency and promote debate that counters terrorist interpretations of Islam. This can raise doubts within the terrorist's constituency by underlining the internal dispute and its implications for strategy, tactics, targets, or goals. The US military has used Sunni scholars in Iraq to promote pro-Coalition aims, such as participating in national elections.[28]

Attempts can also be made to create uncertainty, suspicion, internal dissension, and rivalry between terrorist groups where it does not already exist. As one group of scholars put it, "efforts must be made to reduce the structural integrity, coherence, morale, communication and cooperation within subnational terrorist groups."[29] Disinformation campaigns and black propaganda[30] can plant rumors of spies and informers, allegations of special treatment of officers and/or leaders, and offers of amnesty/incentive programs for terrorists who surrender. Leaking such rumors to the media as hard news or entering internet discussion groups to disseminate such information are two ways that this can be accomplished. Because clandestine organizations are difficult to reach directly, the greatest danger of such an approach is that the main targets of such operations become those groups that are easiest to find, namely radical organizations that may share the goals or ideology of terrorist groups but that do not engage in violence or terrorism. Offensive psyops explicitly directed at such organizations impinge upon democratic principles of freedom of expression and freedom from government interference. The distinction between terrorist operatives, supporters, and sympathizers can be a gray one, so it is often difficult to be sure exactly whom one is targeting. Another danger is that the divisions one creates between groups can backfire. This happened with Fatah and Hamas, where Israeli and US attempts to marginalize Fatah under Yassir Arafat created an opening for Hamas to fill the ensuing vacuum. When Hamas was elected democratically, Western moves to isolate the new government and to deny funding led to increasing conflict and near civil war between the two Palestinian factions. This further destabilized the region and undermined moderates who favored negotiations. When former US President Jimmy Carter met with Hamas officials in Cairo in April 2008, he was strongly criticized by the USA and Israel, but Carter defended his visit, arguing that dialogue with Hamas was essential. He also visited Syria and Israel.[31]

Psychological operations can also be directed at external publics that may possibly identify with or sympathize with terrorist groups. These would be the equivalent of the targets of attention in the typology of terrorist audiences presented above. For example, much more attention could be given to countering terrorist propaganda by answering their ideological writings in a serious way. Terrorist writings, whether of the political or religious persuasion, generally depict the world in black and white terms: one is either on the right side or on the wrong side, part of the solution or part of the problem, and there is no room for doubt, for compromise, or for a middle ground. Those who do opt for that middle ground are often targeted for special vilification. Mediators, moderates, and reform-minded officials are typical targets of terrorist groups. That is why peacekeepers were targeted in Bosnia, and the United Nations was targeted in Iraq. It is also why the UN continues to rank high on Al Qaeda's list of enemies[32] and why aid workers are targeted in Afghanistan by the Taliban.[33] In terrorist propaganda, the opponent is dehumanized and described as being evil beyond redemption. The creation of such an enemy image is important, for it gives the terrorist a moral license to kill those who stand in the way of progress, the revolution, the just cause, the will of some purported god.[34] For radical Islamists, this includes Muslim scholars who reject their narrow and violent interpretations of Islam. Bolstering and disseminating the position of moderate clerics or those who argue that killing innocents will not lead to Paradise is one possible way to counter this polarizing propaganda. The US government is now directing efforts at amplifying the voices of Islamic scholars who explicitly reject or contradict radical Islamist dogma. One example is a recent book by Abdul-Aziz el-Sherif, a top leader of the Egyptian movement Islamic Jihad, and a longtime associate of Al Qaeda's deputy leader, Ayman al-Zawahiri, that renounces violent jihad on religious and legal grounds.[35] That said, however, some have argued that Western interpretations of jihad tend to privilege minority views within Islam that promote spiritual interpretations of jihad over military ones (defensive jihad vs. offensive jihad), as do some Muslims attempting to present Islam in its most favorable light to Western readers.[36]

Terrorist beliefs, teachings, and worldviews should not go unanswered. While imprisoned terrorists or terrorist sympathizers can often be addressed directly, active terrorists in the underground can probably be reached indirectly via postings on the internet. The promulgation of hatred through religious sermons and fatwahs, school textbooks, and parental teaching can be countered by countersermons and counterfatwahs, altering school textbooks, and working with parents and children to foster cross-cultural and inter-ethnic understanding. One researcher analyzed the role of Palestinian school textbooks in promoting anti-Jewish, anti-Israel, and anti-Western sentiments.[37] The Oslo accords required Palestinian and Israeli textbooks to refrain from demonizing the other side. The issue of education has also arisen in the wake of the September 11 attacks, particularly in the context of charges that the Saudi-funded Madrassah schools throughout the Islamic world are breeding grounds for anti-Western and anti-American sentiment. Yet many parents send their children to religious schools because they are free and provide regular meals. Attempts to strengthen public education in these countries could provide an alternative that would foster more desirable values.[38] On the other hand, research has shown that many of the terrorists who launched the most significant anti-Western attacks in recent years were, in fact, college-educated rather than Madrassah graduates.[39] One further caveat is warranted, however. If democratic governments adopt a Manichaean, us vs. them attitude in their counterterrorism discourse, they risk falling into the rhetorical trap that terrorists set for them with their politics of atrocity. Alas, this is exactly what George W. Bush did when he stated that those who are not with us are with the terrorists. Of course, such rhetoric can have its uses (see below).

Defensive external psyops

This variation of psychological operations involves the prevention of undesired perceptions among terrorists and their constituency. Defensive external psyops can be directed to preventing specific beliefs that bind individual members to the terrorist group. Two of the most powerful ones are the idea that once violence has been committed, you cannot go back, and the idea that the group is the only place where a sense of identity, belonging, importance, or existential meaning can be achieved.

A common method for inducting individuals into the world of terrorism is to give new recruits small tasks to perform that are auxiliary to the main mission and typically do not involve the use of violence. Writing and delivering communiqués is one example of a seemingly innocuous task that still makes the individual feel they are making an important contribution to the struggle. In this way, individuals who are sympathetic to the cause and want to help out in some way are not immediately forced to confront their own consciences and their own feelings about violence and victimization. Many people who are attracted to extremist groups are seeking ineffable affective ties as much as they may be seeking instrumental political or cultural goals. They may be seeking a sense of purpose in life, a feeling of doing something important, of being involved in something socially, politically, or even existentially significant.[40] By feeling useful to the group and feeling that they are gradually accepted, these more emotional goals begin to be fulfilled. The new recruit begins to enjoy the *esprit de corps* and begins to feel that s/he belongs. At the same time, of course, they are being tested *by* the group – for their commitment, their particular skills, and their general usefulness to them.

Finally, they are asked to participate in the commission of violence. Once this threshold is crossed, the new member is told that there is no way back, that they will go to jail and that their friends and family will never forgive them for what they have done. In the case of suicide bombers, it can be the reverse: they are told that their families will be honored and rewarded with financial and other community support and privileges when they become martyrs. At this point, those who still may have doubts about the course they have taken commit themselves fully to the cause because they feel that exit is now impossible. Others, who have perhaps found for the first time that sense of belonging or meaning that they were seeking in the first place, accept whatever task they are given so as to maintain their emotional fulfillment.

Laws that provide reduced sentences for cooperation with authorities or that offer amnesty for renouncing violence, coupled with official statements, perhaps publicized through the media, that convey similar messages stating that exit from the group is always possible and that those who cooperate and who renounce the use of violence can be accepted back into society, could help to prevent certain individuals from remaining trapped in the self-contained world of the terrorist. Much as the rehabilitation model within criminal justice attempts to reintegrate offenders into society, so one counterterrorist strategy is to make it possible for ex-terrorists who renounce violence to re-enter society and the communities where they live.

A balance must be struck between the delegitimation of terrorism as a tool in political or cultural life, typical of offensive operations, and leaving open the door to those who wish to come back, typical of defensive operations. To this end, violence and coercion might not always be the best method of coping with terrorism. The more coercive and repressive methods might strengthen the terrorist organization and its hold over its members, since one of the main motivations for engaging in terrorism is revenge for previous attacks and perceived injustice. One member of the Al Aqsa Martyrs' Brigade, whose job it was to dispatch suicide bombers, described his charges as follows: they "are in too much pain to find another way to cope and become totally fixated on carrying out what they view as acts of community defense, expressions of pain and enacting justice in response to 'all that they have seen.' "[41]

Counterterrorist strategies might be directed, on the one hand, at preventing new recruits from joining terrorist organizations and, on the other, at facilitating the exit of older members from existing organizations. To achieve this, positive incentives have to be created so that the conflict can be carried on at a different level, beyond the zero-sum game of victory or defeat. Terrorists are not born. Nobody needs to die a terrorist. A dead terrorist is likely to become a martyr and an inspiration for further violence. This is the central strategy underlying the use of suicide bombers, who are often recruited when they are depressed or suicidal or livid with rage over some perceived injustice or atrocity perpetrated by the other side.[42] Part of defensive external psyops can aim to convince such people – and their families – that martyrdom does not bring its own reward, that they are being used by the terrorist group, and that continuing the struggle by other means can bring greater benefits than dying and killing. The rational image of human beings that underlies the deterrent model of punishment misses the complex range of psychological, cultural, social, and ideological pressures that human beings experience in social and political life. Psychological operations must try to deal with these complex variables. This also means addressing material and economic concerns, creating incentive structures for people to move away from embracing violence and terrorism.

Another way to prevent undesired perceptions among those sympathetic to the terrorist's cause is to engage in debate and dialogue with them.[43] The internet is an excellent medium for such attempts. In its Counterterrorism Communication Center, the US State Department, for example, has created a Digital Outreach Team of Arab-Americans who post comments on mainstream websites where Arabic-speaking people discuss politics and topics such as Iraq and the "war on terror."[44] While some responses to the American postings, which are open about where they come from, have been hostile, others have been quite positive. Many postings exhibit an eagerness to engage with the Americans. While the overall impact is very difficult to assess, such examples of public diplomacy, which targets foreign publics, constitute an important element of counterterrorism strategy. Mass media that enjoy a wide audience with terrorist constituencies or those who sympathize with their cause can also be useful. Al-Jazeera, the Qatar-based 24-hour news channel, is the most prominent example.[45] Giving interviews or presenting the Western position on relevant issues or events on such channels can provide an alternative perspective to the one usually disseminated.[46] When Al-Jazeera English began operations, most cable providers in the USA decided not to add it to their channel line-ups.[47] While this was done with the aim of preventing unwanted images and perspectives from being accessible to an American audience, an opportunity to engage in public diplomacy with those in the USA who might be sympathetic to the jihadi cause or even susceptible to radicalization was thereby lost.

Talking to one's enemies and their constituencies, though anathema to some governments, can serve an important function in challenging and perhaps refuting undesired perceptions whose very existence can be missed in the absence of dialogue and exchange of views. Cultural exchanges, scientific collaboration, international sporting events, and educational outreach to foreign students can all help to prevent undesirable perceptions over the longer term. Even those radical communities who provide a reliable base of support for radical movements and terrorist organizations can be addressed if their dynamics are properly understood. One researcher has shown that there are inherent limits to the support that such communities give.[48] Defensive external psyops can exploit the factors that underlie these limits to accelerate their being reached, for example by demonstrating to these communities that the terrorist organization does not necessarily act in their best interests, but has its own self-perpetuating agenda.

Offensive internal psyops

Offensive internal operations aim to promote desirable attitudes and behavior within one's own constituency to counter the many undesirable reactions that the threat of terrorism provokes. When fear is intense, people willingly sacrifice freedoms for (a sense of) security, rumors spread rapidly and often cannot be verified before they are taken as fact, many people feel an acute need to explain or understand what is happening and this all too often facilitates scapegoating and simplistic explanations. Feelings such as anger or a desire for revenge tend to be intense and seek an outlet. Public pressure on government to do something can also be intense, yet public expectations of what can be done are often unrealistic.

Manichaean pronouncements that "you're with us or with the terrorists" do not help very much, except to promote knee-jerk support for government action, no matter what. One research team has shown experimentally that reminders of death (technically called "mortality salience") and of the 9/11 attacks significantly increased college students' support for George W. Bush and his Iraq policies, as well as the likelihood of voting for him in the 2004 presidential election.[49] Playing on fear of terrorism and death may be a desirable option for opportunistic politicians, but it is clearly counterproductive in a democratic society. The same researchers have shown that support for extreme military solutions to countering terrorism, including preemptive war, and support for the Patriot Act, which impinges on certain freedoms in the interest of broader surveillance, were increased by reminders of death and of the 9/11 attacks, but only among politically conservative college students, not politically liberal ones.[50] This suggests that existential fear drives public support for coercive counterterrorism in a specific segment of the US electorate and that such support can be sustained by constant references to the 9/11 attacks. On the other hand, many people confuse legitimate armed resistance against repressive regimes and clandestine armed attacks by small groups on unarmed civilians in peaceful societies. Freedom fighters do sometimes use terrorism and this can undermine counterterrorism efforts in other contexts if condemnation of terrorism is not universal and double standards are employed. Confusion among the populace also arises when a democratic government uses nondemocratic methods abroad or at home, thereby losing moral superiority and legitimacy vis-à-vis the terrorists. Policies of collective punishment, destruction of homes of suspected terrorists, or targeted assassinations of terrorist leaders may be justified as effective means of combating terrorism, but they open the counterterrorist to charges of sliding into the exercise of state terrorism – of mirroring the terrorist they are fighting. Such practices can also fuel the desire for revenge and can therefore contribute to radicalization and recruitment to terrorist groups.

Democratic regimes of course are not perfect, nor should they be expected to be, especially when faced with persistent threats by intractable and intransigent opponents. By containing the official use of violence and repression within the rule of law, the criminal justice model attempts to maintain legitimacy even as it fights an implacable enemy. By retaining the war model as a means of last resort and by using it only in extreme cases and for a short period of time, according to the principles of just war theory, a government can maintain legitimacy even when using military force. When the war on terrorism is conceived and presented as unending, however, these principles are jeopardized. There is clearly a task to be done in educating the public about the difference between democratic values and terrorist values. But it is also imperative to be open and accountable and honest about the challenges that counterterrorism faces. In order to be credible, a sound human rights policy and a respect for the rule of law are essential points of departure.

An explicit policy to downplay the actual physical impact of terrorism while at the same time condemning the terrorism itself could help to promote the idea that terrorism is unacceptable in democratic society while at the same time minimizing the risk of public calls, fueled by insecurity and terror, for repressive measures that undermine the rule of law and individual rights. Since September 11, unfortunately, the exact opposite has occurred, especially in the USA and its global "war on terror." This is in part understandable, because of the magnitude of the September 11 attacks and the global reach of the threat. Yet it does seem that constant utterances by political authorities and government officials that another massive attack is inevitable simply fuel public anxiety and fear – and apathy stemming from a feeling of helplessness in the face of inevitable catastrophe. The result is that the rule of law and individual rights are increasingly whittled away in the name of increased security.

When terrorists actually do strike, there is a whole new set of parameters that come into play. The organizational needs of first responders can supplant the needs of victims or bereaved relatives and friends as preset disaster response and crisis management plans are put into action. This can fuel further feelings of anger, loss, desire for revenge, and resentment towards the government. Those agencies, such as law enforcement and the military, which are responsible for restoring order may clash with those, such as public health, social work, and other helping agencies, which are responsible for promoting recovery. The former often focus on the danger of further attack or the loss of control, conveying fear-centered messages which can contradict the hope-centered messages of help and recovery promoted by the latter. This clash can be exacerbated by the fear-centered agencies' directive, top-down approach to control, which often predominates over the facilitative, cooperative, and empowering approach of the hope-centered agencies.[51]

The media can amplify or mitigate all of these effects, depending upon the nature of the coverage.[52] If coverage reproduces official views, it may exacerbate public feelings of helplessness and despair or fear of further attack. If coverage is critical of government action, it may put the government on the defensive and trigger spirals of distrust, where authorities invoke the need for secrecy, and the media and the public call for openness and accountability. With its 24-hour news cycle, and the ability to report breaking news "as it happens," the media can sometimes drive public expectations and opinion, making people feel that the government should be on top of new developments at all times, ready to act within minutes of an emerging crisis. Sometimes called "the CNN effect," this can place an added strain on policymakers, who feel pressured to make quick decisions before all the facts are known.[53] The Al-Jazeera effect, whereby other perspectives than Western ones can permeate public consciousness during times of crisis, can also complicate the picture. The role of the internet and the prevalence of conspiracy theories and alternative viewpoints in public discourse make the communicative environment even more complex.[54]

The challenge for counterterrorism in such an environment is to promote and maintain public trust and confidence *before* any terrorist attack occurs. This can be accomplished by maintaining openness and accountability and promoting public knowledge about political affairs through information campaigns, parliamentary debate, and public consultations. Public education about the nature and extent of the terrorist threat, as well as the limits and feasibility of policy options, would help to promote public understanding after a terrorist attack, especially during the recovery phase. The media can serve as a vehicle for disseminating such information. Promoting public awareness without fueling insecurity, apathy, or intolerance and hate is an important part of offensive internal psyops. The amber, orange, and red alerts in the USA only seemed to induce the latter.[55] In 2003, when then US Fire Administrator David Paulison, and first Director of Homeland Security Tom Ridge, called on Americans to stock up on duct tape and plastic sheeting, they only triggered mass panic and hoarding behavior, not an awareness of the real nature of the threat of WMD terrorism.[56] When Mr. Ridge was asked about this in the media, he seemed amused by the public response, apparently oblivious to the fears and anxieties that his government's continual pronouncements and predictions of further and more dire attacks had created.

The availability of foreign all-news channels via satellite and the increasingly important role played by the internet and extremist websites in radicalizing immigrants and citizens in Western countries make the promotion of desired perceptions among one's own that much more important. Muslim youth, for example, must be given an alternative to the radical Salafist–jihadist perspective and made to feel that they have a place in Western society. They should not be automatically treated as potential terrorists or scapegoated by a politics of fear and loathing. Providing them with positive perspectives on Western life as an alternative to the dire visions promulgated on extremist websites can reinforce perceptions that terrorism is not the way to seek change or to achieve a sense of personal worth.

Other less recognized aspects of offensive internal psyops involve strengthening the public health, emergency response, and critical infrastructure protection sectors. This not only projects an image of security and preparedness, but promotes perceptions that the government is aware of the danger and doing something about it. If governments continue to predict the inevitability of biological, chemical, radiological, or nuclear attacks, they must help those professional sectors of their constituency most responsible for dealing with these threats. This includes a full and open discussion of cost issues and related budgetary and level-of-government implications. In the USA, elevated terror alerts risk being ignored by state governments simply because the cost of maintaining levels of vigilance required at higher levels for even short periods of time is prohibitive.[57] As the private sector becomes an increasingly important partner in counterterrorism and prevention, another crucial area is to promote transparency and accountability of private-sector partners. Most of the infrastructure in Western societies is owned by the private sector, so this is an essential part of a good counterterrorism strategy. The role of private contractors in abusing prisoners and in endangering citizens while protecting diplomatic convoys in Iraq underscores this.[58] Working with media to promote all of the above via guidelines and ongoing relations is a critical part of a comprehensive approach to promoting appropriate attitudes and behavior in one's own variegated constituency.

Defensive internal psyops

There are also defensive measures which a government can take to prevent undesired public perceptions. Terrorist attacks are in part symbolic, designed to demonstrate that terrorists are able to strike anywhere at any time, despite governments' superior strength and power. If the terrorist is viewed as strong and omnipresent, public calls to yield to terrorist demands can intensify. If the government stands firm and terrorist violence increases, such demands can intensify further if the public attributes the increased threat to the government's hard line. This seems to have happened in Spain, where the electorate turfed out the Aznar government in the wake of the horrific bombings in Madrid. Clearly, the majority of the population blamed the Aznar government and its support of the US war in Iraq for bringing Islamic terrorism to its shores. Conversely, the public might call for impossible or ill-advised responses from the government, such as a quick end to a hostage siege or a massive crackdown on dissidents, and a cautious government might then be perceived as being cowardly or vacillating. If, on the other hand, a government makes concessions, to prevent violence either immediately or in the future, it can be seen as weak. Such conflicting public perceptions can have a serious impact on public trust and confidence in government.

In order to establish a relationship of trust with the public, democratic governments must be willing to share more and more accurate information about terrorist organizations, their aims, and their capabilities. Only then can the public realistically assess what is possible and impossible for a government to do and what can be done by other sectors of society. This is why it is very dangerous to play politics with intelligence, as seems to have happened in the run-up to the Iraq War.[59] The media also play a central role in this relationship between government and its citizens, since public perceptions are shaped not so much by the terrorist's atrocities themselves as by the way in which the media report on them and on the government's reactions to them. As terrorism provokes a competition for allegiance – either to the terrorists or to the government – the media are in a key position to determine whether the population supports the government or acquiesces to the terrorists. It is unfortunate that some media outlets use their influence to try and skew the political agenda or to bang the drum of patriotism and denigrate democratic dissent. The *New York Times'* admission that it relied too much on unreliable sources and embedded reporters in the months preceding the Iraq War is but one example of how the media can distort the agenda-setting aspect of policymaking.[60] The use of unidentified sources has come under increasing scrutiny as a result.[61] Fox News has often been accused of providing a platform for US Administration doomsday predictions and stoking the fires of war fever, both in the run-up to the Iraq War and during the controversy over Iran's nuclear program. A 2003 study of American perceptions of the Iraq War found that "those who primarily watch Fox News are significantly more likely to have misperceptions, while those who primarily listen to NPR [National Public Radio] or watch PBS [Public Broadcasting System] are significantly less likely."[62]

The mass media, and increasingly the internet, are central players in the terrorism–counterterrorism relationship. Media coverage of terrorist events is fueled by two conflicting ideologies. On the one hand, the concept of newsworthiness leads the media to promulgate official perceptions of the terrorist event and to ignore alternative perspectives. On the other, the media play a watchdog role, criticizing government action and defending the public's right to know. A defensive strategy would therefore do well to address this contradiction by using the privileged access to the media enjoyed by the official perspective to inform the public of the nature and seriousness of the terrorist threat, without spin doctoring for political gain. This might prevent the kinds of panicky and contradictory perceptions that undermine public trust in government and fuel public demands for the quick fix or the impossible solution. On the other hand, officials must be prepared to allow the media to provide objective coverage of terrorist groups and their goals without knee-jerk accusations that the media are thereby legitimizing terrorism. There is a prevalent belief in government circles that truly balanced reporting – a feature of most media guidelines and codes of ethics, by the way – functions to legitimize the terrorist and his cause. Al-Jazeera has suffered the wrath of the US Administration for its coverage of Iraq, including having one of its reporters killed by US missile

fire.[63] Part of a defensive strategy aimed at one's own constituency would be to prevent the legitimation of terrorists and
terrorism from happening without resorting to censorship,
intimidation, or outright violence.

Defensive internal operations could also involve those
groups within society who share ethnic, cultural, or religious
characteristics with the terrorists and who, as a result, feel singled out by counterterrorist activities. Many Muslims in the
USA, Europe, Australia, and Canada feel threatened by the
increased security measures brought in after 9/11. Accusations
and concrete examples of racial profiling abound. Many
Armenians felt nervous during the wave of Armenian terrorism in the 1980s, fearing that they would be lumped in with
the terrorists. Many Chechens in Russia, Irish in England, or
Basques in Spain have feared the same. Communists in many
Latin American countries during the last century felt appre-
hensive about ongoing terrorist campaigns. Many fell victim
to state terrorism as the counterterrorist net widened to
include them. Immigrants, refugees, asylum-seekers, or diaspora communities can feel caught between recruitment and
fund-raising efforts by terrorist groups and their proxies and
intelligence efforts of security and police services, border officials, customs officers, and other control agents in their host
country. The very fact that such people often have a hyphen-
ated identity opens them to suspicions of divided loyalty or
expectations that they should support the terrorist cause.

After it was discovered that British citizens were behind
the 2005 London suicide bombings, the idea of "the enemy
within" increasingly worried lawmakers and decision-makers.
To assume that specific identifiable groups belong to the terrorist camp can function as a self-fulfilling prophecy, driving
alienated individuals into the terrorist fold. If they remain loyal
to their adopted country despite unfair treatment, then legal
redress is all the more imperative to dispel the notion that they

are second-class citizens or outsiders. Governments should encourage other actors within civil society to take a part in preventing undesired perceptions amongst their narrower constituencies. Community leaders within ethnic and religious minorities, as well as immigrant, refugee, and diaspora communities, can keep an eye out for problematic rumors, gossip, or opinions that are fueled by political or religious extremism and try to counter them.[64] In this way, scapegoating, intolerance of minorities, and a politics of fear and loathing can be prevented. Community policing that works with minority leaders and institutions can foster trust and cooperation and prevent suspicion of authority and alienation from the wider society.[65]

Defensive operations can inoculate a population against the fear-driven attitudes that terrorism seeks to provoke or undermine the base of support that terrorist organizations enjoy. Another approach is to focus more directly on the vulnerabilities which terrorists exploit to launch their attacks. Like defensive psyops, this kind of counterterrorism tries to reduce the likelihood of attacks happening in the first place and to lessen the impact of those attacks that do occur. This is the subject of the next chapter.

CHAPTER FIVE

Defensive counterterrorism

While terrorism can strike anywhere, at any time, it is not true that any particular attack is inevitable. It is possible to do some things to reduce the likelihood that an attack will occur in a certain place or at a certain time or in a specific context. Terrorists plan their attacks on the basis of what they are capable of and which opportunities are presented to them. It is not only a question of ideologically driven goals. Sometimes a preferred target is too difficult to reach or a desired tactic is technically unfeasible given the available resources, manpower, or knowledge. The previous chapter looked at ways to alter the perceptions and attitudes of the terrorists and their constituencies, as well as the constituencies of the counterterrorist – the citizens of countries threatened by terrorism. This chapter focuses on the kinds of measures that can be taken regardless of whether a terrorist group can be dissuaded from launching an attack and choosing a particular target for that attack. It is an approach that assumes the inevitability of some kind of terrorist attack and tries to prepare for it by affecting the variables that determine the nature of the attack and identity of its target. There are two basic approaches.

One approach is to minimize the risk of terrorist attack in certain places and at certain times. The principal way to achieve this is through making potential targets less attractive for attack. This is known as target hardening. Given the conservative nature of the terrorist arsenal, with its emphasis on bombings, assassinations, and armed attacks, target hardening has traditionally focused on important people (e.g. VIPs, govern-ment officials) and important places (e.g. government build-ings, military bases) at particular times (e.g. major sporting events, international summits, special anniversaries). As terrorism has become more global and the fear of "superterror-ism" such as CBRN or WMD terrorism has increased,[1] the focus has broadened significantly to include the protection of critical infrastructure. While opinions vary on what infrastruc-ture is critical, the areas of energy, transportation, industry, communications, banking, and urban living are widely recog-nized as key sectors that need to be considered. Another way to minimize the risk of terrorist attack is to closely monitor and regulate the flow of people, goods, and services. This involves a wide range of regulations and controls involving borders, cus-toms, trade, financial transactions, travel, immigration, and refugees and asylum-seekers.

The other approach to defend against terrorist attack is to mitigate the impact of attacks that are carried out. This is designed primarily to take the terror out of terrorism. There are many ways to achieve this, including emergency preparedness, contingency planning and gaming, crisis management, conse-quence management, civil defense, promoting and strengthen-ing citizen resilience, and understanding the social and psychological consequences of terrorist attack. Particularly relevant issues include the impact of terrorist threats on travel, consumer behavior, social cohesion, and citizens' trust in gov-ernment, especially in the case of WMD and CBRN threats. While the more coercive or offensive models of counterterror-ism examined in earlier chapters treat terrorism as a crime or an act of war, more defensive models treat terrorism differently. Two models that will be discussed in this chapter are the natu-ral disaster model and the public health model.

Defensive counterterrorism of this second sort places special emphasis on the first responders who are usually at the front lines when a terrorist attack is in progress or has just occurred. Because of this, it is the local dimension, and most particularly the city or urban center, that has become a central focus for emergency preparedness, crisis management, and contingency planning. Innovative approaches to coordinating national programs with local initiatives and developing best practices that can be shared internationally are being actively pursued, particularly in the EU. In the area of countering WMD or CBRN terrorism, it is increasingly recognized that epidemiological and public health approaches to early warning and detection, promoting public awareness through information campaigns, and inoculating citizens against the corrosive effects of fear and apprehension are central to mitigating the impact of mass-casualty terrorism. All counterterrorism efforts have a local dimension that cannot be divorced from broader initiatives at the national, regional, or international level. Just as all terrorism is ultimately local, so is counterterrorism.

Preventing attacks

Target hardening

One of the measures taken after the 9/11 attacks was the reinforcing of cockpit doors in airplanes. This was because the hijackers on that fateful day forced their way into cockpits, overpowered the pilot and copilot and took over the controls. Now, it would be much more difficult for future hijackers to do the same.[2] Another measure was the introduction of armed air marshals on selected flights, something that the Israeli national airline, El-Al, has been doing for a long time. These measures are examples of target hardening, where potential targets are structurally altered, reinforced, or protected in some way, to reduce the likelihood that they will be attacked or to make it more difficult for anyone to attack if they still choose to do so. In the 1950s and 1960s, family and friends could accompany air travelers to their gate and wave goodbye from balconies overlooking the tarmac as their loved ones boarded their planes in full sight. Those days are long gone, as passengers are segregated from other airport occupants for security checks and channeled to their waiting planes in special secure areas out of sight of everyone else in the airport terminal. The car bomb attack on Glasgow Airport's main terminal building in June 2007 was largely unsuccessful because airport entrances have been reinforced against possible bomb blasts with security posts in front of entrances. The jeep just could not get through. One witness reported that the jeep got jammed in the doorway: "They were obviously trying to get it farther inside the airport as the wheels were spinning and smoke was coming from them."[3] Similarly, embassies have been reinforced and, in the wake of the November 2003 truck bomb attacks against the British Consulate and HSBC Bank in Istanbul, personnel have been relocated away from front offices facing the street.

Target hardening can never prevent all terrorist attacks. Because terrorists learn from experience and innovate, they can always try to circumvent target-hardening efforts. Terrorists and counterterrorists play a cat-and-mouse game, where each countermove can trigger an adaptation designed to get past the barrier created by the new measure. In the airline industry, there have been many such moves and countermoves, particularly surrounding the use of explosives. In December 1994, Ramzi Yousef boarded Philippines Airlines Flight 434, assembled a bomb in the bathroom, planted it in the life jacket under his seat, disembarked at the end of the first leg of the flight, and the bomb exploded on the next leg, killing a Japanese businessman who sat in his seat. No other passengers were killed and the plane successfully made an emergency landing.[4] The batteries for the bomb had been in Yousef's shoes.[5] In December 2001, Richard Reid tried blowing up American Airlines Flight 63, en route from Paris to Miami, using plastic explosives hidden in the lining of his shoes, but was overpowered by passengers before he could light the fuse.[6] Now, many passengers must remove their shoes and have them screened separately.

A major shift occurred with the foiled plot in August 2006 involving liquid explosives which were to be carried onboard separately, disguised as personal care products such as shampoo, and mixed onboard to activate the explosive. While the initial response to the plot was to ban all liquids and gels from carry-on luggage, scientific tests on explosives subsequently determined that the size of the container was critical and so a new rule was developed. The specific rule – no container more than 100 ml (3 oz) and all containers in one 1-litre (1 quart) transparent bag per passenger – reflects the specific chemical requirements to successfully make the explosive onboard.[7]

A new concern is the use of remote-controlled toys. It was triggered in part by the discovery of an Arabic-language video on YouTube that was made by an Egyptian student at South Florida University showing how such toys could be used as detonators. The concern led to a policy of select searches of people carrying remote-controlled toys onto airplanes, including children, and the suggestion that passengers stow them in checked luggage rather than carry-on luggage.[8] The threat was deemed insufficiently precise and imminent to warrant banning these items in carry-on luggage completely. However, with each new innovation or potential plot, the day seems not too far away when carry-on luggage could be banned completely. What makes this eventuality unlikely, however, is the concern of the airline industry over the cost and the impact of security measures.

Many airlines, for example, do not impose the rules concerning liquids and gels in carry-on luggage on domestic travel within one country. These restrictions are typically imposed only on international flights. This leaves a potential loophole to be exploited by future terrorists. Ironically, this disconnect between international and domestic air travel security has happened before and is in a way responsible for making the 9/11 attacks possible. In 1996, TWA Flight 800 exploded in midair off Long Island, killing 230 people. In response, then President Bill Clinton created a Commission on Aviation Security and Safety, chaired by then Vice-President Al Gore. The title was quietly changed to "Commission on Aviation Safety and Security" when it was discovered that defective wiring, not terrorism, had brought the plane down. Nevertheless, the final report of the Commission, published in February 1997, made many recommendations to increase both safety and security against terrorist attack. Recommendations were made for both domestic and international travel, but the airlines in the USA balked at implementing many of them because of the cost or because the increased screening would mean fewer flights per hour. The Commission recommendations became fodder for political commentary and attacks on the Clinton Administration by neo-conservatives and right-wing media outlets.[9] Fiscal conservatives criticized the report on economic and cost-benefit grounds, arguing that the enhanced security was not actuarially justified by the number of lives potentially saved.[10] Several of the recommendations, such as full-match luggage screening, whereby all bags not matching an onboard passenger are searched manually, have not been instituted to this day due to aviation industry resistance. In retrospect, it is no coincidence that the 9/11 hijackings were all on domestic US flights, not international ones. In 2001, domestic US flights were softer targets than international flights. They probably still are today.[11]

The tendency of terrorists to shift their attacks to softer targets highlights the most obvious limit of target hardening: the problem of displacement or target substitution. If one target is made inaccessible, terrorists will simply turn to other more vulnerable targets. When metal detectors were installed in airports in the early 1970s, the incidence of hijackings fell precipitously, but other kinds of terrorist attacks increased.[12] Cruise ships and smaller aircraft were targeted, and other kinds of hostage-taking incidents increased. When embassies were better protected, attacks against embassy personnel increased when they were outside the protected compounds. Because of this displacement effect, some argue that target hardening is useless.[13] On the contrary, however, making certain preferred targets less vulnerable to attack forces terrorists to innovate and to find alternatives, tying up resources and planning. It also serves, quite simply, to deter attacks against obviously important targets and to channel potential terrorists towards less damaging or costly forms of attack. In the area of crime prevention, target hardening has been found to have a "diffusion of benefits" effect as well: when certain targets are hardened, such as frequently burglarized homes, all targets of that class (e.g. other homes in the area) are less likely to be targeted, even if they are not protected.[14] In the area of counterterrorism, this could mean, for example, that if some embassies are protected, attacks against embassies in general might decrease. Of course, there are limits to how much can be protected and this means that societies are always vulnerable in some way. Airline cargo is notoriously vulnerable, since screening of cargo has never matched the level of passenger baggage screening.[15] Nor has screening of airport workers with access to secure areas.[16] Ports, too, are particularly vulnerable because the level of screening of container shipments is ridiculously low: in the neighborhood of 2 percent of all shipments worldwide.[17] This is why target hardening can only be one part of a more comprehensive defensive strategy. It is also why governments should make other partners, such as shipping companies and airlines, share the responsibility – if not the cost – of increased screening and other security measures.

This idea of partnership was a central recommendation in the Final Report of the White House Commission on Aviation Safety and Security:

> Improvements in aviation security have been complicated because government and industry often found themselves at odds, unable to resolve disputes over financing, effectiveness, technology, and potential impacts on operations and pass- engers. Americans should not have to choose between enhanced security and efficient and affordable air travel. Both goals are achievable if the federal government, airlines, air- ports, aviation employees, local law enforcement agencies, and passengers work together to achieve them. Accordingly, the Commission recommends a new partnership that will marshal resources more effectively, and focus all parties on achieving the ultimate goal: enhancing the security of air travel for Americans.[18]

One Commission member, however, formally dissented from the Final Report because she felt that the recommendations were not specific enough and did not incorporate timetables to ensure clear benchmarks and accountability for delays or fail- ure to implement effective measures: "Without specifics, once again we will allow the airlines to lead and the government follow as to what is necessary to secure the flying public."[19] One example she mentioned was training of screeners at airports, where she felt the Commission did not recommend sufficient improvement:

> Currently, screeners typically receive 8 hr. of combined class room and on-the-job training. Most security screeners are minimum wage employees required to buy their uniforms and pay for parking daily. Airlines typically pay airplane clean- ers more than security screeners, hence a 200–400% employment turnover rate exists for security screeners. Security screeners are an integral part of an effective security

system. Security screeners must be selected and trained adequately, paid fairly and given the appropriate technology tools to do their job.[20]

The situation did not improve much after this criticism. A CNN in-depth report of aviation security after the 9/11 attacks revealed that:

> Between 1998 and 2001, the GAO [General Accounting Office], the investigative arm of Congress, published at least five reports critical of security at the nation's major airports, focusing on the low wages paid screeners, what it called inadequate training of security workers and the rapid turnover of screening personnel – an average of 126 percent a year in a study of 19 major airports.[21]

By contrast, screeners in Europe are paid higher wages and turnover rates are lower.[22] Despite objections by hardcore neoliberals in the Republican party, the US Federal government finally took over control of the airport surveillance industry in 2002 under a barrage of criticism directed against the private companies that had been responsible for passenger screening before the September attacks.[23] Within a few years, however, criticism was directed in turn at the Federal agency now responsible for passenger screening, the Transportation Security Administration, with claims that private companies in a few states, and in Europe and Israel, do much better.[24] The adequacy of screening continues to be a contentious issue.[25]

The dissenting Commissioner in 1997 lost her husband in the midair bombing of PanAm Flight 103 over Lockerbie, Scotland, in 1988, and was then president of a victims' lobby group representing families of those lost in that tragic attack. From her particular perspective, the Commission's attempt to balance the needs of the airline industry with the needs of security and safety simply struck her as unacceptable. This highlights the political, economic, and even psychological dimensions of the kinds of security measures central to defensive counterterrorism. The same nexus of problems surrounds the protection of critical infrastructure.

Critical infrastructure protection (CIP)

"Critical infrastructure" generally refers to physical and computer-based systems that are considered vital to the functioning of political, economic, or social life. Many of these systems are favored targets for terrorist attack, including infrastructure related to transport, energy, industry, and urbanization. Potential targets include hydroelectric and nuclear facilities, oil refineries, telecommunications, banks, airports, railways and bridges, and urban centers like shopping malls. Since the March 11, 2004 attacks in Madrid and the July 7, 2005 attacks in London, special attention has been paid to urban transport systems such as subways and buses. The oil industry has been a target in Nigeria and in post-war Iraq.[26] Even before September 11 and the heightened concern about chemical and biological attacks, security experts argued that the agricultural sector is particularly vulnerable to such attacks.[27] The forestry sector is another area where environmental activists have used sabotage to impede logging activities.[28] The box on p. 168 lists the ten sectors identified by the Canadian government as essential components of critical infrastructure. Though the major sectors are basically the same for other countries, lists can vary slightly. For example, the USA added national monuments and icons to its list in 2003.[29]

Media reports regularly "expose" security gaps in a wide spectrum of facilities, be they airports, trains, railyards, chemical plants, subways, the electrical grid, seaports, or nuclear facilities.[30] Add to this ever-growing list the threat of cyberattack on computer systems that control and regulate everything from banking and money transfers to emergency response and air traffic control, and the challenge of protecting all possible

Canada's national critical infrastructure is made up of ten sectors:

1. **energy and utilities** (e.g. electrical power, natural gas, oil production and transmission systems);
2. **communications and information technology** (e.g. telecommunications, broadcasting systems, software, hardware, and networks, including the internet);
3. **finance** (e.g. banking, securities, and investment);
4. **health care** (e.g. hospitals, health care and blood supply facilities, laboratories, and pharmaceuticals);
5. **food** (e.g. safety, distribution, agriculture, and food industry);
6. **water** (e.g. drinking water and wastewater management);
7. **transportation** (e.g. air, rail, marine, and surface);
8. **safety** (e.g. chemical, biological, radiological, and nuclear safety, hazardous materials, search and rescue, emergency services, and dams);
9. **government** (e.g. services, facilities, information networks, assets, and key national sites and monuments);
10. **manufacturing** (e.g. defense industrial base, chemical industry).

Source: Public Safety Canada website: www.publicsafety. gc.ca/prg/em/nciap/about-eng.aspx#01 (last accessed on August 6, 2008).

targets becomes daunting.[31] Because computer-based systems are increasingly integrated and interconnected, the danger of cascading shutdowns of major infrastructural systems is that much greater. The power blackout in the northeastern and midwestern USA and Ontario, Canada, in August 2003 demonstrated how widespread the impact of a cascading computer breakdown can be. By the end of the cascade, which took some four hours, 256 power plants were off-line.[32] In addition to power generation, the blackout affected water supply – triggering advisories in several cities to boil water – as well as transportation, communications, and industry.[33] While no cyberthreat has materialized in any major terrorist incident, cyberattacks in other contexts, such as ethnic strife and political conflict, have increased in recent times. The electronic communications system of the Estonian government, for example, was shut down temporarily in May 2007, allegedly by cyberattacks from Russia.[34] The national banking system was affected for a while. A 20-year-old Estonian student was convicted of taking part in the attack and fined.[35]

How can all these potential targets be protected at the same time? Who pays for such protection? How are priorities to be established if funds are not available to protect everything? Most of the infrastructure deemed critical by security analysts is in the hands of the private sector. Government regulation is often weak or nonexistent and industry resistance to any attempts to strengthen security can be intense. For example, everyone agrees that the chemical industry is vulnerable to terrorist attack. After 9/11, the industry brought in voluntary controls considered by security experts to be insufficient. Nevertheless, the Bush Administration supported industry self-regulation and did not intercede. Subsequent efforts to increase protection of chemical plants and to persuade plants situated near densely populated areas to use less dangerous chemicals met with mixed results: "The private companies that own 80 percent of the most dangerous targets have given varying degrees of cooperation, officials said, and the chemical industry has effectively blocked attempts in Washington to mandate stricter regulations."[36] This failure led the US Department of Homeland Security to call for more Federal regulation, contrary to the Bush Administration's preference for voluntary industry controls.[37] By 2006, legislation was before Congress, but security experts again argued that the controls were insufficient. Furthermore, the Federal legislation would have overridden more stringent state legislation, but this was reversed under pressure from states such as New Jersey.[38]

Like that of the airline industry, the case of the chemical industry underscores the jurisdictional and bureaucratic difficulties that tend to undermine effective infrastructure protection. Efforts to coordinate such programs have led to government restructuring and the creation of new mega-departments, such as the Department of Homeland Security (DHS) in the USA, which was formed out of 22 existing Federal agencies after the 9/11 attacks, the Centre for the Protection of National Infrastructure (CPNI) in the UK, or Public Safety Canada. The latter, created in 2003, coordinates the activities of Federal departments and agencies involved in safety and security issues, including policing, intelligence, corrections, border control, threat assessment, and emergency management. These Federal departments provide advice to industry, and work with provincial and municipal levels of government as well.[39] Allocation of funds for CIP and emergency preparedness has sometimes been politically controversial.[40] In the USA, for example, funds used to be distributed by region, regardless of the level of threat that each region faced. States with large metropolises, such as New York, Seattle, or Washington, received similar funding levels to rural areas with little population and few, if any, potential targets. After protests from various mayors and governors, funding was tied more closely to level of threat. Even with such risk-based funding, there were still complaints about inadequate funding from major urban centers such as New York and Washington.[41] States have also complained that guidelines for Federal counterterrorism grants are too rigid and ignore regional differences and local needs, as well as focusing too narrowly on terrorism, per se, rather than including other risks such as accidents, disasters, or violent crime.[42]

The need to protect critical infrastructure in the face of uncertain threats and certain vulnerabilities has created problems for neoliberal concerns such as fiscal discipline, government spending, and tax cuts. In the rush to prepare for the next attack, there have been examples of waste, misdirection of funds, inaccurate or inappropriate risk assessment, and even corruption. With so much money suddenly made available by anxious legislators intent on doing something, such lapses and errors are probably inevitable. One of the most important lessons for effective and adequate CIP, and one that goes against the grain for the diehard neoliberal, is the importance of maintaining some degree of redundancy in critical systems. This was highlighted in Canada by the SARS pandemic, which hit the country's largest city, Toronto, in April 2003. Hospitals with infected patients had to be quarantined. This meant that new patients with non-SARS-related conditions had to be directed elsewhere. One of the affected hospitals was Toronto's children's hospital, The Hospital for Sick Children. Since there were no other children's hospitals in Toronto, sick children were directed to the one in Ottawa, the Children's Hospital of Eastern Ontario (CHEO). At the time, CHEO's cardiac unit was slated for closure under a provincial plan to cut costs in the medical sector by eliminating perceived redundancies. The government changed hands in a provincial election several months later. The new government decided to keep CHEO's cardiac unit and it was never closed. While there was considerable opposition to the closure even before the SARS epidemic, the need for a second children's hospital during an unexpected health crisis must have been made clear to everyone.

Because not everything can be protected, the most important part of CIP is to develop comprehensive and realistic risk assessment and to share this information across government departments and agencies, across levels of government, and with stakeholders in the private sector, such as managers of buildings that are part of critical infrastructure. The key is to think like the terrorist to determine the modus operandi of particular types of attack. This helps to identify fruitful points of intervention where physical, structural, or procedural changes can be made that reduce the likelihood of attack. This approach is adapted from well-established techniques used in situational crime prevention and offers a fruitful way to out-smart the terrorist.[43] Traditional crime prevention tends to focus on policing and intelligence, as in the criminal justice model of counterterrorism. However, much more can be done in the area of situational crime prevention, which focuses on the patterns and contexts of specific criminal activity and then acts to thwart those activities or to make them harder to engage in successfully. Redesigning the environment, for example installing bullet-proof tellers' windows in banks, changing patterns of activity of potential targets (such as varying the travel routines of diplomats to reduce the likelihood of kidnapping or armed attacks), removing money from cash registers regularly so big sums are never available, and other quite simple things can reduce the likelihood of a crime, including terrorist attack, being committed. Many security professionals in the private sector are former police officers or military personnel. They bring a police or intelligence mentality to the question of pre-vention and preparedness and often lack an appreciation of other approaches.

"September 12 thinkers" often cite suicide bombing as the most "unpreventable" kind of terrorist attack, arguing that sui-cide bombers are undeterrable. Using the principles of situa-tional crime prevention, two criminologists have shown how even suicide bombing can be made less likely.[44] Using the case of Israel and the almost routine suicide bombings in public places such as cafes, nightclubs, and bus stops, they demon-strate how step-by-step analysis of the operational patterns used by terrorist groups to routinize suicide attacks can reveal significant points of intervention for preventive action. Of course, as mentioned in chapter 3 on proactive counterterrorism, this means focusing not just on the suicide bomber, whom these researchers liken – most appropriately – to a "smart bomb," but also on the broader network and context in which suicide attacks are planned and prepared. This includes the physical and human resources needed, such as safe houses, maps, explosives, and "handlers," as well as facilitating conditions, such as community support, money, internet access, and a network of trusted volunteers.[45] This complex and challenging example underscores how defensive measures such as CIP can benefit from approaches not traditionally associated with counterterrorism, such as situational crime prevention, disaster preparedness, and public health emergency response. More will be said about this below.

Regulating the flow of people, goods, and services
Another way to mitigate the risk of terrorist attack is to track the movement of people, goods, and services in an effort to discover plots in the making and thwart them or to impede their preparation. Chapter 3 already looked at how the regulation of banking and money transfers can impact on terrorist financing, which in turn can make the implementation of terrorist attacks more difficult. In this chapter, we are talking more about territorial control that includes border and passport control, customs and immigration, refugee determination, and the monitoring and regulation of the flow of people and goods in and out of a country, as well as within its borders. This form of control has become central to the global "war on terror" and chapter 3 has already examined the surveillance side of things from the perspective of the intelligence function in counterterrorism. The regulation of travel, migration, and asylum-seeking also highlights the divisions referred to in chapter 1, between developed and developing states, North and South,

and the core and periphery, whereby those kept out are often from the latter, while those keeping out are those in the former. More will be said about this aspect in the next chapter.

Terrorists need a lot of things in order to successfully mount attacks. They need food, shelter, training, weapons, explosives, safe houses, communications, travel documents such as passports or identity cards, money. When these are not available or difficult to acquire, the risk of terrorist attack drops. Why, for example, have there not been any terrorist attacks in the shopping malls that constitute the hallmark of Middle American life? A series of such attacks across the Midwest or simultaneous attacks in several states would surely have as great an impact as the 9/11 attacks. Security analysts have long gamed for such an eventuality and some even predict their inevitability. Yet no such attacks have occurred. The reason is that they require the terrorist to be resident in the communities where an attack is to take place, that they know all the ins and outs of the premises, that they can stake out the weaknesses in the security system and the pattern of use of the mall in question. You cannot plan such an attack from afar and just fly into the community to implement it. This is why such attacks have not occurred. American Muslims are generally well integrated into their communities and are better-off than the average American financially and in terms of education and employment.[46] Unlike in Europe, where Muslims tend to experience discrimination and are worse-off than the average European in terms of education and employment, Muslim-American communities have been a bulwark against the spread of radicalism in the USA.[47] Until such time as some homegrown young men become radicalized via the internet and decide to attack their own communities, as happened in the UK, such attacks in the USA will be the exception rather than the rule.

It is for the same reason that hostage-takings and barricaded situations are much easier to carry out than kidnappings. The latter require the same degree of infrastructure and community support as the mall bombings do. The former can be carried out by outsiders with no links to the community or on the spur of the moment, with little planning for afterwards. Hostage-takings are generally designed to gain publicity and to use negotiations as leverage to impose demands of a more tactical nature, rather than broad strategic or political ones. Kidnappings require safe houses, food and supplies for the hostage and guards, and security arrangements that usually involve people in the community. Clearly, an understanding of the logistical requirements of different types of terrorist attack can help inform preventive policy.

The movement and flow of people has become a central focus of counterterrorism policy. Immigrants and refugees are often the first people suspected of terrorist attacks, while foreign students have become suspect since the September 11 attacks, especially in light of the pre-9/11 failure of the upper levels of the American security establishment to heed an FBI agent's alert about Arab men studying at flight training schools.[48] The break-up in early May 2002 of a student fraud ring whereby stand-ins would take English-proficiency exams for foreign students so that the latter could extend their stay in the United States was cited by a US attorney as "part of an overall strategy of arresting potential terrorists before they could strike."[49] In the wake of the murder of Dutch film maker Theo van Gogh by an Islamic extremist in November 2004, Dutch society hardened its attitude towards immigrants and refugees. The Netherlands' traditional tolerance of and openness to outsiders reversed almost overnight.[50] Attitudes in the UK have also hardened and government anti-terrorist policy is coming closer to US policy in the areas of immigration, refugee and asylum policy, and deportation. Following the July 2005 bombings and attempted bombings, the British government sought to toughen its immigration and refugee laws, as well as allowing deportation of those who promote hatred and religious intolerance. In August of that year, British Home Secretary Charles Clarke announced new guidelines on grounds for deporting or excluding foreign-born nationals from the UK. The list included:

> writing, producing, publishing or distributing material, public speaking including preaching, running a website; or using a position of responsibility such as teacher, community or youth leader to express views which foment, justify or glorify terrorist violence in furtherance of particular beliefs; seek to provoke others to terrorist acts; foment other serious criminal activity or seek to provoke others to serious criminal acts; or foster hatred which might lead to inter-community violence in the UK.[51]

There have also been discussions of stripping naturalized Britons of their citizenship after it was revealed that the perpetrators of the July 7 bombings were British citizens and concern about "homegrown" terrorists intensified. In the UK, there is now a lot of pressure on the British Muslim community to police its own youth, its imams, and its mosques. In response, moderate leaders drafted a ten-point proposal designed to combat violent extremism and promote civic responsibility amongst British Muslims.[52]

Borders have always been a major focus of defensive counterterrorism. In North America, the concept of "perimeter defense" promulgated by the Americans has had a considerable impact on Canadian border controls, for example, including the surveillance of seaports, airports, and land routes. After 9/11, Canada–US cooperation on border control was formalized in a Canada–US Smart Border Declaration and a joint Thirty Point Action Plan.[53] There is an inherent tension between the need for stringent customs and border control and the promotion of free trade and free movement of goods and services across borders. Canada and the USA are each other's largest trading partners and they are part of a North American Free Trade Agreement with Mexico. On September 11, 2001, the long US–Canadian border was shut down to all cross-border traffic. The impact on the Canadian trucking industry was devastating. One unanticipated consequence of this is that the Canadian Truckers' Union is now one of the most avid supporters of biometric identification cards for cross-border traffic. In the debate over balancing security with privacy, the truckers have come down on the security side because it will allow them to continue their economic activity despite stringent border security. Similarly, many business travelers are opting for biometric or fingerprint scanning at airports in order to benefit from fast-tracking through security. By consenting to providing biometric and other personal information to a database, such travelers do not have to wait in long lines or be subjected to physical searches. Machine-readable passports are fast becoming the norm and the use of biometric chips seems not too far off either. Passports, like money, are full of special features to reduce the likelihood of counterfeiting and they are continually evolving in an effort to keep ahead of the counterfeiters.

In Europe, the development of "Fortress Europe" that followed the inauguration of the Schengen and Maastricht Treaties has only intensified since September 11, 2001. In Pakistan, the porousness of the Afghanistan–Pakistan border has become a contentious issue in the global "war on terror" and has resulted in the Pakistani state at times allowing American troops to participate in joint operations in the Northwest "tribal zone" of Pakistan to hunt down Taliban and Al Qaeda fighters. This, in turn, has created domestic political problems for the Pakistani government.[54] In Iraq, there are similar concerns about porous borders with Syria and Jordan that help to fuel the persistent insurgency there. In Israel, separation barriers have been built next to the Gaza Strip and in the West Bank, ostensibly to prevent suicide bombers from infiltrating into Israeli territory. It is generally agreed that the barriers have indeed been effective in reducing the incidence of suicide attacks within Israel, sometimes to zero (see chapter 4). The West Bank Barrier remains controversial, as its route sometimes goes deep into Palestinian territory. Many critics feel that it represents a unilateral attempt by Israel to fix the future borders of a Palestinian state to Israel's advantage and it has been declared illegal by the International Court of Justice in The Hague.[55] The most famous historical example of building security walls to keep out invaders is the Great Wall of China. The most infamous example of a wall built to prevent people from leaving a country is the Berlin Wall.

In the area of tracking material that terrorists use in their attacks, such as weapons or explosives, the example of semtex is illustrative of the kinds of things that can be done, as well as the problems that can arise. Semtex is a form of plastic explosive widely used for demolition. For many years, it was almost impossible to detect and was often used by terrorists. The explosive that brought down PanAm Flight 103, for example, used semtex. After this attack, the inventor of the explosive, Czech scientist Stanislav Brebera, added metal components and a distinct odour to make it easier to detect. The problem is that there are large stockpiles of the nondetectable form and thefts from industrial sites are quite common. The Communist government of what was then Czechoslovakia provided large amounts to Libya, Syria, North Korea, Iraq, and Iran. While the current government of the Czech Republic strictly monitors all sales, there have been cases where companies in need of cash have illegally sold weapons to former customers in North Korea, Iraq, and the former Yugoslavia.[56] Volatile organic componds, known as "taggants," are often added to explosives to make them more easily detectable. Dimethyldinitrobutane (DMDNB), for example, is commonly used in the USA and is easily detected by sniffer dogs and by ion mobility spectrometers.[57] In many airports now, passengers are randomly selected and asked to submit to a test for explosives in their carry-on luggage and on their person. If they refuse, they are not allowed to board the plane.

The example of semtex highlights some of the major obstacles to effective control of trade and traffic in weapons, explosives, and other materials favored by terrorists. Lenin said that capitalists would compete with themselves to sell him the rope with which he would hang them all. While all states agree that the proliferation of weapons must be controlled and, in some cases, curtailed, many states profit from manufacturing, exporting, or trading such weapons. As a result, they contribute to proliferation even as they try to control it. This is certainly true in the area of small arms and their use in civil wars and insurgencies, particularly on the African continent, but also in the nuclear and chemical area. Many Western nations sell arms and military technology, only to have them used against them in unconventional "new" wars. Over 1,000 Stinger anti-aircraft missiles were provided by the CIA to *mujahadeen* fighting the Soviets in Afghanistan and, though most of them were reclaimed after the Soviets left, around 300 were not. The CIA then tried to covertly buy back the outstanding Stingers from demobilized *mujahadeen,* but some definitely fell into unsavory hands.[58] Similar concerns surround the export of powerful computers and civilian satellite systems. Many developing countries desire nuclear technology in order to boost their economic development and self-sufficiency, yet the fear is that they are also building up nuclear weapons programs in an effort to deter Western threats to their security. This is the dual-use problem mentioned in chapter 1. Add to this the role of the private sector and its profit-driven modus operandi, and the control of arms traffic and weapons proliferation is made all the more difficult. Illegal arms sales, weapons smuggling, theft of poorly guarded materials, corruption, and collusion to break sanctions or to circumvent tracking and monitoring efforts, or simply seeking profit at the expense of considering the impact of sales on future security, all constitute persistent impediments to reducing the likelihood that dangerous goods fall into terrorist hands. Terrorist groups often engage in auxiliary criminal activity to support their terrorist activities and the possibility that they could cooperate with transnational criminal organizations to procure weaponry or other materiel has long been a concern.[59]

Regulating the flow of people, goods, and services is fraught with other kinds of problems involving privacy rights, the dangers of selective profiling, infringement of human rights, and the creation of a surveillance society akin to that of George Orwell's *Nineteen Eighty-Four*. Many of these issues have been explored in chapter 3. Reducing the likelihood of terrorist attack is possible, but total prevention is not, unless we sacrifice all our freedoms and become closed, totalitarian societies. A comprehensive approach to defensive counterterrorism must therefore also consider how to lessen the impact of terrorist attacks that do succeed.

Mitigating attacks

An Al Qaeda strategy document, dated September 2004, includes the following injunction: "Force the enemy to guard every building, train station, and street in order to plant fear in their hearts and convince Muslims to join and die as martyrs instead of dying as infidels."[60] Clearly, if nations were to try and guard every possible target and protect all infrastructure considered critical to the government and the economy, they would either go bankrupt or create a perpetual crisis atmosphere of hypervigilance, paranoia, and, ultimately, terror. This is obviously part of the terrorist strategy, since a population in constant fear is one that is open to all kinds of panicky solutions that would sooner or later play into the terrorists' hands.[61] As suggested by the Al Qaeda document, one way to play into their hands would be to alienate Muslims at home or abroad, convincing them to take the jihadist path in response to perceived injustice, violence, or discrimination. Chapter 4 showed how preventing undesired perceptions in the counterterrorist's own communities is an essential part of defensive psyops. When faced with uncertain threats and certain vulnerabilities, strong emotions such as fear, hate, anger, and desperation for a quick fix can drive people to demand unrealistic things from their governments or to believe the worst about their neighbors and fellow citizens. When terrorist attacks occur, a crisis atmosphere can quickly develop and escalate out of control if the authorities do not take appropriate care to manage the response properly and to communicate in an open and accountable manner. By expecting the unexpected and developing contingency plans well in advance that can be applied before, during, and after a terrorist attack, crisis managers can be prepared when terrorists do strike. The best way to do this is to create an infrastructure that can respond efficiently and effectively to a whole range of threats, terrorist or otherwise, and to continually train and fine-tune the coordination and interoperability of the different components. This basic approach can take a variety of forms.

The natural disaster model of counterterrorism
Moshe Dayan, Israeli minister of defense from 1967 to 1974, suggested that "terrorist incidents more closely resemble natural disasters than acts of war."[62] This observation underlies one of the basic approaches to responding to terrorist crises. The idea is that a terrorist attack contains many of the same elements that any natural disaster might present to the crisis

manager: dead and wounded people; damaged or destroyed buildings and infrastructure; uncertainty about what may happen next; people fleeing in panic or rushing to the scene to help; an urgent need for rescue workers, ambulances, transportation routes to hospitals, hospital care, medicines, food, water, or other supplies; and intense media coverage that may interfere with rescue operations or create pressure on crisis managers and other authorities. Because many crises do share a lot of these features, it is possible to plan for some of the basic needs that will arise when disaster strikes. Contingency plans can be made, chains of command and communication networks can be established, supplies can be stockpiled, and strategies for dealing with victims, their families, and the media can be developed. In particular, first responders, such as police, fire departments, and medical rescue workers, can be trained and prepared for what to expect, how to deal with various situations, and how to coordinate with other institutional responders and different levels of government.

Good emergency preparedness and crisis management generally require the creation of a central command center that is separate from political control and acts independently to manage the crisis and to advise or inform the local authorities and other levels of government, as well as the media. It also coordinates the activities of first responders, such as rescue services and fire brigades. Each new disaster serves as an opportunity for testing out ideas and developing new ones, for increasing expertise, and learning about new problems or constraints. In the area of earthquakes, for example, many countries now have experienced teams who help out when disaster strikes anywhere in the world. The same is true for firefighting, especially forest fires and oil well fires. More and more, it is true for responding to terrorist attacks as well, especially in the area of forensics. For example, British experts went to Pakistan to help in the investigation of former Prime

Minister Benazir Bhutto's assassination.[63] With the increased concern over mass-casualty terrorism, new efforts are being made to address the special needs of cities.[64] One EU project, "Cities Against Terrorism (CAT): Training Local Representatives in Facing Terrorism," has focused on the urban environment and the threat that terrorism or natural and technical disasters might pose for large events such as sports world cups, competitions, fairs, or mass concerts: in short, crises that involve the "mass accumulation of hurt persons (MAHP)."[65] Because of the changing nature of the threat, such as multiple bomb attacks in different places, serial bombs in the same place, or biological or chemical attack, it has been recognized that certain kinds of experience were lacking:

> The lack of experience is evident when it comes to the problem of self-endangerment of the task forces through explosives, biological, chemical weapons or in case of special injury samples, e.g. amputations, and with the specific characteristic of posttraumatic stress disorder of victims and rescuers alike. Other problems occur in cases with several deployment scenes, destroyed infrastructures, communication and blocked traffic routes.[66]

The public health model of counterterrorism

Because much terrorism, and particularly mass-casualty terrorism, has an impact on public health and the psychological well-being of citizens, another approach is to look at defensive counterterrorism from the perspective of trauma, disease, and health. Concerns about WMD and CBRN terrorism, as well as the general threat of pandemics, pre-date the 9/11 attacks. The mailing of anthrax-laced letters to several American news media offices and two Democratic senators in September 2001, which killed 5 and infected 17 others, intensified the concern.[67] The controversy over the health effects of the 9/11 attacks and the increasing frequency of Ground-Zero-related respiratory illness in a wide variety of first responders, clean-up crews, and area residents has also increased awareness about the wider health implications of mass terrorist attacks.[68] As a result, public health, environmental safety, and local emergency preparedness have all been incorporated into defensive counterterrorism.[69]

Biological or chemical terrorism presents particular challenges for emergency response and crisis management.[70] The first is the problem of determining whether an attack has actually occurred. Most supposed attacks turn out to be hoaxes. In a real attack, the onset of symptoms can be delayed and so it may not even be clear that an attack has taken place until a large number of people are sick. Even then, the cause may be an epidemic, as in the case of SARS, which was spread unwittingly through travel from an infected area in China. For this reason, epidemiological expertise has become a central part of a public health approach to countering CBRN terrorism. Special focus is placed on how to differentiate a CBRN attack from other causes of disease and epidemics. Emphasis is also placed on developing methods to protect first responders from getting infected, decontamination and quarantine procedures, and how to communicate with a frightened population desperate to avoid becoming infected themselves. Much has been learned from historical experiences with epidemics and how different communities have responded.[71] The economic aspects of preparing for CBRN terrorism have led to debates about the wisdom of various options, such as stockpiling of vaccines or mass vaccinations.[72] Many developed countries, for example, are stockpiling smallpox vaccine, as well as flu vaccine, while developing countries are left out in the cold.[73] In the USA, the military and first responders in the health sector, such as hospitals, have been vaccinated against anthrax and/or smallpox, sometimes against the will of individuals.[74] Military personnel who refused vaccinations were punished or court-martialed.[75] The smallpox vaccination program failed because many first responders refused to be vaccinated out of fear of dangerous side-effects.[76]

One government initiative within the Canadian Department of Defence gives an example of the kinds of sophisticated responses to the CBRN threat that are being developed. The CBRNE Research and Technology Initiative (CRTI)[77] was formed in May 2002 to form linkages with science and technology communities in order to increase knowledge about and preparedness for CBRNE threats (the "E" stands for "explosives"). The program coordinates efforts among federal, provincial, and municipal jurisdictions and the private sector to develop or strengthen capabilities for dealing with complex events, be they terrorist attacks, major disasters, or complex emergencies, no matter where they originate. Priorities include capability management, risk assessment and priority setting, explosives (threats and capabilities), emergency casualty management and treatment for CBRNE events, public confidence and sociobehavioral issues, criminal and national security investigation capabilities, food safety, and emerging innovative CBRNE science and technology. This list of priorities highlights the complexity of both the threat and the response and makes it clear that it is no longer sufficient to focus merely on one kind of threat. Again, it relates to creating redundancy – not only in critical infrastructure, but also in the capacity to respond, including those institutions that are central to emergency preparedness and response. Strengthening public health systems, for example, would create an infrastructure that can respond efficiently and effectively to a whole range of threats, whether a disease like SARS, an industrial accident, an environmental disaster, or an intentional release of a pathogen or explosion of a radiological, chemical, or biological device.

Social and psychological defense: citizen resilience
Another way to mitigate the impact of a terrorist attack is to prepare people ahead of time and to strengthen their capacity to cope with the stress, anxiety, and fear that particular kinds of terrorist attack provoke. The terror in terrorism is most directly felt by those who fear terrorist attack themselves because of specific threats or because they belong to the same category as past victims. In the case of indiscriminate, mass terrorism, the terror is much more widespread. Add to that the power of television and the internet to bring images from far away into our homes, constantly barraging us with reports of terror strikes from around the world, and the psychological impact of terrorism can be quite invasive and pervasive. Doomsday predictions of new and frightening attacks can spread the terror even further. Chronic anxiety and stress about the threat of terrorism can be a serious problem in societies geared to expect that an attack is imminent or inevitable. It can even increase the risk of cardiovascular disease.[78] Research on coping behavior during war, imprisonment, torture, and other life-threatening conditions has shown that people vary in the way they cope with stress and trauma. Lessons learned from these contexts can also be applied to terrorism.[79]

Interest in social and psychological defenses and the development of citizen resilience in the face of terrorist threats has increased greatly in recent years.[80] For example, a sister agency of the Canadian CRTI mentioned above, The Centre for Security Science (CSS), works with academia, agencies, and volunteer associations in the development of psychosocial research aimed at increasing the preparedness and resilience of Canadians towards terrorism, emergencies, and crises. In June 2005, a Dutch organization, Impact, began an EU-funded project entitled "Citizens and Resilience: The Balance between Awareness and Fear." Building on expertise from psychiatrists, psychosocial care workers, trauma specialists, and terrorism experts, the program developed a common approach that could be used in all EU countries for increasing citizen resilience in the face of terrorist threats. The three main products of the program were a public information campaign on resilience, a special intervention for primary school children, and the development of strategies for community-based interventions to promote collective resilience and recovery.[81] Figure 5.1 depicts a small pamphlet created by Impact that can be carried on one's person, entitled "Terrorism: How to Move On." It summarizes advice for the general population, for parents, for professionals, and also for professionals working with ethnic minorities. The latter is particularly important in multicultural societies, where the danger of scapegoating and demonization of those who share ethnic, cultural, or religious characteristics with terrorist perpetrators can be intense.

An integrated defensive model: prevention/mitigation, preparedness, response, recovery

Many countries and institutions have adopted what is known as an "all-hazards" or "all-risks" approach to defensive counterterrorism. This is in recognition of the fact that the same basic parameters of prevention and mitigation, preparedness, response, and recovery are shared by a wide variety of risks or threats, be they terrorism, floods, fires, earthquakes, pandemics, industrial accidents, or riots. In practical terms, this means that it can be more cost effective to prepare for a wide spectrum of risks.[82] Lighting of corridors or entrances and exits, for example, can reduce the likelihood of criminal activity or terrorist attack, but it may also mitigate the impact of any emergency by facilitating evacuation, say in the case of fire, a chemical spill, or a terrorist bombing. When the unexpected happens, a contingency plan is in place that can deal with the

terrorism
how to move on...

advice for parents	advice for professionals
Reactions from parents to situations strongly influence the behaviour and feeling of children	People have a natural instinct for survival which makes them strong and resilient
do • Go on with your normal daily activities • Keep things calm • Be honest about the situation • Adjust information to suit your children's age • Switch off the TV and do something with your children	**do** • Normalise reactions • Foster social support • Monitor groups at risk • Look after yourself **do not** • Offer single session debriefing • Medicalise needlessly
www.impact-kenniscentrum.nl	www.impact-kenniscentrum.nl

terrorism
how to move on...

terrorism
how to move on...

advice for professionals working with ethnic minorities	general advice
do • Actively offer psycho-social care • Act as normal as possible, as culture-specific as necessary • Pay attention to language problems • Have eye for culture-specific (mourning) rituals • Connect to key figures **do not** • Discriminate • Stereotype	**do** • Seek out other people • Look after yourself (rest, drinks, food) • Split big problems up into little clear bits • Ask for help if you need it **do not** • Watch news bulletins all day • Take your feelings out on the people around you • Suppress your feelings and stay on your own • Over-indulge in alcohol and drugs
www.impact-kenniscentrum.nl	www.impact-kenniscentrum.nl

Figure 5.1 Terrorism: how to move on

most common kinds of things that need to be done. Local managers and first responders on the scene can then innovate and adapt the basic plan according to the particular kind of threat being faced. The all-hazards approach also facilitates training, since gaming and desktop simulation exercises for senior management can address a wide range of risks and threats in order to highlight commonalities and identify differences. The all-hazards approach is also uniquely suited to assessing and preparing for the long-term impact of terrorist attack and the trauma that derives from it. This is because there are not only health effects, such as post-traumatic stress or long-term exposure to pathogens or toxic substances, but also economic, social, cultural, political, and environmental effects that can play out and evolve over a long period of time.

It can be argued that terrorism is not suited to an all-hazards approach because of its man-made origin, the element of terror or fear, and the criminal nature of the actual attack, which necessitates the gathering of forensic evidence. It is true that the criminal nature of terrorist attacks imposes specific demands on response and recovery. These include the legal and forensic requirements of criminal investigation, such as protecting evidence at the scene, interviewing witnesses, and guarding suspected perpetrators who survive while they are treated. Victims of terrorism also need special handling that may differ somewhat from victims of other kinds of trauma. Yet terrorist attacks contain elements that do overlap with other kinds of threats or emergencies. As such, preparing for terrorism can benefit from other kinds of preparedness, and vice versa. The Israeli practice of response and recovery after suicide bombings is designed in part to normalize the scene of the attack as quickly as possible, by routinizing the response and clean-up as much as possible. This performs a double function. First, it professionalizes response and recovery to a challenging kind of terrorism. Second, it deprives suicide bombing of its particularly pernicious impact precisely by treating it as just another kind of disaster. A third benefit is that this particular response capability can easily be applied to other kinds of emergency.

In defensive counterterrorism, the greatest challenge is to maintain a balance between overreaction and fear-mongering and underreaction and blindness to threats and dangers. Isolated events, such as an individual terrorist attack, can have a much wider scope than initially expected, impacting far beyond the original source of the event. These broader repercussions can be quite intense, moving very rapidly through systems and subsystems, and they can have quite long durations, lasting as long as several years. One analyst calls these kinds of crises "cascades."[83] Cascading crises can be triggered not only by actual events, such as a terrorist attack, but also by discourse, such as policy statements, threat prediction, or even a political cartoon. The Danish cartoons that depicted Muhammed, for example, were published in late 2006, but protests erupted only in early 2007.[84] After a lull, the controversy reemerged in early 2008 after Danish newspapers republished one of the cartoons on February 13 in response to the arrest by Danish police of three suspects accused of plotting to kill the man who drew the cartoon – an image of the prophet with his turban in the shape of a bomb with a lit fuse.[85] In March, an audio message purportedly from Osama bin Laden was posted on the internet. In it, bin Laden threatened the EU over the Danish cartoon controversy.[86] In April, Danish embassies in Afghanistan and Algeria were evacuated and staff moved to secret locations in response to terror threats related to the cartoons.[87] This example demonstrates how cascades can persist over years and take on a life of their own.

The challenge is to avoid snowballing crises and triggering public reactions or institutional responses that can become problems in themselves, looping back to create chains of action and reaction that escalate and spread quickly and uncontrollably. The best way for governments to deal with such complex kinds of crisis is the "all-hazards approach." In terms of government structure and response capability, the term "system-of-systems" best captures the complexity of what is required: an ability to respond to large-scale, cross-disciplinary problems with multiple, heterogeneous, distributed systems that are embedded in networks at multiple levels and across multiple domains. Table 5.1 provides one example of how a government's defensive counterterrorism requirements can be conceived of in terms of mission, functions, tasks, capabilities, and technologies.

If the public understands the limitations within which crisis management must operate *before* a terrorist attack occurs, then public trust can be maintained despite the constraints that a crisis inevitably imposes on government openness and accountability, and even in the face of emergency measures that suspend the rule of law in certain areas. On the other hand, in an era of deficit reduction and cost-cutting, publics who vote for governments promising tax cuts, deregulation, and privatization should be educated in the consequences these trends may hold for public safety and security. If those agencies and companies that take over government responsibilities are less publicly accountable or less subject to legal controls, and if profitability and the interests of stockholders take precedence over the public interest, people should not be surprised when governments have little control over the prevention of future terrorist attacks. The real key to effective counterterrorism is to complement defensive measures with broader, strategic measures that take a long view and address the wider structural context in which terrorism incubates, develops, and evolves. This is the subject of the next chapter.

Table 5.1 A System-of-systems approach to counterterrorism capability management

The proposed table of functions below serves as a "checklist" for a balanced assessment of mission requirements, as well as a guide to the capability analysis process.

Functional groups	Sub-functional groups
Planning and management	Contingency plans Processes and procedures Management Policies Liaison and coordination Equipment and technical standards Lessons learned and after-action reporting
Surveillance and situation awareness	Surveillance Forensics Common operating picture
Information management	Data fusion Information exchange – multi-agency Data integration and correlation Data warehousing
Communications	Communications – multi-agency Public information and awareness Telecommunications and IT support Incident response communications system
Detection and identification	Potential threat detection Detection of illicit access Detection of hazardous materials
Positioning and localization of threats	Hazardous material localization Hazardous material control Hazardous material transport and storage Hazardous material disposal
Incident response	Protection – first responders Protection – general population Incident investigation Search and rescue
Public care	Medical care and prophylaxis distribution Mass care Fatalities Long-term care
Incident command	Incident resource management Emergency operations center
Site restoration	Site clean-up Site remediation Disposal of materials

Table 5.1 (cont.)

Functional groups	Sub-functional groups
Training, education, and exercises	Training, exercises, and simulation Education – hazardous materials Education – behavioral and physiological
Assessment and modeling	Integrated risk assessment Vulnerability assessment Threat forecasting and prediction Incident hazard assessment

Source: adapted from *CRTI – Call For Proposals: Guidebook For Fiscal Year 2007– 2008* (Ottawa: Defence Research and Development Canada, 2007), Annex A: Specific CRTI Investment Priority Areas, p. 32, available at www.css.drdc-rddc.gc.ca/crti/proj-prop/call-appel/2007_crti_guide-eng.pdf (last accessed on August 6, 2008).

CHAPTER SIX

Long-term counterterrorism

The previous chapters make it clear that there is no quick fix to the problem of terrorism. Coercive strategies can take individual terrorists out of circulation or even lead to the demise of particular terrorist groups. But they can produce backlash and fuel resentment among target populations, creating new grievances and facilitating recruitment to new or reinvigorated causes. Much of the "war on terror" has led to the erosion of the rule of law, the civil liberties of citizens, and their trust in government. The reliance on proactive strategies such as pre-emption has played a major role in this trend. The unintended consequence has been to make it more difficult to pursue persuasive strategies that might reduce the necessity of coercive ones in the first place. Despite this, persuasive strategies hold out hope for changing hearts and minds, but they require persistence and a sensitivity to other perspectives that is difficult to promote or to sustain in the face of uncertainty and the seductive power of fear and loathing. As for defensive strategies, the problems of target displacement, cost, and jurisdictional conflict all make it very difficult to achieve optimum results in preventing terrorist attack. Reducing the impact of those attacks which do succeed can help in the short run, during a terrorist crisis, but achieving the goal of building resilience and taking the terror out of terrorism takes time and requires policymakers and decision-makers to desist from exploiting the fear of terrorism for political or budgetary purposes. Building trust and assuring accountability can pay dividends, but these can always be washed away by the next election, when the slate is wiped clean and a new administration brings in its own priorities and practices. Institutional memory and bureaucratic procedures are designed to ensure continuity, but can often be ignored by incoming leadership. This is, in part, what happened when the second Bush Administration took over from the Clinton Administration in January 2001. The threat of Al Qaeda slipped down the policy agenda, despite dire warnings from the intelligence and national security communities.[1]

Just as policymakers tend to fight the last war, so they tend to focus on the past attack, the immediate threat, or the most feared doomsday prediction. This limits not only their policy options, but also their imagination. This chapter focuses on initiatives that do not hold out promise for quick returns on the investment of time, money, resources, manpower, or training that long-term counterterrorism demands. Their impact is not immediate, but develops over time. Combating terrorism over an extended period requires thinking outside the box and keeping an eye out for the new development, the new point of friction, the new twist in the prevailing pattern. "September 12 thinkers" have certainly tried to do this, arguing that we are in a "long war" against a new form of global terrorism. The problem is that they have created a new box – the "new terrorism." They miss the point that there are many terrorisms and many contexts in which they occur. They miss the trees for the forest, ignoring local variation, internal dissension, and completely unrelated threats. Salafist–jihadist terrorism may be the flavor of the moment, but it will not always dominate the policy agenda, despite the alarmist rhetoric that continues to prevail in some circles; and then what? "September 10 thinkers" on the whole recognize this, stressing the need to understand the root causes of terrorism so as to be able to construct policies with lasting impact across many contexts and situations.

While they usually point to structural problems such as endemic poverty and injustice or the persistent gap between rich and poor, they tend to attribute terrorism to one favored "root cause" to the exclusion of all others. As such, they, too, create their own boxes.

Some terrorist movements last decades, others centuries. Some are very localized, others have a global reach. One analyst suggests four waves, beginning in the late nineteenth century with the Russian anarchists.[2] Yet tactics that we associate with terrorism date back much further than that. Hostage-taking, for example, was a central part of building alliances: monarchs would "host" each others' offspring to "underwrite" the alliance and forestall unexpected betrayal or surprise attacks.[3] Arranged marriages performed a similar function – until romanticism injected individual choice into the equation and fathers' diplomatic alliances were trumped by "true love." The Jewish Zealots in the first century AD used terror tactics against the Roman Empire. The Muslim Assassins who used stealth and surprise to kill their victims began their reign of terror in the ninth century AD and persisted into the eleventh century.[4] Causal links between "root causes" and terrorist behavior are not usually linear or unidimensional, nor are they stable over place or time. For this reason, to develop meaningful counterterrorism policies over the long term, it is important to combine levels of analysis and try to address the complexity of the environment in which terrorism develops and evolves. This brings us back to the complex security environment described in chapter 1.

Terrorism and root causes

In June 2003, an international panel of leading terrorism experts met in Oslo, Norway, to discuss the root causes of terrorism. Their main conclusions serve as a state-of-the-art consensus on the question of root causes.[5] The panel generally agreed that poverty, state sponsorship, religion (and in particular Islam), and psychopathology (or a specific terrorist personality) were not root causes of terrorism, including suicide terrorism.[6] Distinguishing between "preconditions" and "precipitants," the panel concluded that "terrorism is better understood as emerging from a process of interaction between different parties, than as a mechanical cause-and-effect relationship."[7] This is consistent with the definition of terrorism offered in the Introduction. Since terrorism is defined as a communicative tool of coercive persuasion, causation really is about what factors play a role in driving some individual, group, or organization to adopt this particular tool rather than others. What are often assumed to be causes, for example, poverty, alienation, personality, discrimination, ideology, are usually either facilitating factors (preconditions), which are usually structural, or triggering factors (precipitants), which are usually ideational in that they involve interpretations of an event, situation, or conflict. It is these interpretations that are then used to mobilize and recruit people to adopt terrorist violence. Here, ideological justifications, legitimation processes, ways of perceiving and thinking, all come into play. Radicalization, mobilization, and recruitment processes become central to understanding how the terrorist option comes to be seen as the appropriate tool for achieving particular goals and how it is justified to those who are recruited and trained to carry it out.[8]

Viewed in this way, causation is not a linear, one-way path from cause to effect, but a nonlinear relationship that involves feedback and interaction over space and time between agency and structure. This interactive process includes the formation and maintenance of allegiances, the institutionalization of means of collective action and advocacy, the legitimation of such means, and the attempts to marshal support for one side and to discredit the other side. Terrorists can be considered to be free agents and rational actors who decide whether and when to adopt violence to achieve their goals, but they are also determined to some degree by structural variables that constrain their freedom of action and direct them along certain paths and not others. For example, democratization does not necessarily reduce the likelihood of terrorism, since people can choose a violent path despite the existence of nonviolent options, as Iraq, Palestine, and Lebanon have shown. However, the availability of other options, usually institutionalized in some way, may make it less likely that such a path will be pursued. Extreme poverty may preclude terrorism as a viable option for those struggling to maintain the bare essentials of existence, but others may choose the terrorist path as a means of mobilization and recruitment in their name. Motivations of individual actors may change during the lifetime of a particular conflict and the structure of the conflict may also change over time as the context evolves.[9] It is important to understand the relationship between micro variables, such as individual choice, motivation, career trajectories, and life history, and macro variables, such as organizational, social, economic, or political structure, and to identify important structural variables that may constrain or facilitate movement towards or away from terrorism and mass violence.

When we enter the realm of "root causes," we must therefore confront these more structural factors that can create a suitable climate for the promotion and use of terrorism by ideologues and zealots. Poverty, personality, or structural inequalities do not lead inexorably to terrorism. The majority of poor people are not terrorists; there is no terrorist personality; and the gap between the rich and poor, the haves and the have-nots, is not, in and of itself, a necessary precondition for terrorism. Addressing the root causes of terrorism involves understanding the processes of alienation, radicalization, glorification and justification of violence, and the creation of enemies deserving of terrorism and violence. While chapter 4 looked at this from the perspective of communications, ideology, and propaganda, this chapter will examine these issues from a more structural point of view. Because structural factors usually change and evolve very slowly, action taken now may not have a clear and discernible impact until much later. Short-term successes can evolve into long-term failures, and vice versa. Interventions can have unintended consequences and doomsday scenarios that become the basis of policy can become self-fulfilling prophecies. "September 10 thinking" tends to recognize the importance of root causes of terrorism, but this has often led to sterile debates about the definition of terrorism, and how one man's terrorist is another man's freedom fighter. Largely because of this, "September 12 thinking" shows little patience with such discussions and tends to brush aside the issue of root causes and to focus on what can be done now. This chapter tries to move beyond these two positions by focusing on long-term strategies that can make choosing pathways to terrorism more difficult and less attractive.

Development, resource utilization, trade, and aid

Trade, foreign aid, and development projects can play an important role in counterterrorism efforts aimed at undercutting the ideological fuel that drives terrorist radicalization and recruitment in a world of haves and have-nots. Left-wing terrorism in Western democracies has often revolved around issues of exploitation, anti-capitalism, workers' rights, and class conflict – issues that are part and parcel of ideological critiques of the increasing commodification of resources, the free-market system, the consumer society, and globalization. Radical Islamists also see Western consumerism and other aspects of Western culture as a sign of moral decay.[10] The commodification of resources opens up the possibility of their being over-exploited, leading to irreversible depletion or environmental degradation. This has led to conflict between aboriginal peoples, who use resources for their basic survival needs and in the context of longstanding cultural traditions, and non-natives, who use resources primarily for economic purposes. The Zapatista rebellion in Mexico was triggered by the Mexican government's suspension of land reform and redistribution in the wake of the North American Free Trade Agreement (NAFTA) with the United States and Canada.[11] In the Amazon rainforests of Brazil, natives fight to protect their way of life from loggers who use intimidation and violence, even against government agents, to continue their illegal activities.[12] The development and utilization of resources in one state by multinational enterprises can also lead to violent conflict, as with Shell in Nigeria.[13] Western dependency on fossil fuels, such as oil, has led to complex policy problems aimed at reducing such dependency. One analyst argues that the Bush Administration's National Energy Policy is doomed to failure and will only increase dependency on unstable suppliers in dangerous parts of the world, increasing the risk of US military involvement and resulting in continuing threats to American security.[14] Policies such as the development of biofuels, which depend on grains such as wheat and corn, have led to food shortages and the rapid rise in food prices, triggering hunger, riots, and hoarding in poor countries and an escalating conflict between developed and developing nations.[15] The spread of the McDonald's restaurant chain to many countries, both developed and developing, has sometimes spawned violent attacks or protests related, in part, to the broader anti-globalization movement.[16] The settler movement in Israel shows how land policy can fuel radicalization and terrorism in defense of those whose land is expropriated. Many national separatist movements have emerged in the context of longstanding economic, social, and infrastructural inequities between two ethnic groups sharing a common territory, such as the Catholics and Protestants in Northern Ireland, the Basques and Spanish in Spain, and the Kurds and Turks in Southeastern Turkey. The continuing conflict in Sudan is in part a struggle between two different lifestyles: nomadic herders and sedentary farmers. The genocidal violence is a tool in a longstanding struggle over land and resources, as much as between two different cultures (see chapter 1).

All these examples show how development issues and resource utilization can have social and political repercussions that go far beyond purely economic concerns, and how violence can become part of the equation. In developing counterterrorism policy, issues such as land distribution and reform, environmental management, market regulation, and commodity markets should therefore complement the more territorially based issues of border control, customs and immigration, and refugee and migration flows that were examined in chapter 5. Such issues have become increasingly important ideological motors in areas such as WMD proliferation, anti-globalization movements, environmental activism and protest, and anti-Western, anti-capitalist, and religious fundamentalist movements.

There have been signs that Western states do recognize the importance of more long-term solutions in the fight against terrorism that address the structural inequities that divide rich nations and poor ones. The G8 summit in Kananaskis, Canada, in June 2002, for example, pledged to reduce debt for the most heavily indebted poor countries, though to a much lesser extent than those countries had requested, and focused in particular on development in Africa. The next G8 summit in France also focused on Africa. At the G8 summit at Gleneagles, Scotland, in July 2005, debt was indeed cancelled for the most heavily indebted poor countries. In March 2002,

US President Bush announced a $5 billion increase in foreign aid to poor countries, though he made this increased aid conditional on recipient countries "improving their governance, rule of law, social safety nets, investment climates and anticorruption practices."[17] This list of conditions highlights the complexity of development and aid projects and the many variables that can impede effective implementation.

The promotion of free trade has also been suggested as a means of countering the inequities and resentments that fuel sympathy and support for Al Qaeda's terrorist activities, particularly in the Muslim and Arab world.[18] This approach is consistent with the thesis that trading states tend not to go to war with each other.[19] Free trade agreements could be a valuable tool in a global counterterrorism strategy if they are promoted in a way that accommodates the concerns of developing states as well as developed ones. Unfortunately, this is not always the case. One analyst suggests, for example, that economic competition has driven developed states to cut costs in the area of social protection so as to be more competitive in the global market.[20] This trend has led to resistance by developing countries to the establishment of global rules on social clauses in free trade agreements. Western demands for such rules are seen as a disguised form of economic protectionism that would undermine the competitive advantage provided in part by lower wages and weaker labor standards.[21]

In the fight against terrorism, similar contradictions and conflicts have arisen in areas such as free trade agreements, tariffs and subsidies, and the regulation of international financial flows. It has been argued, for example, that Central American countries only joined the US "war on terror" because of ongoing negotiations surrounding the Central American Free Trade Agreement (CAFTA), as well as bilateral migration agreements, particularly with Honduras and El Salvador, that allowed those countries' citizens to work in the

USA and send their pay home. According to the Stockholm International Peace Research Institute (SIPRI), "these remittances are the most important source of capital flows for Central America, and for Latin America in general."[22]

In a world characterized by economic and communicative interdependence, the argument has been made that military conquest for territorial gain is unwarranted or increasingly counterproductive, since gaining territory is not a prerequisite for benefiting from globalization. A central question in an era of proliferating free trade agreements is whether trading states can create security regimes that cross the divide between core and periphery, North and South, and developed and developing states. One analyst argues that there are cultural differences in the socioeconomies of more and less developed countries that create unintended consequences when trade occurs between them.

> [C]omparatively speaking, individuals in the developing world are more likely to be economically dependent on in-groups integrated with reciprocity; individuals in the developed world are more likely to be economically dependent on strangers in a society integrated with contracts. These distinctive economic conditions form routines and habits that promote distinctive political habits. Social integration with contracts promotes respect for individual choice, the equal rights of strangers, and religious and cultural tolerance – the norms that stabilize the liberal democratic state. Social integration with reciprocity promotes acceptance of in-group beliefs and values, loyalty to in-group leaders, and distrust of outsiders – the norms that support authoritarianism and sectarianism.[23]

Because "freer trade between the developed and developing world can hurt the local economy and worsen the conditions of the urban jobless – increasing the dependence of millions on extremist in-groups who blame the foreigners for their conditions,"[24] the unintended consequence of free trade can be to strengthen the influence of extremist groups and increase the likelihood of their using terrorism and directing it against Western targets.

Identity politics can lead to a proliferation (and persistence) of irredentist claims on ethnically similar enclaves in neighboring states – a trend that could further impede or counter the spread of free trade and economic interdependence. The constitutional impasse in post-war Iraq during the summer of 2005 and the persistent danger that Iraq will splinter into three ethnically defined autonomous regions underscore the inherent artificiality of many post-colonial states, especially in the Middle East and Africa. Most of the current conflicts in today's world center around ethnic or tribal claims for autonomy within arbitrarily defined borders or merging with contiguous groups situated in neighboring states. One analyst has demonstrated how the civil wars that stem from such conflicts have been prolonged in large part because of the infusion of foreign aid and weapons from the international community.[25] Another analyst has argued that NGOs, as well as donor states, are often coopted by violent groups since they can only bring in and deliver aid by cooperating with such groups.[26] Because of these complexities, state making and capacity building in weak and failed states have become significant challenges in the development of long-term counterterrorism strategies.

The EU, in particular, has tried to focus more on the African continent as a whole, in the belief that promoting development there will in the long run impede the growth of failed states that become breeding grounds for terrorism, organized crime, and other transnational threats, such as pandemics or mass migration flows. Failed states can become terrorist havens or conduits for terrorist acquisition of WMD. They can also generate spillover of terrorism and violent conflict into neighboring states or into the integrated network of international trade, commerce, tourism, and travel that is characteristic of our globalizing world. Pakistan, with its confluence of Islamic extremism and violence, political turmoil, lawless frontiers, nuclear weapons, and increasing influence of Al Qaeda, is currently a hot spot for such concerns. One Pakistani observer argues that the resurgence of the Taliban and Al Qaeda in Pakistan's Northwest Frontier Province is the direct result of the failure to make nation-building a central part of the "war on terror."[27] The integration of development and foreign aid into counterterrorism strategies is all the more imperative when an important ally in the war looks increasingly like a failed state with rogue elements. The EU strongly endorses this approach and is intimately involved in reaching out to other countries as a central part of its contribution to the international coalition against terrorism.[28]

At the 2002 EU summit in Seville, Spain, for example, the EU declared that it would focus on political dialogue with third countries in the fight against terrorism, as well as on nonproliferation and arms control; provide technical assistance to third countries in order to reinforce the capacity to respond effectively to the international threat of terrorism; and include anti-terrorism clauses in EU agreements with third countries.[29] In consultation with the United Nations Counter-Terrorism Committee, the EU selected Indonesia, Pakistan, and the Philippines as priority countries for technical assistance and began assessment missions at the end of 2002 and the beginning of 2003. Anti-terrorism clauses were included in agreements with Chile, Algeria, Egypt, and Lebanon by the end of the 2003 EU summit in Thessaloniki, Greece, while the EU completed threat assessments for 9 regions and 55 countries. Providing assistance and expertise to other regional organizations, such as the OSCE, ASEAN, ASEM,[30] and the African Union, has been another key priority. According to one analyst, "This . . . helps to lock a growing number of countries into an international counter-terrorism regime of laws, technical requirements, and training assistance."[31]

One analyst who has looked more closely at the relationship between weak and failed states and the organization of terrorist activities has concluded that a clear causal relationship does not exist. He suggests that terrorist activity is most likely to occur in contested states, with some state capacity, rather than weak or failed states. He argues that

> State-building assistance should therefore remain a part of the development assistance sector rather than counter-terrorism or terrorist prevention. Where international state-building is a potentially effective counter-terrorism policy is in states – such as Thailand, Afghanistan, and the Philippines – where governments are genuinely engaged in counter-terrorism, where there is an obvious terrorist threat, but a lack of state capacity hinders counter-terrorism.[32]

Clearly, attempts to infuse counterterrorism strategies with development and aid initiatives are fraught with difficulties. Over and above the problems of funding, political will on the part of developed countries, and the unintended consequences of aid programs noted above, there are the perennial problems in developing countries of waste, mismanagement, corruption, and the dominance of military over social spending. For example, of $10 billion in US aid to Pakistan since 2002, less than 10 percent went to education, health, and democracy promotion, while the bulk of the rest went to the military.[33] Then there are the suspicions that Western largesse is merely a disguised form of imperialism. Problems can also arise when international agencies publish research in an attempt to raise consciousness about existing inequities and how to remedy them. When the first Arab Human Development Report came out in 2003, the response among some Arab commentators was extremely negative:

The report, the first of its kind, was practically an exercise in advertising the Arab dirty laundry around the world, for all to see, and then used by various parties as they saw it fit. In effect, it was used to further humiliate Arabs, confirm their backwardness and support the argument that reform of the Arab world from within is not possible, and that external intervention is not only justified but also a condition for change.[34]

While the report was conducted in the previous year and provided data for 2002, it came out when the USA and its allies were invading and occupying Iraq and justifying this as a means of bringing democracy to Iraq and reordering the Middle East. Clearly, the Iraq intervention made it easier for some to see any attempt to address problems in Arab societies as part of the same strategy. This highlights how long-term initiatives aimed at redressing structural problems can be undermined by coercive, short-term campaigns such as military interventions.

Those called on to implement aid and development programs can also become terrorist targets themselves. Events in post-war Iraq have shown how aid agencies and their workers can become terrorist victims. The most notorious attack was the August 2003 bombing of UN headquarters in Baghdad, which killed 22 people, including top UN envoy, Sergio Vieira de Mello.[35] Aid workers have been targets of attacks or kidnappings in Afghanistan and Somalia as well. Attacks on aid workers and contractors involved in reconstruction aim to dissuade international agencies from getting involved. Yet the very fact that they are targeted suggests that terrorists recognize their value in undermining the appeal of terrorism. A related danger is in the area of intelligence gathering. Intelligence agencies can either infiltrate aid or humanitarian organizations themselves or recruit informers to collect intelligence for them in areas where state agencies fear to tread. Using humanitarian intervention to serve the needs of military intelligence in complex emergencies can undermine their acceptance by local populations and compromise their effectiveness. This link between humanitarian aid and intelligence gathering – perceived, suspected, or real – has become an issue in several areas other than Iraq, such as Afghanistan and the Aceh province of Indonesia, especially after the December 2004 tsunami.[36]

Anti-immigration sentiment in Europe could also be addressed by working to improve conditions in those countries from which economic migrants flow. Some in the anti-immigrant camp have even argued as such, suggesting that helping developing countries would reduce the incentive for migration to developed countries. A strategy to raise the standard of living in impoverished countries would certainly have long-term benefits not just for citizens in those countries, but globally as well. But with the demographic realities of developed countries, where the graying of the population means a lack of young workers to provide a tax base for social benefits, immigration will always be necessary. Developed countries that subsidize their own farmers and industries and place tariffs on agricultural or manufactured products from Africa only perpetuate the inequities that aid programs attempt to address. When the EU buys fishing rights from corrupt West African governments anxious for cash and European trawlers then overfish African waters, stripping local fishermen of their livelihood, these fishermen then join the flow of illegal migrants to Europe.[37] When developed countries offer professional education for foreign students from developing countries, this often results in a brain drain when graduates decide to stay in their host countries rather than return home. If the living standards in developing countries were improved, including the educational system, then people could study and practice at home, without the need to

study abroad. Attempts to stop child labor in certain developing countries have come up against the harsh reality that the
meager incomes earned by children help to support their families. Legal remedies must therefore be complemented by
economic incentives for families to allow their children to
have childhoods and go to school. All these examples demonstrate how interconnected different problems and their
solutions really are. Local solutions can create problems elsewhere, and action in one area can have an impact on another
policy domain. This is why long-term strategies are so
difficult, but they are not intractable.

Consider poverty reduction. One economist identifies four
traps that befall the most impoverished countries of the world,
mostly in Africa: civil war, a "resource curse" which creates a
dependence on the extraction and export of some natural
resource such as oil or diamonds, a landlocked geography
which creates a dependence on neighboring countries for
transportation in order to trade, and bad governance.[38] He
identifies three factors that explain the first trap, the recur-
rence of civil war: a preponderance of uneducated young men;
one ethnic group that outnumbers all others; and an abundance of some natural resource which obviates the need to
raise taxes, thereby reducing government accountability, while
encouraging and financing conflict. The solutions that he pro-
poses emphasize preferential trade policies by the most developed countries, which must exempt the poorest countries
from protectionist tariffs; legal regimes against corruption,
fraud, resource exploitation, and media censorship; and even
limited military intervention, such as was done in Sierra Leone
to end the civil war there. While the last solution is the most
controversial in the wake of the Iraq fiasco, it highlights once
again how long-term approaches may have to combine a variety of strategies, including, but not exclusively so, coercive
ones.

Promoting human rights

Promoting social and economic rights can reduce the dispari-
ties and inequities that fuel radicalization and facilitate terrorist recruitment. Many of the UN conferences held during
the 1990s, such as those dealing with social development,
women's rights, population, and habitat, all came up with recommendations and specific time-frames for Member States to
enact specific proposals. Many of these proposals deal explicitly with the issue of human rights and the need to strengthen
legal regimes that require states to protect different baskets of
rights. In the global fight against terrorism, these highly complex and recalcitrant issues are often ignored or sidestepped in
the interests of short- or medium-term solutions, such as are
found in the domains of policing, security intelligence, criminal justice, and military action – in other words, the exercise of
the state's monopoly on physical violence (internally) and the
projection of military power (externally). The fact that Russia,
India, and Israel have all concentrated their efforts primarily
on coercive counterterrorism in their conflicts with Chechen,
Kashmiri, and Palestinian terrorists respectively – and have all
justified these actions as part of the global "war on terror" –
suggests that democracies, when faced with serious terrorist
violence, will tend to emphasize judicial and military control
over other control models that emphasize root causes and
long-term solutions. While this was true before 9/11, the trend
has been exacerbated since.

It is striking, for example, that the Colombian government
broke off negotiations with the Revolutionary Armed Forces of
Colombia (FARC) in the wake of the 9/11 attacks and returned
to a primarily military response to the insurgency. The immediate result was a marked increase in violence, including
alleged massacres by paramilitaries and extra-judicial killings
by the military. The USA continued to aid the Colombian

military in its fight with the FARC – again in the name of the "war on terror" – despite concerns by human rights groups that serious human rights violations could intensify.[39] Since the inauguration of the International Criminal Court, however, and Colombia's refusal to sign a bilateral immunity agreement with the USA, US training of Colombian military personnel has been cut back. This punitive policy was applied to over two dozen countries, with 12 of them in Latin America and the Caribbean.[40] While an emphasis on military and judicial control of terrorism and political violence is also characteristic of authoritarian and totalitarian regimes, for example China and its Uighur insurgency,[41] the difference post-9/11 is that Western criticism of abuses or human rights violations is more muted or absent altogether. The Abu Ghraib scandal in Iraq has also shown that democracies can abuse human rights in the name of counterterrorism or counterinsurgency. There have been many scathing critiques of the "war on terror" from the perspective of the erosion of human rights, civil liberties, personal privacy, and other democratic values and constitutional freedoms.[42]

Efforts have been made to find nonviolent solutions to various conflicts, such as in Israel/Palestine, Kashmir, and Sri Lanka, but successes tend to be short-lived. The promotion of political and civil rights can clearly have an impact on the attractiveness of the terrorist option. By giving voice to disenfranchised or oppressed groups, other options are provided that make the terrorist option less compelling. In the short term, however, allowing excluded groups access to the political process can increase conflict and even violence. It is only when rights are fully entrenched and, in a sense, institutionalized and routinized, that the use of violence becomes counterproductive. This is what happened in Northern Ireland, though it can be very difficult for those who have relied on violence for so long to give it up. A related challenge is the problem of anti-democratic political or religious movements and whether there are acceptable limits to the right to free expression, assembly, and participation in political life: the balance between freedom of expression and freedom *from* expression.[43] Violent rhetoric, such as sedition or hate propaganda, creates special policy problems. Freedom of expression collides with freedom from threat and intimidation. While most civil liberties organizations are loath to criminalize such activities in the interests of protecting free speech, many realize that some limits should be placed on the free expression of hateful, demagogic speech and the outright promotion of violence or the glorification of terrorism.

There are clear links between propaganda, the promotion of hate and violence, and the mobilization and recruitment of terrorists and their supporters and sympathizers. However, they do not always follow a linear, top-down model of indoctrination and recruitment. One researcher who studied the Hamburg cell that carried out the 9/11 attacks identifies eight phases in their pathway to terrorism:

1. individual alienation and marginalization;
2. spiritual quest;
3. process of radicalization;
4. meeting and associating with like-minded people;
5. gradual seclusion and cell formation;
6. acceptance of violence as legitimate political means;
7. connection with a gatekeeper in the know;
8. going operational.[44]

The first phase underscores the importance of addressing those factors that create feelings of alienation and marginalization. The promotion of human rights is one way to accomplish this, though it certainly cannot provide a panacea. The sixth phase refers to the legitimation of violence and terrorist action. This, too, would be much more difficult if human rights were respected and nonviolent political means were available.

A rights-based approach to counterterrorism that respects the rule of law, is nondiscriminatory in its application, and accountable and transparent can contribute significantly to the building of trust and confidence in government, particularly in communities that are vulnerable to radicalization and terrorist recruitment. In Australia, for example, Victoria State Police have applied a community-policing approach to counterterrorism. This involves developing and maintaining long-term relations with community leaders in culturally and linguistically diverse communities. In the area of intelligence gathering, this has led to a recognition that intelligence gathering methods built on trust and community engagement pose fewer risks than covert or coercive methods, which can often fuel resentment and radicalization, increasing the risk of terrorist recruitment.[45] Research by the Victoria Police and university researchers has concluded that the Australian Federal approach to counterterrorism, which is primarily coercive and directed at discovering plots and conspiracies and apprehending offenders, has undermined more long-term efforts aimed at preventing or reducing the risk of radicalization and recruitment in sensitive communities.[46]

Promoting cross-cultural dialogue

Related to the overall attempt to embed counterterrorism in a human rights framework, and to reach out to communities where radicalization and terrorist recruitment are significant risks, is the promotion of dialogue between cultures. In response to Samuel Huntington's thesis of a "clash of civilizations,"[47] many have called for a dialogue of civilizations instead. The belief is that if peoples of different cultures, traditions, religions, or worldviews could engage in dialogue, misunderstandings could be cleared up and common ground could likely be found. At the international level, the Alliance of Civilizations (AoC) was created by the UN in 2005, based on an initiative by the governments of Spain and Turkey. Its stated mission is "to improve understanding and cooperative relations among nations and peoples across cultures and religions and, in the process, to help counter the forces that fuel polarization and extremism."[48] In January 2008, the AoC held its first International Forum in Madrid; the second will be held in Turkey in 2009. At the civil society level, there has been an explosion of "dialogue studies" and the establishment of centers for dialogue which specialize in bringing diverse groups together to share their perspectives and strive for mutual understanding and appreciation.

Many of these programs emphasize "faith-based" dialogue in particular, reflecting the current fashion of focusing on Islamist terrorism and Salafist–jihadist extremism. The result, according to some analysts, has been to privilege religious leaders and thinkers over other kinds of experts, particularly secular ones.

> Attempts to tackle terrorism through the aid of religion has had the effect of magnifying in Britain and America the voice of Islamic clerics and other members of the religious establishment on matters that are not in the domain of religion, at a time when the political and social roles of Muslims in civil society, including in the practice of democracy, need emphasis and much greater support. What religious extremism has done to demote and downgrade the responsible political action of citizens (irrespective of religious ethnicity) has been, to some extent, reinforced, rather than eradicated, by the attempt to fight terrorism by trying to recruit the religious establishment on "the right side." In the downplaying of political and social identities as opposed to religious identity, it is civil society that has been the loser precisely at a time when there is a great need to strengthen it.[49]

This observation underscores the kind of unintended consequences that reactive strategies focused on the latest threat can create. By emphasizing religion, its role in other aspects of social and political life is strengthened and the secular values that underlie liberal democracy are thereby undermined, quite unintentionally. This was highlighted at a conference on counterterrorism in Melbourne, Australia, when a spokeswoman for the Muslim community of Melbourne pointed out that 80 percent of Muslims did not attend mosques. The result was that the majority felt excluded when religious community leaders were called upon to speak for all Muslims.[50]

Education

In chapter 4, education was stressed as an important element in efforts to improve public understanding of the nature of the terrorist threat and the feasibility and practicality of different counterterrorism measures, as well as in countering undesirable beliefs and perceptions in the terrorists' constituency. These are necessarily long-term efforts. Education can also help in creating a social and political environment that is sensitive to human rights and mutual understanding across cultures and civilizations. Counterterrorism policy that favors the development of anti-racist education and fosters the dissemination of human rights training to social control agents could provide a sociopolitical climate conducive to long-term prevention rather than quick fixes that more coercive policies offer. The most important values or skills that might be included in such programs include:

- tolerance and mutual understanding of differences between racial, ethnic, and religious groups;
- the ability to formulate or discuss misunderstandings and to maintain communication;

- acceptance of unusual or different behavior with regards to language, non-verbal communication, and social rules;
- knowledge and recognition of different concepts, viewpoints, ways of life;
- focusing on common work and interests and on cooperation;
- the ability to combat racist behavior and other forms of prejudice;
- building awareness of racism, racist and other forms of exclusionary, us/them propaganda, and extremist thought via critical thinking, media literacy, and content analysis.

Many international conventions on human rights single out education as a fundamental right and emphasize education as a vehicle for promoting democratic, pluralistic, and anti-racist values. Both the Universal Declaration of Human Rights (Article 26) and the International Covenant on Economic, Social and Cultural Rights (Article 13) refer to the right to education, the access to various levels of education, and the purposes of education. The purposes of education are also referred to in the UN Declaration on the Elimination of All Forms of Racial Discrimination (Article 8), the International Convention on the Elimination of All Forms of Racial Discrimination (Article 7), the Declaration on the Elimination of All Forms of Intolerance and of Discrimination Based on Religion or Belief (Article 5, para. 3), and the UNESCO Declaration on Race and Racial Prejudice (Article 5, para. 2, and Article 6, para. 2). The purposes of education include:

- strengthening respect for human rights;
- promoting understanding, tolerance, and friendship among all nations and racial, ethnic, or religious groups;
- furthering the maintenance of peace;
- enabling people to participate effectively in a free society;
- combating prejudices and racist attitudes which lead to racial discrimination; and

- the prevention and eradication of racism and racist propaganda.[51]

There are three areas in which the inculcation of such values is most relevant for long-term counterterrorism: (1) the schools (both students *and* teachers); (2) social control agencies that deal with immigrants, refugees, asylum-seekers, and culturally and linguistically diverse communities; and (3) police colleges and military academies. Each can be viewed as an important link in a broad, long-range and preventive approach to counterterrorism that addresses the wider sociopolitical context in which terrorism waxes and wanes.

The schools

Albert Einstein suggested that the spell of nationalism can be broken by teaching history in such a way as to avoid instilling in students "an obsession with the past." He argued that the teaching of geography and history could promote pacifism by fostering sympathetic understanding for the national characteristics of the different countries in the world, "especially of those whom we are in the habit of describing as 'backward.' "[52] Einstein's emphasis on the teaching of history and geography and on habits of description suggests a concrete way that the values and skills listed above might be incorporated into school curricula. Lessons are too often taught in ways that obscure understanding of other cultures, that mystify the practices and beliefs of other civilizations, and that pathologize or demonize the behavior of historical or political enemies. It is an "obsession with the past" that often lies at the root of intractable conflicts, particularly of an ethnic nature. Nostalgia for past glories of empire also drives many conflicts. Rather than focusing on the present and attempting to foster harmonious relations in the conduct of everyday life, many people dwell on real or perceived injustices from the past. This is especially true when justifying war, invasion, political violence, terrorism, or communal violence. In doing so, they expend much energy and talent in perpetuating enmity, suspicion, misunderstanding, and, ultimately, injustices of their own. Teaching methods that foster an understanding of the interdependence of human beings and an appreciation of ethnic, linguistic, cultural, religious, and historical diversity can contribute to reducing the fear and cultivated ignorance that lie at the root of much hatred and violence. Such ways of thinking can also diminish the attractiveness of hate rhetoric and us/them thinking. People would become inoculated to demagoguery and violent rhetoric. Recruitment would become more difficult and support for extremist and terrorist groups would become harder to sustain. Experimental research suggests that such an approach is not merely wishful thinking or an idealistic pipedream. Reminders of death tend to trigger negative evaluations of those with different attitudes. This is why scapegoating of minorities is so easy in time of war or during political conflict. However, when subjects were first "primed" to affirm the value of tolerance by indicating their level of agreement with statements that espoused tolerance, this effect of death reminders disappeared completely. The authors conclude: "These studies provide hope that emphasizing the value of tolerance could be one antidote to hostility toward those who are different."[53]

This said, it is obvious that education can also inform people of injustices and inequities around the world. Much of the left-wing terrorism of the 1970s was driven by awareness of such problems. Students were often at the center of such terrorist movements, and intellectuals were at the vanguard of the ideologies that inspired and sustained them. Many separatist terrorist movements recruit students as well, such as the Basque ETA and the Kurdish PKK. As people become exposed to the realities of our complex world, they search for answers and solutions and can become vulnerable to the simplistic explanations offered up by ideologues and fanatics. Many seek refuge in the past or in the rigid authoritarianism of political or religious dogma. This is why education must stimulate critical thought as well as mere awareness of issues and facts. The ability to think for oneself and to research issues by collecting data from many sources is a good antidote to the propensity to succumb to ideological fads or exclusionary, racist theories.

Agents of social control

Control agents who deal on a daily basis with the very people who are presently perceived as most likely to be involved in terrorism must receive training that will help them see beyond the stereotypes and the demonology. These include those working within the criminal justice model, such as prosecutors, public defenders, judges, correctional officers, prison guards, and parole officers. But it also includes social workers, hiring or job placement agents, employers, members of refugee or immigration boards, customs officials, government bureaucrats, medical professionals, and school and adult education officials. Because the post-9/11 security mandate has broadened so much and because a moral panic about illegal immigrants, refugees, Muslim extremists, and "the enemy within" is in full swing, governments should work all the more diligently to ensure that agents of the State, at all levels, are able to deal with their clients as human beings, not simply as potential terrorists.

Police and military

It is those control agents who are imbued with the right to exercise the State's monopoly on violence that are most in need of special training in the area of human rights and the rule of law. These include police, security intelligence agents, private security professionals, and military personnel. Many police academies do include courses on the rights of the accused and the nature of police powers and their judicial controls, while military academies sometimes include courses on human rights. The question is how such training translates into actual practice. It is one thing to teach these subjects at the academy and quite another to ensure that the lessons are followed in the field. Specialized training for counterterrorist police units has created better understanding of the complexities and sensitivities involved in policing terrorism.[54] The same is probably true for specialized military units. The challenge is to spread this understanding to all personnel so as to create a subculture of human rights norms. If such a subculture exists, then when higher authorities demand extraordinary procedures that undermine these values, such as happened in Iraq and the "war on terror," then the likelihood of orders being refused or whistle-blowing occurring may be increased. This might constitute a defense against the corruption of counterterrorist efforts for political or ideological purposes that undermine effectiveness and make a mockery of democratic governance.

Gender

One area that is too often neglected in counterterrorism strategies is the issue of gender. The majority of terrorists are young males. With many scholars and practitioners focusing on Asia as a major hub of Al Qaeda activity, and China and India emerging as major world powers, it is striking that few have made the connection between sex selection policies in this region and the abundance of young males for indoctrination and recruitment to extremist or terrorist groups. Researchers have identified "offspring sex selection" as one of the most compelling measures of gender inequality.[55] Two examples of this practice are female infanticide and sex-selective abortion, where female fetuses are aborted while male fetuses are allowed to come to term. Sex-selective abortion is made possible by ultrasound technology, which can reveal the sex of a fetus. The result of extreme forms of offspring sex selection, particularly in China – where a one-child policy has been in effect for some time – and India, but throughout Asia as well, is a drastic increase in the male/female sex ratio. In rural China, for example, where the scarcity of girls is most acute, girls as young as 16 are kidnapped and sold to desperate bachelors, who force them into marriage or even prostitution. In the cities, educated girls find jobs and often defer marriage in favor of pursuing their careers and living the good life that regular salaries make possible. This only exacerbates the poor marriage prospects of young men.[56]

This surfeit of males means that many young men in these countries will never have a hope of finding a mate, marrying, or raising a family. These "bare branches," as the Chinese call them, are perfect fodder for terrorist recruitment. Imagine a young man who can never have sexual relations with a woman, who is forever shut out of the institutions of marriage, family, school (other than religious), and job. As militaries around the world have known for centuries, teenage males are extremely susceptible to indoctrination, to bonding rituals, and to organized channeling towards sanctioned and condoned violence supported by appropriate appeals to God, country, or fraternity.[57] Add to this the sexual and social frustrations of a "bare branch," and you have a perfect candidate for the commission of indiscriminate violence, including suicide bombing.

Studies by the United Nations Development Program (UNDP) and others have shown a significant inverse correlation between a woman's educational level and the number of children she bears.[58] The more educated and empowered a woman is, the less likely it is that she will have a lot of children. In the long term, then, the best antidote to the bare branch problem would be the promotion of education and empowerment of women throughout the world and particularly in those regions where the sex ratio significantly favors males. In South Korea, for example, an age-old preference for baby boys is being reversed and there is a decrease in the abortion of female fetuses. While the government has long banned the use of ultrasound to reveal the sex of fetuses and has funded advertising campaigns extolling the virtues of daughters, the main reason behind the reversal has been the economic boom and the entry of women into the workforce.[59] An unintended consequence of this empowerment of South Korean women has been an overall decline in the birth rate to the point where the average birth rate is less than two. The government has tried to encourage larger families of three to five children through economic incentives and promises of better daycare, but women are loath to give up their new-found independence in the workplace.[60] Given the global problem of population growth, however, it might be better to encourage immigration rather than more births. Unfortunately, as in some European countries, ethnocentrism, nationalism, and downright racism can make such a solution unpalatable or even unthinkable, despite its potential benefits.

In countries where the sex ratio may be more balanced than in Asia, but women are denied access to education or the workforce, the bare branch problem is manifested differently. Overpopulation and failing economies mean lack of job opportunities for young men and therefore a reduced likelihood of finding a mate and raising a family, since husbands are expected to provide for their own and even their extended families. Idle, unemployed young men are ideal targets for radicalization and recruitment. In such countries, traditional women's roles emphasize child-rearing at the expense of other contributions that a woman might make to the society or the economy. Young women are confined to traditional roles and transgressions bring shame on the entire family or tribe.

Honor killings of women who have brought shame onto their family are common. Women in such situations can also be convinced to become suicide bombers to redeem themselves and spare their families social exclusion. Empowering women in these countries would reduce the birth rate overall, addressing the bare branch problem, but also allow half the population to contribute to social, political, and economic life and to resist the pressure of family and tribal traditions that can sometimes drive "deviant" girls and women along the terrorist path.

This approach has its own challenges and problems. The UNDP has found that attempts to address the empowerment of women, particularly in Arab societies, have met with resistance:

> The spread of the concept of "women's empowerment" in the Arab region has excited the rancour of certain socio-political forces. They have tended to see it as "imposed" by the West and not emerging from either the realities or needs of Arab societies, which are based on the entrenched role of the family as society's basic building block. This has driven some to resist development plans that adopt the gender perspective and to resist the government and the women's organizations which work in accordance with it."[61]

Ironically, the UNDP found that in Arab countries girls did better than boys in school, over 50 percent of top-scoring students being girls despite female enrollment figures below 50 percent.[62] The obvious waste of human capital because of traditional, archaic views of women is striking. From a counterterrorist perspective, empowering and educating women could have an impact over the long term, especially if it is implemented locally, with the support of local authorities. In the short term, however, violent backlash by men who feel threatened or displaced by empowered women can make the long-term strategy seem ineffective. The Taliban in Afghanistan and Islamist extremists in Pakistan exemplify this point. That said, one small-scale initiative to build schools for girls in Afghanistan and Pakistan has found that educated mothers have at times been instrumental in convincing their sons to quit the Taliban and become teachers in these schools.[63]

Democratization

For post-conflict states or states that are undergoing a transition from a nondemocratic past and are in the process of democratization, market liberalization, and state-building, there are a whole series of challenges that can have a serious impact on efforts to create a globally coordinated and integrated counterterrorism regime, especially since many such states constitute actual or potential allies in the current "war on terror." Many of these states have an authoritarian/totalitarian or an imperial/colonial past. State institutions are weak and there is endemic corruption. Their state-run economies are also weak and often compete with or are completely supplanted by underground economies that involve organized crime, mafia, drug trafficking, or narcoterrorism. Civil society is weak and there is limited democratization, if any. The promotion of democracy, human rights, and open and transparent government can often appear to such states as a form of cultural imperialism. Efforts at policy harmonization can be perceived as a disguised form of subordination. A long-term strategy of democratization should take into consideration how Western values are perceived in other societies and cultures and how homologous concepts in those societies, perhaps in a different form, can create points of contact for harmonization efforts. The impact of democratization policy within one country on neighboring states and regions is also an important consideration. Consider the case of Iraq. One commentator has argued that the democratization efforts in

Iraq have had a negative impact on democracy in some of Iraq's neighbors: "Although the Bush administration has cited the need for democratic change in the Middle East as a reason for going to war in Iraq, the threat of instability on Jordan's border may actually be restricting democratic freedoms there."[64]

The assumption that democratization will bring peace and prosperity to previously oppressed peoples ignores the often central role that violence can play in electoral politics.[65] In Gaza, the Hamas electoral victory led to a power struggle between the new guard (Hamas) and the old guard (Fatah). While this was probably exacerbated by the US and EU decision to withhold funding from the democratically elected Hamas government, the conflict had its own internal dynamics, culminating in Hamas taking over Gaza and Fatah retreating to the West Bank. In post-war Iraq, a democratic election brought the previously repressed Shia majority to power and led to a Sunni insurgency fueled in part by a desire to maintain a role in the power structure. Al Qaeda in Iraq launched a terror campaign against the Shia population in an attempt to trigger civil war. The result was sectarian violence on a horrific scale. In Pakistan, when President Pervez Musharraf announced that elections would be held in January 2008, the ensuing electoral campaign was marred by violence, including the assassination of former prime minister and leading contender Benazir Bhutto. The election was postponed until February and ultimately went off fairly smoothly. Widespread violence erupted in Kenya in the wake of an election at the end of December 2007 that many perceived as being rigged by the incumbent president:

> Within the span of a week, one of the most developed, promising countries in Africa has turned into a starter kit for disaster. Tribal militias are roaming the countryside with rusty machetes, neighborhoods are pulling apart, and Kenya's

economy, one of the biggest on the continent, is unraveling – with fuel shortages rippling across East Africa because the roads in Kenya, a regional hub, are too dangerous to use.[66]

Historically, electoral violence has been a regular feature of democratic life in Europe and America as well. The role of violence in democratic renewal has often been praised as a "cleansing" element, as in Thomas Jefferson's famous dictum that "the tree of liberty must be refreshed from time to time with the blood of patriots and tyrants." Whether violence is an inevitable and salutary aspect of democratic life has been disputed, especially when violence becomes so commonplace and normative that a cultural of violence emerges.[67]

The emphasis on free and fair elections as a key indicator of democratization is problematic simply because it ignores the complex process of institutionalization and bureaucratization that underlies "deep" democracy. Smooth and peaceful electoral transition involves numerous elements, including a free press which allows equal access to all parties, well-functioning political parties that represent all sectors of society, a level of literacy that allows citizens to understand the issues and differentiate between ideology and fact, a transparent and accountable system for registering and counting votes, and a functioning infrastructure, especially transportation, that permits all citizens to get out and vote. Even in the USA, a paragon of democracy, this ideal was far from being achieved in the 2000 US presidential election.[68] As for the 2004 campaign, it was marred by fear-mongering related to the threat of terrorism, which colored the electoral discourse and obscured many important issues that might have influenced voters. Democratization campaigns that merely focus on elections risk triggering unexpected results and unintended consequences if they do not also address wider structural issues such as education, access to services, distribution of resources, and overall quality of life.[69] One analyst draws the following rather pessimistic conclusion about the transition to democracy worldwide:

> There is no format, or many times not even an identifiable starting point, for a democratic evolution to begin. . . . The process is messy, uneven in timing, often facing setbacks in policies or leadership, and extraordinarily difficult to achieve and maintain. Add to this that the international community often loses interest as time passes, and as long as the forms of the democratic process are honored, regardless of the reality of the situation, it is normally satisfied. Perception is the key to politics; unfortunately, it may also be the key to maintaining semiauthoritarian, or even fully authoritarian, states.[70]

Environmental protection

The Intergovernmental Panel on Climate Change (IPCC), which shared the 2007 Nobel Peace Prize with former US Vice-President Al Gore, has warned in its Fourth Assessment Report, *Climate Change 2007*, that more than 60 nations, mostly developing countries, face a risk of tensions and conflicts over resources being exacerbated by climate change. The threat of environmental refugees fleeing natural disasters, flooding, severe storms, and scarcity of resources is also increased. Countries that are now at peace, such as the USA, China, and most European nations, risk the emergence of conflict triggered by the impact of climate change.[71] The UNDP's *Human Development Report 2007/2008* warns that the world needs to focus on the development impact of climate change, which could bring unprecedented reversals in poverty reduction, nutrition, health, and education.[72] These warnings highlight the interdependency and interrelatedness of the different policy areas related to the complex security environment described in chapter 1. They suggest that many of the long-term strategies discussed above are vulnerable to being undermined over time by the impact of climate change. As such, even this seemingly remote policy area has to be considered in any long-term counterterrorism strategy.

Disturbances brought on by climate change, such as flooding, drought, wildfire, insects, and ocean acidification, and factors that drive global changes in climate, such as changes in land use, pollution, and over-exploitation of resources, all have important implications for the broader sociopolitical climate in which terrorism develops. In the area of health, climate change carries an increased risk of malnutrition and susceptibility to diarrhea, cardiovascular disease, and infectious disease. Heat waves, floods, and droughts are expected to increase illness and death. Europe has already seen its elderly citizens succumb to extreme heat waves during the summer months.[73] Italy has recently reported cases of a tropical disease carried by tiger mosquitoes migrating from Africa.[74] All this will increase the burden on health services. "Critically important will be factors that directly shape the health of populations such as education, health care, public health initiatives and infrastructure and economic development."[75]

Environmental issues have increasingly been recognized as potential security issues.[76] Solutions for many of the threats posed by environmental change are usually sought in areas that are familiar to security analysts:

> Security experts . . . are not well versed in the intricacies of ecological theory, soil erosion, population dynamics, hydrological regimes, and natural resource management; their eyes have been focused elsewhere: on evil empires, rogue states, international terrorists, arms build-ups, fundamentalist movements, resurgent nationalisms, etc. Their attention has also been directed towards the large-scale actors: nation-states, in particular. Clearly they have not been peering down into the grassroots, but that of course is where they should be looking if it is environmental degradation that is the cause of all the trouble in the world.[77]

One example of "grassroots" is the subsistence farmer who chops down trees and burns forests to create fields for planting crops. To tackle the problem of deforestation, then, incentives to find other means of subsistence must be offered to such farmers. As with poverty reduction, women's empowerment, human rights, and civilizational dialogue, the answers lie in complex systems that tend to elude the power of states to deal effectively with them. Nonstate actors, such as those identified in chapter 1, are part of the equation. As Al Gore has argued in promoting solutions to climate change, an individual can make a difference over time.[78] Just as the "butterfly effect" reveals how occurrences at the micro level can produce effects at the macro level, so local initiatives and individual efforts can sometimes lead to major change. The inexorable spread of non-smoking policies and practices from North America to Europe and beyond took decades, but the trend seems to be continuing slowly and steadily. Human rights, such as homosexual rights, have spread from North America to Latin America and beyond.

International cooperation

It has been an axiom for at least 30 years that international cooperation is essential in the fight against all forms of terrorism. One analyst describes a three-pronged strategy of the United Nations, outlined in the September 2002 report of the High-Level Policy Working Group on the United Nations and terrorism, in which cooperation is the third prong: "UN Strategy 3 is to sustain broad-based international cooperation in the struggle against terrorism."[79] This third prong includes making cooperation between the UN and other international actors more systematic; ensuring an appropriate division of labor based on comparative advantage; developing an international action plan; ensuring a higher degree of internal coordination and coherence within the United Nations; and strengthening some UN offices, most notably the Office for Drug Control and Crime Prevention of the UN Secretariat.[80] All this takes time. Not only do alliances have to be maintained, sometimes with less than friendly partners as well as longstanding allies, but legislative and institutional frameworks have to be developed and implemented.

Among the main enduring obstacles to international cooperation are the continuing supremacy of sovereignty in international affairs, which makes intervention a tricky business (see chapter 1), and the failure to achieve a universal definition of terrorism (see Introduction). The question remains how to counteract nonstate enemies while keeping cohesive and cooperative relations in the interest of international order. This is the crux of the matter. If individual states in the international system cannot agree on a universal definition of terrorism, and resist or undermine cooperation in the name of sovereignty and national interest, then effective international cooperation in the fight against terrorism will remain a dream. Differences in structure (institutional and jurisdictional), culture, ideology, and interests, as well as perceptions of the terrorist threat and how to combat it, can all make international cooperation difficult to sustain, even among allies. For example, four areas in which EU–US cooperation in the "war on terror" has experienced the most strain are human rights, the death penalty, intelligence sharing, and data protection.[81] There are also cooperation problems within the EU itself.[82]

The examples of EU–US and intra-EU cooperation demonstrate how difficult it can be for states to cooperate without sacrificing principles, circumventing established procedures, or failing to remain open and accountable to their domestic constituencies. Furthermore, when electoral change brings new priorities and new concerns about neighbors, promises made by defeated administrations can be reversed by incoming leaders.

In the October 2007 election in Poland, the opposition party won, ousting the former nationalist government that sent troops to Iraq and supported the US missile defense plan that would have missile-interceptor bases stationed on Polish territory in conjunction with a radar station in the Czech Republic. The new government expressed doubts about the missile-defense project, arguing that Iran poses no threat to Poland, and promised to pull its troops out of Iraq.[83] In the environmental field, when a new Australian prime minister, Kevin Rudd, was elected at the end of 2007, his first official act was to sign the Kyoto Protocol, reversing a longstanding policy of global warming skepticism and isolating the USA as one of the last holdouts. The problems multiply when cooperation is required between states that are not traditional allies. The role of Pakistan as a key ally in the "war on terror" has been fraught with difficulties. Because of the Pakistani government's inability to effectively control its Northwestern Frontier Province, where Al Qaeda is suspected to operate with the support of local tribes and increasing numbers of foreign fighters,[84] the USA has periodically considered covert operations inside the country. The situation became even more critical following the December 2007 assassination of former Prime Minister Benazir Bhutto. US intelligence believes that Al Qaeda has a new mission to try and destabilize Pakistan, and Pakistani intelligence has suggested that an Al Qaeda associate was behind the assassination. The problem is that covert US operations inside Pakistan risk undercutting the authority of the Pakistani military and the legitimacy of the Pakistani government, exacerbating internal tensions and violence.[85]

As discussed in chapter 1, nonstate actors from the private sector and civil society have also become important players in world affairs and interact with state actors and international institutions in a wide variety of policy domains, including counterterrorism. The preceding chapters of this book have provided numerous examples. If tourists, businessmen, and citizens are to be more vigilant; if private schools and universities are to monitor their foreign students more; if banks, investment firms, and charitable organizations are to be more transparent and accountable; if religious institutions are to be more vigilant about extremist ideology and indoctrination of people who come to worship; if NGOs are to be more responsible for peacekeeping and humanitarian assistance, as well as inquiries into human rights violations; if consulting firms and transnational corporations are to provide advice, auxiliary services, and even battalions for military interventions; if airline companies and other transportation agencies, hydroelectric and nuclear plants, computer industries, and agricultural enterprises are expected to watch out for terrorist attacks or hire private security companies to do it for them – then counterterrorism has clearly become the province of many more actors than just the State.

In view of this explosion in actors, partners, and stakeholders, international cooperation in the fight against terrorism cannot rely solely upon a supranational legal order or regime, but must be able to function at several levels at once – supranational, regional, national, and subnational, including the very local. This kind of "multicentric regime" would include "multiple sets of public and private, national and international rules, contributing to an integrated and orderly . . . system."[86] Such "transnational" cooperation, as opposed to purely international, state-to-state cooperation, better reflects the nature of the terrorist threat, as well as the kind of response framework that can more effectively meet it. In a post-Westphalian world order, domestic politics plays an important role, and transnational interaction between multinational enterprises, private businesses, NGOs, civil society organizations (CSOs), and media organizations complement the more traditional domains of diplomacy and international summitry. International cooperation as traditionally conceived is increasingly complemented by these kinds of transnational cooperation, for example in peacekeeping, conflict resolution, and state-building. It should also happen in the area of counterterrorism.

This multicentric view recognizes the complexity of today's security environment and tries to match the networked nature of the security threats that characterize it. The EU idea of subsidiarity, whereby action should be taken at lower levels unless a collective response is justified, can be applied to the area of international cooperation in countering terrorism. The idea is that any central authority should have a subsidiary function, performing only those tasks which cannot be performed effectively at a more immediate or local level. This means that much more emphasis should be placed on cooperation at the community level or between localities or regions where a common or sufficiently similar threat, risk, or vulnerability exists. The idea would be to synchronize activities of both state and nonstate actors or stakeholders, through the exchange of best practices and their adaptation to local needs, rather than to compel all local or regional efforts to conform to some Procrustean, harmonized framework common to all.

If a comprehensive long-term strategy of counterterrorism is to truly become a reality, it will probably be by small changes at the local level that evolve and adapt over time and space until they become widespread and normalized as a universal value or practice. But they need to be allowed the space to develop and spread by legal frameworks that protect rights and provide opportunities to all. This can only be done by States, but non-state partners will increasingly play a central role in the process as well, and state actors will increasingly cooperate transnationally.[87] From the perspective of long-term counterterrorism strategies, a human security model best describes what might be entailed. By working to ensure the quality of life and the security of all individuals, no matter where they live, it may just be possible for state and nonstate actors, working in concert, to make it increasingly difficult for ideologues and zealots to mobilize and recruit people to use terrorism and violence in the name of some purportedly noble cause.

Conclusion. A comprehensive counterterrorism strategy

Having surveyed the various kinds of options that are available for counterterrorism, it now remains to bring them all together into a comprehensive counterterrorism strategy that takes advantage of the full array of possibilities. In a world where boundaries are blurring between internal and external security, international and domestic jurisdictions, and state and nonstate actors, it is important to cast our eyes wide in developing an effective approach to counterterrorism that can apply across a broad variety of policy domains and can outlive the electoral horizon of individual governments.

Bringing it all together

Can democratic states under threat from serious or persistent terrorist attack maintain their freedoms and their values while assuring their security or must the very principles which define them as democracies be cast aside in the battle against anti-democratic forces? The answer lies in combining the various approaches to counterterrorism presented in the preceding chapters at the local, the national, the regional, and international levels. Counterterrorism cannot be merely reactive or coercive, otherwise it risks creating a bunker mentality, triggering resentment and backlash that risks promoting terrorist recruitment as a result, and missing the next new development. It must therefore be proactive, looking ahead and trying to out-think the terrorist, and plan ahead, thinking preventively. It must also be persuasive, convincing terrorists to abandon their destructive paths and supporters and sympathizers to seek other, nonviolent ways to achieve their goals. Counterterrorism must think in the long term, even as it acts in the short term to respond to attacks and outwit terrorist planning and targeting. And it must go beyond legal and military approaches, to include political, social, cultural, and economic initiatives aimed at undermining the viral spread of radicalizing and violence-glorifying ideas that fuel the use of terrorism in social and political life. The only way to achieve this is to move beyond the polarized discourse between "September 10 thinking" and "September 12 thinking" and to look for ways to operate on several levels at once: locally and globally; tactically and strategically; politically and economically; publicly and privately; institutionally and individually; offensively and defensively.

Figure C.1 summarizes the variety of preventive strategies that are available. They include examples of coercive and persuasive, short-term and long-term, legal and military, national and international. They are presented across two different pairs of variables: space–time and offensive–defensive. Horizontally, the different approaches range from shorter-term initiatives that apply across jurisdictions or borders, i.e. space (lefthand side), to longer-term initiatives that play out over time (righthand side). Vertically, they range from offensive (upper half) to defensive (lower half) initiatives. In the upper left quadrant one finds offensive strategies that can be expected to have some results in the immediate or medium term. Preemption, economic blockades, and blocking terrorist financing are examples. In the upper right quadrant are offensive strategies that can take considerable time to develop and that yield results only after an extended period of time. They include international legal regimes, intelligence sharing and cooperation, and offensive psyops, though some psychological

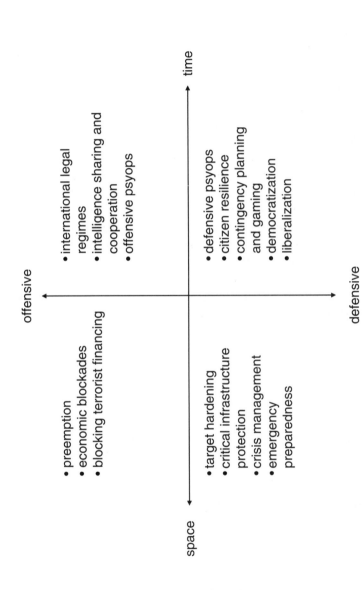

Figure C.1   Prevention and counterterrorism

operations such as counter-propaganda, enacting certain reforms to undercut terrorist rhetoric, or mediation could have a shorter-term impact as well. The lower left quadrant depicts shorter-term defensive strategies that can be expected to have a more immediate impact. They include target hardening, critical infrastructure protection, crisis management, and emergency preparedness. The lower right quadrant depicts defensive strategies that only promise dividends in the longer term. They include defensive psyops, building citizen resilience, contingency planning and gaming, democratization, and market liberalization. Again, some psychological operations, such as granting amnesties to those who renounce violence or working with the media to reduce sensationalism, rumors, and fear-mongering during terrorist crises could also have a shorter-term impact.

Figure C.2 summarizes the variety of options that involve the use of hard power. Along the horizontal axis, they are again classified according to whether they are shorter-term (space) or longer-term (time). Along the vertical axis, they are divided between the criminal justice model (upper half) and the war model (lower half). In the upper left quadrant, one finds the elements of criminal justice – from arrest and detention to prosecution, trial, and punishment – with a more immediate impact. International elements, such as extradition and international law and policing, are also included. The upper right quadrant includes longer-term elements of the criminal justice model, including proactive policing, criminal intelligence, and anti-terrorism legislation. It also includes peacekeeping, which is closer to international policing and the maintenance of law and order even though it usually involves military forces. In the lower left quadrant, one finds examples of the use of military force that can be expected to have an immediate impact. These include retaliatory strikes, military invasions, gunboat diplomacy, and economic blockades. The lower right

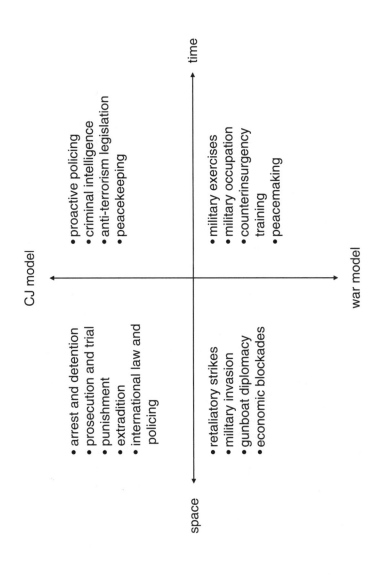

Figure C.2   Hard power and counterterrorism

quadrant includes military training exercises, including joint operations among allies, military occupation, counterinsurgency training, and peacemaking, which usually requires greater use of force than peacekeeping. All these examples either require more time to develop and maintain or pay dividends after an extended period of investment of resources and manpower.

Figure C.3 summarizes the range of options involving the use of soft power. The horizontal axis divides them according to space and time; the vertical axis separates them according to whether they focus primarily on the economic domain (upper half) or the political, social, and cultural domain (lower half). The upper left quadrant depicts those strategies that can be applied in the short term across a range of national jurisdictions. They include regulation of resource utilization, trade, foreign aid, and employment policies. In the upper right quadrant, one finds the longer-term initiatives that focus on the economic sphere, such as promoting economic growth, market liberalization, and development programs. The lower left quadrant lists those issues that are most important for social policies that aim in the shorter term to promote tolerance of diversity and to reduce the tensions that typically provide opportunities for radicalization and terrorist recruitment. They include culture, ethnicity, religion, and identity, as well as the role of diaspora, refugee, and immigrant communities in social, cultural, and political life. Then there are initiatives that undercut the appeal of terrorism, such as amnesties for those who renounce violence, or negotiations and reforms that address grievances that terrorists exploit to draw people onto the terrorist path. In the lower right quadrant, one finds longer-term strategies that focus on the social, cultural, religious, or political dimension. They include psychological operations aimed at changing attitudes and beliefs, education, countering radicalization, community policing that aims to promote trust and open dialogue

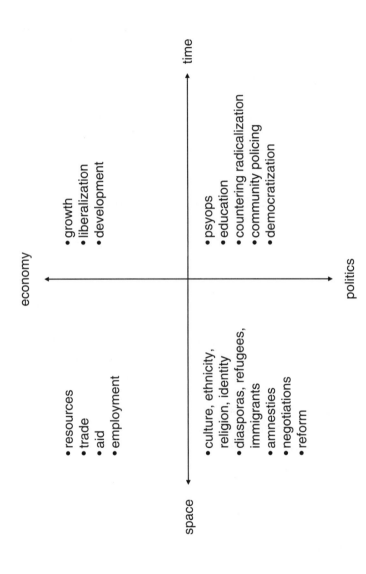

Figure C.3   Soft power and counterterrorism

between culturally and linguistically diverse communities and the police, and democratization.

Finally, figure C.4 combines both hard power and soft power. The horizontal axis differentiates between shorter-term and longer-term initiatives, while the vertical axis differentiates between coercive ones (upper half) and persuasive ones (lower half). The upper left quadrant depicts the range of shorter-term coercive strategies. They include the operations of criminal justice, including reactive policing, preemptive military strikes, economic blockades, and retaliatory strikes. The upper right quadrant lists those strategies that need more time to produce results. They include proactive policing, criminal and security intelligence, and counterinsurgency operations. In the lower left quadrant, one finds those persuasive strategies that could have a short-term impact on terrorist decision-making and terrorist incidents. These include deterrence, amnesties, negotiations, and reforms, emergency preparedness and crisis management, and well-developed relations with the media designed to lessen the risk that media coverage of terrorism might exacerbate its effects. The lower right quadrant lists those strategies that require more time to yield results. These include many psychological operations designed to alter perceptions and beliefs of terrorist constituencies and citizens, education, building citizen resilience, foreign aid and development projects, democratization, and market liberalization.

Taken together, these four figures depict the full range of options available for countering terrorism in a security environment where interdependence, connectivity, and complexity necessitate multiple and overlapping solutions that look beyond electoral horizons, national borders, jurisdictional frameworks, institutional mandates, and individual policy agendas. The question remains as to how all this works in reality.

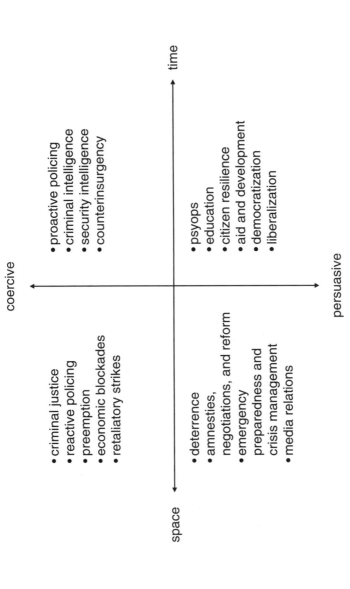

Figure C.4   Hard and soft power combined

Delicate balances

Counterterrorism clearly poses specific challenges to liberal democratic states. In the words of Israeli Supreme Court President Aharon Barak, it is like fighting with one hand tied behind one's back. If the fight against terrorism undermines or reverses the basic tenets of a democratic state, then the terrorist wins. This means that counterterrorism policy in democratic states and in a globalizing world order where democratization is a valued norm must try to achieve a balance between effectiveness and a variety of other values that underlie the social contract in democratic societies. Yet juxtaposing acceptability and effectiveness as two criteria that must be "balanced" in the fight against terrorism "encourages the view that the problem inevitably involves 'trade-offs' between our values and security."[1] A similar argument was made some ten years earlier:

> Any dichotomy [between democratic acceptability and effectiveness] remains heuristic only insofar as it helps us understand how the two sides of the coin interact. The danger is that we treat the two sides as separate entities that behave independently of each other. The very effectiveness of any *democratic* solution to the terrorist problem must include a determination of the political dimension and the impact of that solution on democratic political life. If terrorism is eliminated at the expense of democracy or the rule of law, via either too much repression (dictatorship) or too much accommodation (anarchy), is it really effective?[2]

In other words, "effectiveness" is a relative term and merely reducing or preventing terrorist attacks is not – and should not be – the sole measure of response effectiveness. Arguing that the rule of law diminishes the effectiveness of counterterrorism, by, for example, allowing those charged with terrorist offenses the right to a defense, misses the larger context within which counterterrorism must operate. The rule of law can be an effective means of preserving democratic values in the face of terrorist threats, attacks, and systematic campaigns. By standing firm on democratic procedure and principles, democracies project an image of integrity and determination in the face of those who wish to undermine the very system that makes them democratic in the first place. This is also why opinion polling in time of crisis is a potentially misleading and even dangerous exercise. It opens the way to justifying extreme measures and self-defeating policies in the name of public demand for security at the expense of freedom. Terrorism is designed to herd people towards supporting violent and repressive responses so that recruitment to the cause can be stimulated and constituencies can be enlarged. In authoritarian and totalitarian regimes, the people do not even have a say, so this political variable cannot be manipulated by terrorists intent on provoking repression.

One analyst uses the metaphor of a puzzle, arguing that figuring out how to balance different and often conflicting values represents dilemmas needing to be solved.[3] This is an apt metaphor, since puzzles can sometimes have several solutions, depending on how one approaches the problem (see Introduction). Sometimes, one thing has to be done first, before another thing can succeed, or several things should be done in concert, since doing each separately will not provide a solution. These "delicate balances" include the balance between:

1. collective security and individual freedom;
2. necessity and proportionality: the dual problems of overreacting and underreacting to uncertain threats and certain vulnerabilities;
3. the need for operational secrecy and political openness and accountability: the issue of judicial and political oversight;
4. freedom of expression and freedom from threat and intimidation;

5. the needs of security and legitimate activities of fundraising and banking;
6. the need for stringent customs and border control and the promotion of free trade and free movement of goods and services across borders;
7. promoting international trade and the economic development and self-sufficiency of developing countries and the control of conventional arms, WMD proliferation and the spread of other dangerous technology;
8. the demands of state-building, democratization, and market liberalization in weak states and states in transition from authoritarian to democratic rule and maintaining stability and respecting cultural and political sensitivities within the target state;
9. the promotion of universal human rights and respect for cultural and religious differences.

Maintaining these delicate balances is not an easy task and there are clearly many obstacles to solving the dilemmas that they present to policymakers and decision-makers, as the preceding chapters have tried to demonstrate. Taken together, they clearly go well beyond a simple dichotomy between a criminal justice model and a war model or between democratic acceptability and effectiveness. How these delicate balances play out in the international arena and how they affect national or domestic counterterrorism policy determines to a large extent whether the threat of terrorism succeeds in undermining the very nature of democratic governance. The basic choice is really between a comprehensive approach that recognizes the complete range of options and understands when to use which, how and for how long (see box on p. 247) and a reductionist one which focuses exclusively on one option, remaining blind to all others.

> It's not which to use,
> but when to use which,
> in what combination or order,
> and for how long.

Global governance vs. global war

"Governance" refers to the sets of rules, decision-making procedures, and programmatic activity that serve to define social practice and to guide the interactions of those participating in these practices. "Global governance" refers to the global rules, procedures, and programs that typically are institutionalized as legal regimes within international organizations such as the WTO, the EU, the OSCE, and the United Nations and its agencies. Examples include:

- refugee determination;
- immigration rules;
- border and passport controls;
- sustainable development;
- environmental protection;
- control of international trade, investment, and foreign aid;
- human rights and minority rights (individual and collective rights);
- rule of law;
- rules of war;
- peacekeeping/making;
- conflict resolution.

While chapter 2 described the set of international anti-terrorism conventions that have emerged over the past several decades to compel all states to adopt national legislation reflecting the contents of these treaties, other chapters make clear that all the above areas are relevant to counterterrorism.[4]

The challenges of counterterrorism in the current world environment are clear. Proliferating actors at the local, regional, national, and international levels, and the ability of groups to act across a variety of frontiers in a complex array of variations and possibilities renders the environment in which terrorism may occur a complicated one. Waging a global war against terrorism limits the response to a particular mindset of which "September 12 thinking" is a prime example. If you use a hammer, you see everything as a nail. If you use military force and a doctrine of preemptive war, you see every challenge as an enemy in waiting. Global governance, by contrast, requires flexibility and cooperation across the many divides that characterize today's world. It provides a framework within which state and nonstate actors can work. It poses challenges of course, but it provides direction and a sense of common purpose. For dictatorships and totalitarian regimes, counterterrorism really does not pose the same set of challenges. Given the closed nature of their political systems and their societies, they can make up their own rules, as the Nazis did, and ignore the outside world and its carefully calibrated mechanisms of governance, as does Myanmar (Burma) today. The Soviet Union had no significant nonstate terrorism until, ironically, the period of *glasnost* and *perestroika*.

Counterterrorism is easy in a totalitarian regime. All it takes is to seal off borders (both to insiders and outsiders); repress all political and social opposition; offer social and economic incentives for informing on neighbors and dissidents; create a secret police to control all aspects of social and political life; centralize the economy and create an autarky; control the media and deny the public alternative visions, viewpoints, and vistas. In short, create a reign of terror and become a terrorist state that resists or disrupts global governance at every possibility. The result: homeland security via unilateralism and isolationism. For democracies, counterterrorism will always be more difficult. This is because it requires states to respect the rule of law; sign, ratify, and adhere to all international conventions against terrorism and related acts; extradite or prosecute suspected terrorists; participate in international regimes that control trade, aid, finance, arms control, and WMD proliferation; complement police, military, and legal control of terrorism (the exercise of "hard power") with economic, social, cultural, and environmental measures that address the root causes of political, social, and religious grievances (the exercise of "soft power"); work both domestically and internationally to reduce the gap between rich and poor peoples and nations and to create a better world for all human beings. In short, create a rules-based regime that promotes and strengthens democratic regimes and encourages or supports global governance at every possibility. The result: homeland security via multilateralism and multicentric cooperation.

The choice is clear. If the easy path to counterterrorism is taken, then the beliefs of those fanatics, zealots, and ideologues who claim that their terrorism and violence are legitimate responses to tyranny, oppression, and state terrorism will simply be confirmed. If the difficult path to counterterrorism is taken, those beliefs will ultimately be undermined among the vast majority of people, isolating the fanatics, zealots, and ideologues and facilitating their being brought to justice, and wearing down the radical communities that support them. The key word here is "ultimately." Short-term solutions and "quick fixes" may work for a while – until the next terrorist attack or the next terrorist movement. Coupled with long-term efforts, their impact will be much more long-lasting.

If the difficult path is chosen, the major opportunities for an effective global response to terrorism lie in the same factors that produce the challenges. For example, the private sector can become a partner in counterterrorism and crisis management, provided that the same standards applied to governments and states apply: accountability, respect for the rule of law, and openness (if not during a crisis, then afterwards). The internet can be a source of early warning indicators, as well as a vehicle for promoting public understanding of the threats that exist in today's turbulent world. Countering racist propaganda or pernicious conspiracy theories with sound research and reliable data could serve to reinforce public support for measured responses and preparedness. Moral panics created by fearmongers, whether in government, the media, or the terrorist's constituency, can be prevented or at least mitigated. The greatest challenge that faces the counterterrorism community in today's complex world is to avoid the simplifications that were so easy to propagate in a simpler, bipolar world – and which are so favored by totalitarian regimes – and to learn to deal with the complexities with which we are faced, both rationally and competently. This may not be easy, but it is certainly not impossible. Understanding the wider political, economic, social, and cultural issues which underlie the delicate balances outlined above and discussed in previous chapters can ultimately help to make a global consensus on a comprehensive counterterrorism strategy more likely.

Notes

INTRODUCTION. TERRORISM AND
COUNTERTERRORISM BEFORE AND AFTER 9/11

1. See Alex P. Schmid and Janny de Graaf, *Violence as Communication: Insurgent Terrorism and the Western News Media* (Beverly Hills: Sage, 1982); Ronald D. Crelinsten, "Terrorism as Political Communication: The Relationship between the Controller and the Controlled," in Paul Wilkinson and A. M. Stewart (eds.), *Contemporary Research on Terrorism* (Aberdeen: University of Aberdeen Press, 1987), pp. 3–23; Ronald D. Crelinsten, "Power and Meaning: Terrorism as a Struggle over Access to the Communication Structure," in Wilkinson and Stewart (eds.), *Contemporary Research on Terrorism*, pp. 419–50.

2. See David C. Rapoport, "The Politics of Atrocity," in Yonah Alexander and Seymour Finger (eds.), *Terrorism: Interdisciplinary Perspectives* (New York: John Jay, 1977), pp. 45–61.

3. Lorenzo Vidino, *Al-Qaeda in Europe: The New Battleground for International Jihad* (Amherst, NY: Prometheus Books, 2006); Petter Nesser, "How did Europe's Global Jihadis Obtain Training for their Militant Causes?" *Terrorism and Political Violence* 20(2) (2008): 234–56.

4. For a critique of how the Chinese/Uighur conflict is being depicted as a problem of Islamist terrorism by the Chinese, see Michael Clarke, "China's 'War on Terror' in Xinjiang: Human Security and the Causes of Violent Uighur Separatism," *Terrorism and Political Violence* 20(2) (2008): 271–301. Seventeen Uighurs have been detained in Guantánamo Bay as enemy combatants since they were picked up in Afghanistan in 2001. They claim that they are not enemies of the USA at all, but were escaping oppression in China and were planning attacks there. In 2008, a US Federal Court rejected government evidence suggesting that

one of the Uighur detainees was an enemy combatant, citing the evidence as unverifiable.The Court ordered that the man be released or given a new military hearing. See William Glaberson, "U.S. Court, in a First,Voids Finding by Tribunal on Guantánamo Detainee," *New York Times*, June 24, 2008; William Glaberson, "Evidence Faulted in Detainee Case," *New York Times*, July 1, 2008.

5. Mariya Y. Omelicheva, "Combating Terrorism in Central Asia: Explaining Differences in States' Response to Terror," *Terrorism and Political Violence* 19(3) (2007): 369–93, at p. 385.

6. See Edward S. Herman, *The Real Terror Network: Terrorism in Fact and Propaganda* (Boston: South End Press, 1982). He distinguishes between "wholesale" and "retail" terrorism to refer to state terrorism and insurgent terrorism, respectively.

7. For a comparative analysis of international and some national definitions, see Beril Dedeoglu, "Bermuda Triangle: Comparing Official Definitions of Terrorist Activity," *Terrorism and Political Violence* 15(3) (2003): 81–110. For a historical review, see Bruce Hoffman, *Inside Terrorism* (New York: Columbia University Press, 1998), ch. 1.

8. Kofi Annan, "A Global Strategy for Fighting Terrorism," Keynote Address to the Closing Plenary of the International Summit on Democracy, Terrorism and Security, Madrid, March 10, 2005. Available at http://english.safe-democracy.org/keynotes/a-global-strategy-for-fighting-terrorism.html (last accessed on August 7, 2008).

9. Michael Mousseau, "Terrorism and Export Economies: The Dark Side of Free Trade," in James J. F. Forest (ed.), *The Making of a Terrorist: Recruitment, Training, and Root Causes*, Vol. III: *Root Causes* (Westport, CT: Praeger Security International, 2006), at pp. 196–7.

10. Crelinsten, "Terrorism as Political Communication," in Wilkinson and Stewart (eds.), *Contemporary Research on Terrorism*, p. 5. For a similar view, see Arie Kruglanski and Shira Fishman, "The Psychology of Terrorism: 'Syndrome' versus 'Tool' Perspectives," *Terrorism and Political Violence* 18(2) (2006): 193–215.

11. For more detailed analyses of the use of torture, see Ronald D. Crelinsten, "The World of Torture: A Constructed Reality," *Theoretical Criminology* 7(3) (2003): 293–318; Ronald D. Crelinsten and Alex P. Schmid (eds.), *The Politics of Pain: Torturers and Their*

Masters (Boulder, CO: Westview Press, 1995). For the definitive study of modern torture, its history, its social, political, and psychological impact, and its reputed effectiveness, see Darius Rejali, *Torture and Democracy* (Princeton, NJ: Princeton University Press, 2007). For two highly critical accounts of how the Bush Administration came to adopt torture as a central feature of the "war on terror," see Philippe Sands, *Torture Team: Rumsfeld's Memo and the Betrayal of American Values* (New York: Palgrave Macmillan, 2008); Jane Mayer, *The Dark Side: The Inside Story of How The War on Terror Turned into a War on American Ideals* (New York: Doubleday, 2008).

12. Ian S. Lustick (2006), *Trapped in the War on Terror* (Philadelphia: University of Pennsylvania Press, 2006).

13. For a polemical discussion of the supposed superiority of a war approach to counterterrorism, see Richard H. Shultz and Andreas Vogt, "It's War! Fighting Post-11 September Global Terrorism through a Doctrine of Preemption," *Terrorism and Political Violence* 15(1) (2003): 1–30. For a critique and refutation, see Paul R. Pillar, "Metaphors and Mantras: A Comment on Shultz and Vogt's Discussion of Terrorism, Intelligence and War," *Terrorism and Political Violence* 15(2) (2003): 139–51.

14. Cited in Adam Litvak, "In War of Vague Borders, Detainee Longs for Court," *New York Times*, January 5, 2007.

15. Cited in George F. Will, "The Triumph of Unrealism," *Washington Post*, August 15, 2006, p. A13.

16. For a good review, see Matthew J. Morgan, "The Origins of the New Terrorism," *Parameters* (Spring 2004): 29–43, available at www.carlisle.army.mil/usawc/parameters/04spring/morgan.htm (last accessed on August 7, 2008).

17. The idea that terrorism is fundamentally changing predates the 9/11 attacks. See, for example, Bruce Hoffman, *Inside Terrorism* (New York: Columbia University Press, 1998), and Walter Laqueur, *The New Terrorism: Fanaticism and the Arms of Mass Destruction* (Oxford: Oxford University Press, 1999) for two early proponents. See also Ian O. Lesser, Bruce Hoffman, John Arquilla, David Ronfeldt, and Michele Zanini, *Countering the New Terrorism* (Santa Monica, CA: Rand, 1999). For a post-9/11 anthology, see Andrew Tan and Kumar Ramakrishna (eds.), *The New Terrorism: Anatomy, Trends and Counter-strategies* (Singapore: Eastern University Press, 2002). For a nuanced critique, see

David Tucker, "What is New about the New Terrorism and How Dangerous is It?" *Terrorism and Political Violence* 13(3) (2001): 1–14. For an empirical refutation of the claim that a "new terrorism" is responsible for terrorism's increasing lethality, see Daniel Masters, "The Origin of Terrorist Threats: Religious, Separatist, or Something Else?" *Terrorism and Political Violence* 20(3) (2008): 396–414.

18. See, for example, Paul Wilkinson, *Terrorism and the Liberal State* (London: Macmillan, 1977), which includes discussions of the role of force and the role of the military, and Grant Wardlaw, *Political Terrorism: Theory, Tactics and Counter-Measures. Second Edition* (Cambridge: Cambridge University Press [first published in 1982], 1989), which includes a discussion of the role of the military in counterterrorism.

19. Ronald D. Crelinsten and Denis Szabo, *Hostage-Taking* (Lexington, MA: Lexington Books, D. C. Heath, 1979).

20. Paul Wilkinson, "The Laws of War and Terrorism," in David C. Rapoport and Yonah Alexander (eds.), *The Morality of Terrorism: Religious and Secular Justifications* (New York: University of Columbia Press, 1982), pp. 308–24. See also M. Sassoli, "International Humanitarian Law and Terrorism," in Wilkinson and Stewart (eds.), *Contemporary Research on Terrorism*, pp. 466–74.

21. See, for example, Gabor Rona, "Interesting Times for International Humanitarian Law: Challenges from the 'War on Terror,' " *Terrorism and Political Violence* 17(1–2) (2005): 157–73.

22. See, for example, Paul Johnson, "The Seven Deadly Sins of Terrorism," *New Republic*, September 15, 1979; Neil C. Livingstone and Terrell E. Arnold (eds.), *Fighting Back: Winning the War Against Terrorism* (Lexington, MA: Lexington Books, 1986).

23. Richard Clutterbuck, "Negotiating With Terrorists," in Alex P. Schmid and Ronald D. Crelinsten (eds.), *Western Responses to Terrorism* (London: Frank Cass, 1993), pp. 263–87.

24. The identification and contrast of these two control models was first proposed in Ronald D. Crelinsten, "International Political Terrorism: A Challenge for Comparative Research," *International Journal of Comparative and Applied Criminal Justice* 2(2) (1978): 107–26. Reprinted as ch. 18 in Rosemary H. T. O'Kane (ed.), *Terrorism*, vol. II (Northampton, MA: Edward Elgar Publishing, 2005).

25. Fernand Braudel, *On History* (Chicago: University of Chicago Press, 1980); Fernand Braudel, *Civilization & Capitalism:*

15th–18th Century, vol. III: The Perspective of the World (New York: Harper & Row, 1984), esp. pp. 71–88.

CHAPTER I. THE CONTEXT FOR COUNTERTERRORISM: A COMPLEX SECURITY ENVIRONMENT

1. Claire Sterling, *The Terror Network: The Secret War of International Terrorism* (New York: Henry Holt & Co., 1981); Ray S. Cline and Yonah Alexander, *Terrorism: The Soviet Connection* (New York: Crane Russak, 1984).
2. For a discussion of right-wing terrorism from the 1990s, see Tore Bjørgo (ed.), *Terror from the Extreme Right* (London: Frank Cass, 1995). Also a special issue of *Terrorism and Political Violence* 7(1) (Spring 1995).
3. For an excellent analysis of both regimes of terror, see Darius Rejali, *Torture and Modernity: Self, Society, and State in Modern Iran* (Boulder, CO: Westview Press, 1994).
4. Noam Chomsky and Edward S. Herman, *The Washington Connection and Third World Fascism* (Boston: South End Press, 1979); Edward S. Herman, *The Real Terror Network: Terrorism in Fact and Propaganda* (Boston: South End Press, 1982).
5. Benjamin Netanyahu, *Terrorism: How the West Can Win* (New York: Avon Books, 1987).
6. For a discussion of the militarization of counterterrorism in the late 1980s, see Ronald D. Crelinsten and Alex P. Schmid, "Western Responses to Terrorism: A Twenty-Five Year Balance Sheet," in A. P. Schmid and R. D. Crelinsten (eds.), *Western Responses to Terrorism* (London: Frank Cass, 1993), pp. 307–40, esp. pp. 315–22.
7. For an extensive bibliography of the early literature (pre-1988), see Alex P. Schmid and Albert J. Jongman, *Political Terrorism: A New Guide to Actors, Authors, Concepts, Data Bases, Theories, and Literature* (New Brunswick, NJ: Transaction Books, 1988), pp. 237–483. For a more recent review of the psychological literature, see Jeff Victoroff, "The Mind of the Terrorist: A Review and Critique of Psychological Approaches," *Journal of Conflict Resolution* 49(1) (2005): 3–42.
8. For one attempt to transcend some of these Cold-War-inspired distortions and to view terrorism in its historical, social,

political, and economic context, see Martha Crenshaw (ed.),
Terrorism in Context (Philadelphia: University of Pennsylvania
Press, 1995).

9. For a comparison of American and Soviet views on terrorism at
the end of the 1980s, see Brian Jenkins, "Setting the Scene," in
John Marks and Igor Beliaev (eds.), *Common Ground on Terrorism:
Soviet–American Cooperation Against the Politics of Terror* (New
York: W. W. Norton, 1991), pp. 30–49.

10. See, for example, Andrew T. Price-Smith, "Infectious Disease
and State Failure: Developing a New Security Paradigm,"
unpublished paper prepared for the annual meeting of
the International Studies Association, Toronto, March 18–22,
1997.

11. See, for example, Matthew G. Devost, "National Security in the
Information Age," MA thesis in Political Science, The
University of Vermont, May 1995. See also Matthew G. Devost,
Brian K. Houghton, and Neal Allen Pollard, "Information
Terrorism: Political Violence in the Information Age," *Terrorism
and Political Violence* 9(1) (1997): 72–83.

12. Didier Bigo, "The Möbius Ribbon of Internal and External
Security(ies)," in Mathias Albert, David Jacobson, and Yosef Lapid
(eds.), *Identities, Borders, Orders: Rethinking International Relations
Theory* (Minneapolis: University of Minnesota Press, 2001),
pp. 91–116.

13. Richard Clutterbuck, *Terrorism in an Unstable World* (London:
Routledge, 1994).

14. For a detailed look at the impact of globalization on the
development of terrorism, see Brynjar Lia, *Globalization and the
Future of Terrorism: Patterns and Predictions* (London: Routledge,
2005).

15. David Held, Anthony McGrew, David Goldblatt, and Jonathan
Perraton, *Global Transformations: Politics, Economics and Culture*
(London: Polity Press, 1999); Jan Aart Scholte, *Globalization: A
Critical Introduction* (New York: Palgrave, 2000); Gordon S. Smith
and Daniel Wolfish (eds.), *Who Is Afraid of the State? Canada in a
World of Multiple Centres of Power* (Toronto: University of Toronto
Press, 2001).

16. James N. Rosenau, *Along the Domestic–Foreign Frontier: Exploring
Governance in a Turbulent World* (Cambridge: Cambridge
University Press, 1997).

17. James N. Rosenau, *Turbulence in World Politics: A Theory of Change and Continuity* (Princeton: Princeton University Press, 1990).
18. Yale H. Ferguson and Richard W. Mansbach, *Polities: Authority, Identities and Change* (Columbia, SC: University of South Carolina Press, 1996).
19. Margaret E. Keck and Kathryn Sikkink, *Activists Beyond Borders: Advocacy Networks in International Politics* (Ithaca: Cornell University Press, 1998).
20. Ronald D. Crelinsten, "Policy Making in a Multicentric World: The Impact of Globalization, Privatization and Decentralization on Democratic Governance," in Smith and Wolfish (eds.), *Who Is Afraid of the State?*, pp. 89–130.
21. The UN Global Compact's website is www.unglobalcompact.org (last accessed on August 7, 2008).
22. Office of the High Commissioner for Human Rights, United Nations Environment Programme, International Labour Organization, United Nations Development Programme, United Nations Industrial Development Organization, United Nations Office on Drugs and Crime.
23. See, for example, the blog, "Global Compact Critics," at www.globalcompactcritics.net (last accessed on August 7, 2008), for links to many critiques.
24. Anja Dalgaard-Nielsen and Daniel S. Hamilton (eds.), *Transatlantic Homeland Security: Protecting Society in an Age of Catastrophic Terrorism* (London: Routledge, 2006).
25. Barry Buzan, *People, States and Fear: An Agenda for International Security Studies in the Post-Cold War Era, Second Edition* (Boulder, CO: Lynne Rienner, 1991).
26. One analyst has argued that this traditional view of war between states has become an anachronism under the impact of globalization. See Mary Kaldor, *New and Old Wars: Organized Violence in a Global Era, Second Edition* (Cambridge: Polity, 2006).
27. Barry Buzan, Ole Waever, and Jaap de Wilde, *Security: A New Framework for Analysis* (Boulder, CO: Lynne Rienner Publishers, 1998), p. 8.
28. William B. Werther, Jr. and David Chandler, *Strategic Corporate Social Responsibility: Stakeholders in a Global Environment* (Thousand Oaks, CA: Sage, 2005); Peter Singer, *One World: The Ethics of Globalization, Second Edition* (New Haven, CT: Yale University Press, 2004).

29. Buzan, Waever, and de Wilde, *Security,* p. 8.
30. Rob McRae and Don Hubert (eds.), *Human Security and the New Diplomacy: Protecting People, Promoting Peace* (Montreal: McGill-Queen's University Press, 2001). See also the website of the Canadian Consortium on Human Security (CCHS) at www.humansecurity.info (last accessed on August 7, 2008) for a link to its *Human Security Bulletin.*
31. David E. Sanger, "N. Korea Reports 1st Nuclear Test," *New York Times,* October 9, 2006.
32. Peter Maass, "Radioactive Nationalism," *New York Times Magazine,* October 22, 2006. For a similar view on how terrorism, including the 9/11 attacks, reinforces existing trends in international politics, see Kenneth N. Waltz, "The Continuity of International Politics," in Ken Booth and Tim Dunne (eds.), *Worlds in Collision: Terror and the Future of Global Order* (New York: Palgrave Macmillan, 2002), pp. 348–53.
33. William J. Broad, David E. Sanger, and Raymond Bonner, "A Tale of Nuclear Proliferation: How Pakistani Built His Network," *New York Times,* February 12, 2004; David Rohde and David E. Sanger, "Key Pakistani Is Said to Admit Atom Transfers," *New York Times,* February 2, 2004.
34. Joby Warrick and Peter Slevin, "Probe of Libya Finds Nuclear Black Market," *Washington Post,* January 25, 2004; Elise Labott, "U.S. to Restore Relations with Libya," CNN.com, May 15, 2006, available at www.cnn.com/2006/US/05/15/libya (last accessed on August 7, 2008).
35. Lawrence Scott Sheets and William J. Broad, "Smuggler's Plot Highlights Fear Over Uranium," *New York Times,* January 25, 2007.
36. David S. Cloud, "U.S. Airstrike Aims at Qaeda Cell in Somalia," *New York Times,* January 9, 2007; Michael R. Gordon and Mark Mazzetti, "U.S. Used Base in Ethiopia to Hunt Al Qaeda in Africa," *New York Times,* February 23, 2007. For a broader assessment of Al Qaeda activity in Africa, see Reuven Paz and Moshe Terdman, "Africa: The Gold Mine of Al-Qaeda and Global Jihad," *The Project for the Research of Islamist Movements (PRISM) Occasional Papers,* 4(2) (June, 2006), available at www.e-prism.org/images/PRISM_no_2_vol_4_-_AQ_and_Africa.pdf (last accessed on August 7, 2008).
37. David Rohde, "Al Qaeda Finds Its Center of Gravity," *New York Times,* September 10, 2006; Mark Mazzetti and David Rohde, "Al

Qaeda Chiefs Are Seen to Regain Power," *New York Times*, February 19, 2007; Mark Mazzetti and David Rohde, "Amid Policy Disputes Qaeda Grows in Pakistan," *New York Times*, June 30, 2008.

38. Hassan M. Fattah, "Uneasy Havens Await Those Who Flee Iraq," *New York Times*, February 8, 2006.

39. Michael T. Klare, *Resource Wars: The New Landscape of Global Conflict* (New York: Metropolitan Books, Henry Holt, 2001); Phili Le Billon, *The Geopolitics of Resource Wars* (London: Routledge, 2008).

40. See, for example, A. Ghaffar Ahmed and Leif Manger (eds.), *Understanding the Crisis in Darfur: Listening to Sudanese Voices* (Bergen, Norway: Centre for Development Studies, University of Bergen, 2006); Edmund Sanders, "Another Disaster Brews in Darfur," *LA Times*, October 1, 2007.

41. *New York Times*, "Editorial: Ensuring Progress at Ground Zero," May 26, 2007.

42. Julia Preston, "Public Misled on Air Quality After 9/11 Attack, Judge Says," *New York Times*, February 3, 2006.

43. Jonathan B. Tucker (ed.), *Toxic Terror: Assessing Terrorist Use of Chemical and Biological Weapons* (Cambridge, MA: MIT Press, 2000).

44. Dan Smith and Janani Vivekananda, *A Climate of Conflict: The Links Between Climate Change, Peace and War* (London: International Alert, 2007).

45. Andrew C. Revkin , "Poor Nations to Bear Brunt as World Warms," *New York Times*, April 1, 2007.

46. See, for example, John Mueller, *Overblown: How Politicians and the Terrorism Industry Inflate National Security Threats, and Why We Believe Them* (New York: Free Press, 2006).

47. See, for example, Ole Waever, "Securitization and Desecuritization," in Ronnie D. Lipschutz (ed.), *On Security* (New York: Columbia University Press, 1995), pp. 46–86.

48. The Canadian Government defines RMA as follows: "A Revolution in Military Affairs (RMA) is marked by a fundamental transformation in military affairs that results from changes in weapon technology and equipment, operational concepts and military organizational methods. RMAs usually take place over a few decades and profoundly affect, and often replace, existing warfighting practices." Accessed at www.vcds. forces.gc.ca/dgsp/pubs/rep-pub/dda/rma/primer_e.asp on July 29, 2008.

49. Beverly Crawford, "Hawks, Doves, but no Owls: International Economic Interdependence and Construction of the New Security Dilemma," in Lipschutz (ed.), *On Security*, pp. 149–86.

50. Barry Buzan and Gerald Segal, "Rethinking East Asian Security," in Michael T. Klare (ed.), *World Security: Challenges for a New Century. Third Edition* (New York: St. Martin's Press, 1998), pp. 96–112.

51. C. J. Chivers and Mark Lander, "Putin Suspends Arms Treaty," *New York Times*, April 27, 2007.

52. Thomas Harding, "Terrorists 'use Google maps to hit UK troops,' " *Telegraph*, January 13, 2007, available at www.telegraph.co.uk/news/main.jhtml?xml=/news/2007/01/13/wgoogle13.xml (last accessed on August 7, 2008).

53. Gwynne Dyer, *The Mess They Made: The Middle East After Iraq* (Melbourne: Scribe, 2007), pp. 164–5.

54. Robin Bromby, "Desalination now a word on everybody's lips," *Weekend Australian, Water: Special Report*, October 13–14, 2007, p. 3.

55. Kenneth D. Bergeron, *Tritium on Ice: The Dangerous New Alliance of Nuclear Weapons and Nuclear Power* (Boston: MIT Press, 2002).

56. Richard Rosecrance, *The Rise of the Trading State: Commerce and Conquest in the Modern World* (New York: Basic Books, 1986); Robert O. Keohane and Joseph S. Nye (2001), *Power and Interdependence, Third Edition* (London: Longman, 2001).

57. See, for example, David C. Rapoport and Leonard Weinberg (eds.), *The Democratic Experience and Political Violence* (London: Frank Cass, 2000); Ekaterina Stepanova, *Anti-terrorism and Peacebuilding During and After Conflict* (Stockholm: SIPRI, 2003).

58. Luc Huyse, "Justice after Transition: On the Choices Successor Elites Make in Dealing with the Past," *Law & Social Inquiry* 20(1) (1995): 51–78; Stanley Cohen, "State Crimes of Previous Regimes: Knowledge, Accountability, and the Policing of the Past," *Law & Social Inquiry* 20(1) (1995): 7–50; A. James McAdams (ed.), *Transitional Justice and the Rule of Law in New Democracies* (Notre Dame, IN: University of Notre Dame Press, 1997).

59. International Commission on Intervention and State Sovereignty (ICISS), *The Responsibility to Protect: Report of the International Commission on Intervention and State Sovereignty* (Ottawa: International Development Research Centre for ICISS, 2001); Jennifer M. Welsh, "Review Essay: From Right to Responsibility: Humanitarian Intervention and International Society," *Global Governance* 8(4) (2002): 503–21.

60. Simon Chesterman, *Just War or Just Peace? Humanitarian Intervention and International Law* (Oxford: Oxford University Press, 2001).
61. Barry Buzan and Ole Waever, *Regions and Powers: The Structure of International Security*, Cambridge Studies in International Relations (Cambridge: Cambridge University Press, 2004).
62. Barry Buzan, "The Security Dynamics of a 1 + 4 World," in Ersel Aydinli and James N. Rosenau (eds.), *Globalization, Security, and the Nation-State: Paradigms in Transition* (Albany: State University of New York Press, 2005), pp. 177–98.
63. Robert S. Chase, Emily Hill, and Paul M. Kennedy (eds.), *The Pivotal States: A New Framework for U.S. Policy in the Developing World* (New York: W. W. Norton, 1998). The editors also include Algeria, Egypt, Turkey, Pakistan, and Indonesia, for a total of nine pivotal states.
64. Buzan, "Security Dynamics," in Aydinli and Rosenau (eds.), *Globalization, Security, and the Nation-State*.
65. Mohammed Ayoob, *The Third World Security Predicament: State Making, Regional Conflict and the International System* (Boulder, CO: Lynne Rienner, 1995); Stephanie G. Neuman (ed.), *International Relations Theory and the Third World* (New York: St. Martin's Press, 1998).
66. Thomas M. Kane, *Theoretical Roots of U.S. Foreign Policy: Machiavelli and American Unilateralism* (London: Routledge, 2006), esp. ch. 1.
67. Alyson J. K. Bailes and Isabel Frommelt (eds.), *Business and Security: Public–Private Sector Relationships in a New Security Environment* (Oxford: Oxford University Press, 2004).
68. David Barboza, "My Time as a Hostage, and I'm a Business Reporter," *New York Times*, June 24, 2007.
69. Robert H. Jackson, *Quasi-States: Sovereignty, International Relations and the Third World* (Cambridge: Cambridge University Press, 1993).
70. Christopher Clapham, *Africa and the International System: The Politics of State Survival* (Cambridge: Cambridge University Press, 1996); Kevin C. Dunn and Timothy A. Shaw (eds.), *Africa's Challenge to International Relations Theory* (New York: Palgrave Macmillan, 2001).
71. See John Mueller, "Six Rather Unusual Propositions about Terrorism," *Terrorism and Political Violence* 17(4) (2005): 487–505, for a critical view. In the same volume of this journal, see also the

Comments on this article by Richard K. Betts, "Maybe I'll Stop Driving": 507–10; Daniel Byman, "A Corrective That Goes Too Far?": 511–16; and Martha Crenshaw, "A Welcome Antidote": 517–21, as well as Mueller's Response: 523–8.

72. Ronald D. Crelinsten, "Terrorism as Political Communication: The Relationship between the Controller and the Controlled," in Paul Wilkinson and A. M. Stewart (eds.), *Contemporary Research on Terrorism* (Aberdeen: University of Aberdeen Press, 1987), pp. 3–23; Ronald D. Crelinsten, "Analysing Terrorism and Counter-terrorism: A Communication Model," *Terrorism and Political Violence* 14(2) (2002): 77–122.

73. On the limited efficacy of deterrence, see, for example, Richard K. Betts, "The Soft Underbelly of American Primacy: Tactical Advantages of Terror," in Demetrios James Caraley (ed.), *September 11, Terrorist Attacks and U.S. Foreign Policy* (New York: The Academy of Political Science, 2002), pp. 33–50, at pp. 45–6. See also Paul K. Davis and Brian Michael Jenkins, *Deterrence & Influence in Counterterrorism: A Component in the War on al Qaeda* (Santa Monica, CA: Rand, 2002).

74. Henry Schuster and Mike Boettcher, "The Al Qaida Tapes – What Have we Learned," in Lars Nicander and Magnus Ranstorp (eds.), *Terrorism in the Information Age – New Frontiers?* (Stockholm: Swedish National Defence College, 2004), pp. 73–82.

75. Jerrold M. Post, Ehud Sprinzak, and Laurita M. Denny, "The Terrorists in Their Own Words: Interviews with 35 Incarcerated Middle Eastern Terrorists," *Terrorism and Political Violence* 15(1) (2003): 171–84.

76. Mark Sedgwick, "Al-Qaeda and the Nature of Religious Terrorism," *Terrorism and Political Violence* 16(4) (2004): 795–814, at p. 808.

77. See, for example, Bruce Hoffman, "Terrorism Trends and Prospects," in Ian O. Lesser, Bruce Hoffman, John Arquilla, David Ronfeldt, and Michele Zanini, *Countering the New Terrorism* (Santa Monica, CA: Rand, 1999), pp. 7–38.

78. Sedgwick, "Al-Qaeda and the Nature of Religious Terrorism."

79. For an analysis of the Moscow incident, based on firsthand accounts of surviving hostages, see Anne Speckhard, Nadejda Tarabrina, Valery Krasnov, and Khapta Akhmedova, "Research Note: Observations of Suicidal Terrorists in Action," *Terrorism and Political Violence* 16(2) (2004): 305–27.

80. See, for example, Barry Wellman, "Little Boxes, Glocalization, and Networked Individualism," in Makoto Tanabe, Peter van den Besselaar, and Toru Ishida (eds.), *Digital Cities II: Computational and Sociological Approaches* (Berlin: Springer-Verlag, 2002), pp. 11–25.

CHAPTER 2. COERCIVE COUNTERTERRORISM

1. For the full text of Common Article 3, see the website of the Office of the UN High Commissioner for Human Rights, at www. unhchr.ch/html/menu3/b/92.htm (last accessed on August 7, 2008).
2. Adam Roberts, "The Laws of War," in Audrey Kurth Cronin and James M. Ludes (eds.), *Attacking Terrorism: Elements of a Grand Strategy* (Washington, DC: Georgetown University Press, 2004), pp. 186–216.
3. Ronald D. Crelinsten, "Terrorism as Political Communication: The Relationship between the Controller and the Controlled," in Paul Wilkinson and A. M. Stewart (eds.), *Contemporary Research on Terrorism* (Aberdeen: University of Aberdeen Press, 1987), pp. 3–23, at pp. 16–17.
4. John Collins and Ross Glover (eds.), *Collateral Language: A User's Guide to America's New War* (New York: New York University Press, 2002).
5. Ronald D. Crelinsten, Danielle Laberge-Altmejd, and Denis Szabo, *Terrorism and Criminal Justice* (Lexington, MA: Lexington Books, D. C. Heath, 1978).
6. Bradley, W. C. Bamford, "The United Kingdom's 'War Against Terrorism,'" *Terrorism and Political Violence* 16(4) (2004): 737–56, at p. 747.
7. For a review of French counterterrorism efforts, see Gregory Shaun, "France and the War on Terrorism," *Terrorism and Political Violence* 15(1) (2003): 124–47.
8. UK Foreign and Commonwealth Office (FCO), "Counter-Terrorism Legislation and Practice: A Survey of Selected Countries," research paper published on October 13, 2005. See www.fco.gov.uk/en/newsroom/latest-news/?view=PressR&id=4186457 for details (last accessed on August 7, 2008).
9. Ibid.

10. See http://untreaty.un.org/English/Terrorism.asp (last accessed on August 7, 2008).

11. The OAU was replaced by the African Union (AU) in 2002.

12. Donatella della Porta, "Institutional Responses to Terrorism: The Italian Case," in Alex P. Schmid and Ronald D. Crelinsten (eds.), *Western Responses to Terrorism* (London: Frank Cass, 1993), pp. 151–70, esp. pp. 165–7.

13. Alan Cowell, "London Finds Linked Bombs, a Qaeda Tactic," *New York Times*, June 29, 2007.

14. Tasia Scolinos, Justice Department spokeswoman, cited in Adam Liptak, "In Terror Cases, Administration Sets Own Rules," *New York Times*, Nov 27, 2005.

15. *Copenhagen Post Online (English)*, "Judges Overturn Terrorism Trial Verdict," February 15, 2007.

16. Sheryl Gay Stolberg, "President Moves 14 Held in Secret to Guantánamo," *New York Times*, September 7, 2006.

17. Mathias Gebauer, "Sept 11 Helper Gets 15 Years: Motassadeq to Appeal as Judge Gives Maximum Sentence," *Spiegel Online International*, January 9, 2007, at www.spiegel.de/international/0,1518,458610,00.html (last accessed on August 7, 2008); BBC News, "Profile: Mounir al-Motassadek," December 4, 2006, at http://news.bbc.co.uk/2/hi/europe/2223152.stm (last accessed on August 7, 2008); Mary Wiltenburg and Daryl Lindsey, "German Terror Trial: Motassadeq Guilty of 247 Counts of Abetting Murder," *Spiegel Online International*, November 16, 2006, at http://www.spiegel.de/international/0,1518, 448921,00.html (last accessed on August 7, 2008).

18. See, for example, Jerry Markon, "Moussaoui Loses Right to Represent Himself," *Washington Post*, November 14, 2003.

19. Stephen Schafer, *The Political Criminal: The Problem of Morality and Crime* (New York: Free Press, 1974).

20. Scott Anderson, "The Hunger Warriors," *New York Times Magazine*, 21 October, 2001.

21. See, for example, Thom Shanker, "Abu Ghraib Called Incubator for Terrorists," *New York Times*, February 15, 2006.

22. Tim Pat Coogan, *On the Blanket: The Inside Story of the IRA Prisoners' "Dirty" Protest* (New York: Palgrave Macmillan, 2002).

23. Tim Golden, "The Battle for Guantánamo," *New York Times Magazine*, September 17, 2006.

24. Ronald D. Crelinsten, "Power and Meaning: Terrorism as a Struggle over Access to the Communication Structure," in Wilkinson and Stewart (eds.), *Contemporary Research on Terrorism*, pp. 419–50, at p. 434.

25. See Christine van den Wijngaert, *The Political Offence Exception to Extradition* (London: Kluwer International, 1980); Ethan A. Nadelmann, *Cops Across Borders: The Internationalization of U.S. Criminal Law Enforcement* (University Park, PA: The Pennsylvania State University Press, 1993), pp. 419–26.

26. Richard Clutterbuck, "Negotiating With Terrorists," in Schmid and Crelinsten (eds.), *Western Responses to Terrorism*, pp. 261–87, at p. 270.

27. Ibid., p. 277.

28. BBC News, "Fugitive on the Run: Ocalan Mystery Tour," February 16, 1999, at http://news.bbc.co.uk/2/hi/europe/280473.stm (last accessed on August 7, 2008); BBC News, "How Turkey Got its Man," February 19, 1999, at http://news.bbc.co.uk/2/hi/europe/280817.stm (last accessed on August 7, 2008); Jeremy Bowen, "The Story of Ocalan's Arrest," BBC News, May 28, 1999, at http://news.bbc.co.uk/2/hi/programmes/from_our_own_correspondent/283189.stm (last accessed on August 7, 2008).

29. Colin Freeze, "Torture Fears Stop Deportation of Suspect," *Globe and Mail*, October 16, 2006.

30. Clare Dyer, "Court Bans Deportation of Terror Suspect," *Guardian*, February 28, 2008, at www.guardian.co.uk/uk/2008/feb/28/terrorist.deportation (last accessed on August 7, 2008).

31. Kirk Makin and Tenille Bonoguore, "Court Puts Security Certificates in Limbo," *Globe and Mail*, February 23, 2007; Ian Austen, "Canadian Court Limits Detention in Terror Cases," *New York Times*, February 24, 2007.

32. BBC News, "Control Orders Explained," March 12, 2005, at http://news.bbc.co.uk/1/hi/uk_politics/4343081.stm (last accessed on August 7, 2008).

33. Barnaby Mason, "Terrorist Legislation Shambles," BBC News, March 14, 2005.

34. BBC News, "Judge Quashes Anti-terror Orders," June 28, 2006, at http://news.bbc.co.uk/1/hi/uk/5125668.stm (last accessed on August 7, 2008); Jon Silverman, "Government's Control Order 'Problem,'" BBC News, June 28, 2006, at http://news.bbc.co.uk/2/hi/uk_news/politics/5127388.stm (last accessed on August 7,

2008); Alan Travis, "Reid's Curfew Orders on Six Terror Suspects are Illegal, say Judges," *Guardian*, August 2, 2006, at www.guardian.co.uk/uk/2006/aug/02/terrorism.humanrights (last accessed on August 7, 2008).

35. Matthew Tempest, "MPs Renew Control Order Powers," *Guardian*, February 22, 2007, at www.guardian.co.uk/politics/ 2007/feb/22/immigrationpolicy.terrorism (last accessed on August 7, 2008); James Sturcke, "The Control Order Detainees," *Guardian*, October 31, 2007, at www.guardian.co.uk/uk/2007/oct/ terrorism.politics1 (last accessed on August 7, 2008).

36. United Nations, "UN Special Rapporteur Calls for Changes to the Philippines' Human Security Act," March 12, 2007, press release.

37. Gabor Rona, "Interesting Times for International Humanitarian Law: Challenges from the 'War on Terror,' " *Terrorism and Political Violence* 17(1–2) (2005): 157–73, at p. 164.

38. For the texts, see Bruce Lawrence (ed.), *Messages to the World: The Statements of Osama bin Laden*, trans. James Howarth (London: Verso, 2005): the first at pp. 23–30 (ch. 3); the second at pp. 58–64 (ch. 6). For an interesting review of the evolution of bin Laden's thinking as evidenced in this collection, see Noah Feldman, "Becoming bin Laden," *New York Times*, February 12, 2006.

39. Crelinsten, "Power and Meaning," in Wilkinson and Stewart (eds.), *Contemporary Research on Terrorism*. The War Measures Act was replaced by the Emergencies Act in 1988.

40. William Stevenson, *90 Minutes at Entebbe* (New York: Bantam Books, 1976).

41. George Jonas, *Vengeance: The True Story of an Israeli Counter-Terrorist Team* (New York: Simon & Schuster, 2005); Aaron J. Klein, *Striking Back: The 1972 Munich Olympics Massacre and Israel's Deadly Response* (New York: Random House, 2005). Steven Spielberg's 2005 film, *Munich*, also tells the story of Israel's counterterrorist operation.

42. For a critique of Israel's policy, see Michael L. Gross, "Fighting by Other Means in the Mideast: A Critical Analysis of Israel's Assassination Policy," *Political Studies* 51(2) (2003): 350–68.

43. Joseph T. Stanik, *El Dorado Canyon: Reagan's Undeclared War with Qaddafi* (Annapolis, MD: US Naval Institute Press, 2003); David C. Martin and John Walcott, *Best Laid Plans: The Inside Story of America's War Against Terrorism* (New York: Simon & Schuster, 1988).

44. CNN.com, "U.S. Missiles Pound Targets in Afghanistan, Sudan," August 21, 1998, at www.cnn.com/US/9808/20/us.strikes.02 (last accessed on August 7, 2008).

45. For a comprehensive look at the nature and meaning of victory and defeat in modern warfare, including contemporary insurgencies and the "war on terror," see Jan Angstrom and Isabelle Duyvesteyn (eds.), *Understanding Victory and Defeat in Contemporary War* (New York: Routledge, 2007).

46. See, for example, Norman Podhoretz, *World War IV: The Long Struggle Against Islamofascism* (New York: Doubleday, 2007). For an intelligence perspective, see James W. Harris, "Building Leverage in the Long War: Ensuring Intelligence Community Creativity in the Fight Against Terrorism," *Policy Analysis* 439 (May 16, 2002): 1–14. For a devastating critique of the consequences of this argument, published on the fourth anniversary of the 9/11 attacks, see Mark Danner, "Taking Stock of the Forever War," *New York Times Magazine*, September 11, 2005.

47. For a balanced discussion of the legal challenges posed by a "war on terror" that sees no quick end, see Benjamin Wittes, *Law and the Long War: The Future of Justice in the Age of Terror* (New York: Penguin Press, 2008).

48. In a speech following the capture of the terrorists who took over a cruise ship, the *Achille Lauro*, in 1985.

49. G. Pascal Zachary, "The Big Thought Is Missing in National Security," *New York Times*, July 1, 2007.

50. Mark Mazzetti, "Spy Agencies Say Iraq War Worsens Terrorism Threat," *New York Times*, September 24, 2006; Office of the Director of National Intelligence, "Declassified Key Judgments of the National Intelligence Estimate 'Trends in Global Terrorism: Implications for the United States' dated April 2006," at www.dni.gov/press_releases/Declassified_NIE_Key_Judgments. pdf (last accessed on August 7, 2008).

51. See, for example, Wolfgang S. Heinz and Hugo Frühling, *Determinants of Gross Human Rights Violations by State and State-Sponsored Actors in Brazil, Uruguay, Chile, and Argentina 1960–1990* (The Hague: Kluwer Law International, 1999).

52. Menachem Hofnung, "States of Emergency and Ethnic Conflict in Liberal Democracies: Great Britain and Israel," *Terrorism and Political Violence* 6(3) (1994): 340–65. See also John E. Finn,

Constitutions in Crisis: Political Violence and the Rule of Law (New York: Oxford University Press, 1991).

53. See, for example, Brian Jenkins, Janera Johnson and David Ronfeldt, *Numbered Lives: Some Statistical Observations from 77 International Hostage Episodes* (Santa Monica, CA: Rand, 1977).

54. Jonathan Eyal, "Analysis: Russia's Caucasus Quagmire," BBC News, September 6, 2004, at http://news.bbc.co.uk/2/hi/europe/3632332.stm (last accessed on August 7, 2008); John B. Dunlop, *The 2002 Dubrovka and 2004 Beslan Hostage Crises: A Critique of Russian Counter-Terrorism*, Soviet and Post-Soviet Politics and Society 26 (Stuttgart: ibidem-Verlag, 2006).

55. Peter C. Sederberg, *Terrorist Myths: Illusion, Rhetoric, and Reality* (Englewood Cliffs, NJ: Prentice-Hall, 1989), at pp. 149–50.

56. CNN interactive, "26 Sentenced to Death in Rajiv Ghandi Assassination," January 28, 1998, at www.cnn.com/WORLD/9801/28/india.gandhi (last accessed on August 7, 2008).

57. For an assessment of the impact of coercive measures, in general, see Tom Parker, "Fighting an Antaean Enemy: How Democratic States Unintentionally Sustain the Terrorist Movements They Oppose," *Terrorism and Political Violence* 19(2) (2007): 155–79. See also Seth G. Jones and Martin C. Libicki, *How Terrorist Groups End: Lessons for Countering al Qa'ida* (Santa Monica, CA: Rand, 2008).

58. Michael Walzer, *Just and Unjust Wars: A Moral Argument With Historical Illustrations* (New York: Basic Books, 1977); Paul Robinson (ed.), *Just War in Comparative Perspective* (Aldershot: Ashgate, 2003); Jean Bethke Elshtain, *Just War Against Terror: The Burden of American Power in a Violent World* (New York: Basic Books, 2003).

59. George W. Bush, "Military Order: Detention, Treatment, and Trial of Certain Non-Citizens in the War Against Terrorism," issued on November 13, 2001. Full text available at www.whitehouse.gov/news/releases/2001/11/20011113–27.html (last accessed on August 7, 2008).

60. George W. Bush, September 11, 2001, Address to the Nation, at www.whitehouse.gov/news/releases/2001/09/20010911–16.html# (last accessed on August 7, 2008).

61. Grant Wardlaw, *Political Terrorism: Theory, Tactics, and Counter-measures. Second Edition* (Cambridge: Cambridge University Press, 1989), pp. 97–100.

62. Rosie Cowan, Duncan Campbell, and Vikram Dodd, "New Claims Emerge over Menezes Death," *Guardian*, August 17, 2005.

63. Haim Watzman, "When You Have to Shoot First," *New York Times*, July 28, 2005.
64. Ronald D. Crelinsten, "The Discourse and Practice of Counterterrorism in Liberal Democracies," *Australian Journal of Politics and History* 44(3) (1998): 389–413.
65. Vincenzo Ruggiero, "Criminalizing War: Criminology as Ceasefire," *Social & Legal Studies* 14(2) (2005): 239–57.
66. Christopher Coker, "The Long War: The Transatlantic Rift," in Dan Hansén and Magnus Ranstorp (eds.), *Cooperating Against Terrorism: EU–US Relations Post September 11* (Stockholm: Swedish National Defence College, 2007), pp. 23–9, at p. 28.
67. Commission of Inquiry into the Actions of Canadian Officials in Relation to Maher Arar, *The Report of the Commission of Inquiry into the Actions of Canadian Officials in Relation to Maher Arar*, 3 vols. (Ottawa: Queen's Printer, 2006), accessible from http://epe. lac-bac.gc.ca/100/206/301/pco-bcp/commissions/maher_arar/ 07-09-13/www.ararcommission.ca/eng/index.htm (last accessed on August 7, 2008).
68. Hofnung, "States of Emergency."
69. For an electronic copy of Seymour Hersh's original reports for the *St. Louis Post Dispatch*, see www.pierretristam.com/Bobst/ library/wf-200.htm (last accessed on August 7, 2008). See also Seymour Hersh, *My Lai 4: A Report on the Massacre and Its Aftermath* (New York: Random House, 1970).

CHAPTER 3. PROACTIVE COUNTERTERRORISM

1. For a good introduction to intelligence studies, see Mark Phythian and Peter Gill, *Intelligence in an Insecure World* (Cambridge: Polity, 2006).
2. Leaderless resistance was initially associated with the American radical right. See Jeffrey Kaplan, "Leaderless Resistance," *Terrorism and Political Violence* 9(3) (1997): 80–95. More recently, it has been applied to the radical environmental movement and the Islamist jihadi movement. See Paul Joose, "Leaderless Resistance and Ideological Inclusion: The Case of the Earth Liberation Front," *Terrorism and Political Violence* 19(3) (2007): 351–68; Marc Sageman, *Leaderless Jihad: Terror Networks in the Twenty First Century* (Philadelphia: University of Pennsylvania Press, 2007).

3. Ronald D. Crelinsten, "Terrorism, Counter-Terrorism and Democracy: The Assessment of National Security Threats," *Terrorism and Political Violence* 1(2) (1989): 242–69, at pp. 254–5.

4. Peter Whoriskey and Dan Eggen, "7 Held in Miami in Terror Plot Targeting Sears Tower," *Washington Post*, June 23, 2006; John O'Neil, "New York Tunnel Plot Is Uncovered in Early Stage," *New York Times*, July 7, 2006. Later reports on the New York plot revealed that the target was actually JFK Airport. See Cara Buckley and William K. Rashbaum, "4 Accused of Plot to Blow Up Facilities at Kennedy Airport," *New York Times*, June 3, 2007.

5. Eric Lipton, "Recent Arrests in Terror Plots Yield Debate on Pre-emptive Action by Government," *New York Times*, July 9, 2006.

6. Philip Shenon and Neil A. Lewis, "Tracing Plots, British Watch, Then Pounce," *New York Times*, August 13, 2006.

7. Alan Travis, "Watchdog's Threat to 42-day Terror Law," *Guardian*, March 31, 2008.

8. Jeff Sallot, "Terror Vote Fails as Dion Reins in Liberals: Conservative Bid to Renew Measures Voted down 159–124," *Globe and Mail*, February 28, 2007.

9. For a classic discussion, see Otto Kirchheimer, *Political Justice: The Use of Legal Procedure for Political Ends* (Westport, CT: Greenwood Press, 1980).

10. Dina Temple-Raston, *The Jihad Next Door: The Lackawanna Six and Rough Justice in an Age of Terror* (New York: PublicAffairs Books, 2007).

11. Alan Cowell and Dexter Filkins, "British Authorities Say Plot to Blow Up Airliners Was Foiled," *New York Times*, August 10, 2006.

12. In this case, the prosecutions were *not* very successful. See John F. Burns and Elaine Sciolino, "No One Convicted of Terror Plot to Bomb Planes," *New York Times*, September 8, 2008.

13. For some case studies of politicization of intelligence, see Loch K. Johnson and James J. Wirtz (eds.), *Strategic Intelligence: Windows Into a Secret World* (Los Angeles: Roxbury, 2004), Part IV: "The Danger of Intelligence Politicization," pp. 167–217.

14. Juan Cole, "The Outing of Muhammed Naeem Noor Khan," Antiwar.com, August 19, 2004, at www.antiwar.com/cole/?articleid=3382 (last accessed August 2, 2008); Jim Lobe, "From One Blunder to the Next," *Asia Times Online*, August 11, 2004; Charlie Savage and Brian Bender, "Leak of Qaeda Suspect Name

Criticized," *Boston Globe*, August 10, 2004; Tom Regan, "Did US Blow Cover on Al Qaeda Mole?" *Christian Science Monitor*, August 9, 2004; CNN.com, "U.S. Leak 'Harms Al Qaeda Sting,' " August 9, 2004, at www.cnn.com/2004/WORLD/asiapcf/08/09/terror. wrap (last accessed August 2, 2008).

15. Laurence Lustgarten and Ian Leigh, *In From the Cold: National Security and Parliamentary Democracy* (Oxford: Clarendon Press, 1994), p. 292.

16. Dave Lindorff, "Chertoff and Torture," *Nation*, February 14, 2005, at www.thenation.com/doc/20050214/lindorff (last accessed on August 21, 2008).

17. Rosie Cowan, Duncan Campbell and Vikram Dodd, "New Claims Emerge over Menezes Death," *Guardian*, August 17, 2005; Al-Jazeera.net, "Doubts Cast on London Police Killing," August 17, 2005.

18. Ronald V. Clarke and Graeme R. Newman, *Outsmarting the Terrorists* (Westport, CT: Praeger Security International, 2006), at p. 266, n. 7.

19. A. B. Hoogenboom, "Grey Policing: A Theoretical Framework," *Policing and Society* 2(1) (1991): 17–30. See also Trevor Jones and Tim Newburn, *Private Security and Public Policing* (Oxford: Oxford University Press, 1998).

20. The word "sunlighting" was first used in John Darnton, "Madrid's New Working Class: The Bureaucrats," *New York Times*, February 7, 1983. See the entry for "sunlighting" at wordspy.com, at www.wordspy.com/words/sunlighting.asp (last accessed on August 7, 2008).

21. Sabrina Tavernise, "U.S. Contractor Banned by Iraq Over Shootings," *New York Times*, September 18, 2007; Sabrina Tavernise and James Glanz, "Iraqi Report Says Blackwater Guards Fired First," *New York Times*, September 19, 2007.

22. Associated Press, "U.S. Renews Blackwater Contract in Iraq," *International Herald Tribune*, April 5, 2008.

23. CNN Interactive, "CIA Tries New Strategy to Deter Terrorism," March 1, 1999; Vernon Loeb, "U.S. Tip to Turkey Led To Capture of Ocalan," *Washington Post*, February 21, 1999, p. A27; Tim Weiner, "U.S. Helped Turkey Find and Capture Kurd Rebel," *New York Times*, February 20, 1999, p. 1.

24. Scott Shane and David Johnston, "Mining of Data Prompted Fight Over U.S. Spying," *New York Times*, July 29, 2007; Scott

Shane and Eric Lichtblau, "Cheney Pushed U.S. to Widen Eavesdropping," *New York Times*, May 14, 2006.

25. Philip Bobbitt, "Op-Ed Contributor: Why We Listen," *New York Times*, January 30, 2006.

26. Carl Hulse and Edmund L. Andrews, "House Approves Changes in Eavesdropping," *New York Times*, August 5, 2007.

27. For a recent survey of the extent of surveillance in various European countries, see BBC News, "The Most Spied Upon People in Europe," February 28, 2008, at http://news.bbc.co.uk/2/hi/europe/7265212.stm# (last accessed on August 7, 2008).

28. Cara Buckley, "New York Plans Surveillance Veil for Downtown," *New York Times*, July 9, 2007.

29. Keith Bradsher, "China Enacting a High-Tech Plan to Track People," *New York Times*, August 12, 2007.

30. National Commission on Terrorist Attacks Upon the United States, *The 9/11 Commission Report: Final Report of the National Commission on Terrorist Attacks Upon the United States* (New York: W. W. Norton, 2004), pp. 385–90. For a critique of such "identity policies" and related "risk profiles," see Kim Rygiel, "Protecting and Proving Identity: The Biopolitics of Waging War through Citizenship in the Post-9/11 Era," in Krista Hunt and Kim Rygiel (eds.), *(En)Gendering the War on Terror: War Stories and Camouflaged Politics* (Aldershot: Ashgate, 2006), pp. 145–67, esp. pp. 154–8.

31. See, for example, Jeffrey Rosen, *The Naked Crowd: Reclaiming Security and Freedom in an Anxious Age* (New York: Random House, 2004); Christian Parenti, *The Soft Cage: Surveillance in America from Slavery to the War on Terror* (New York: Basic Books, 2003).

32. Robert Baer, *See No Evil: The True Story of a Ground Soldier in the CIA's War on Terrorism* (New York: Crown, 2002). See also Mark Phythian and Peter Gill, *Intelligence in an Insecure World* (Cambridge: Polity, 2006), pp. 77–8.

33. For a case study of the use of informers in the Israeli/Palestinian conflict, see Hillel Cohen and Ron Dudai, "Human Rights Dilemmas in Using Informers to Combat Terrorism: The Israeli–Palestinian Case," *Terrorism and Political Violence* 17(1–2) (2005): 229–43. See also Gary T. Marx, "Thoughts on a Neglected Category of Social Movement Participant: The Agent Provocateur and the Informant," *American Journal of Sociology* 80(2) (1974): 402–42.

34. Kirk Semple, "Closing Arguments Begin in Trial of Men Charged in Plot to Destroy the Sears Tower," *New York Times*, November 30,

2007. For another case where paid informers were used to monitor mosques in New York City, see William K. Rashbaum, "Trial Opens Window on Shadowing of Muslims," *New York Times*, May 28, 2006.

35. Gary T. Marx, *Undercover: Police Surveillance in America* (Berkeley: University of California Press, 1988).

36. Stephen Jay Gould, *The Mismeasure of Man* (New York: W. W. Norton & Co, 1981). A revised edition of this classic exploration of racism within the positivist tradition was published in 1996.

37. George Orwell, *Nineteen Eighty-Four* (Toronto: S. J. Reginald Saunders & Co. Ltd., 1949).

38. Alan Cowell, "Blair Wins Parliament Vote Criminalizing 'Glorification' of Terror," *New York Times*, February 16, 2006. But see also Souad Mekhennet and Dexter Filkins, "British Law Against Glorifying Terrorism Has Not Silenced Calls to Kill for Islam," *New York Times*, August 21, 2006.

39. Peter Taylor, "Real Spooks," *Panorama*, BBC 1, broadcast on April 30, 2007, transcript made from broadcast available at http://news.bbc.co.uk/1/hi/programmes/panorama/6692741.sm (last accessed on August 2, 2008).

40. Colin Freeze and Jeff Sallot, "Fast-food Encounter Drew Attention to Arar," *Globe and Mail*, November 11, 2003; Colin Freeze, "Arar Case Began Amid Fear of Attack on Ottawa," *Globe and Mail*, January 16, 2004.

41. Ian Austen, "Canada Reaches Settlement With Torture Victim," *New York Times*, January 26, 2007.

42. Victor E. Kappeler and Aaron E. Kappeler, "Speaking of Evil and Terrorism: The Political and Ideological Construction of a Moral Panic," in Mathieu Deflem (ed.), *Terrorism and Counterterrorism: Criminological Perspectives* (Amsterdam: Elsevier, 2004), pp. 175–97.

43. Ronald D. Crelinsten, "Terrorism and Counter-Terrorism in a Multi-Centric World: Challenges and Opportunities," in Max Taylor and John Horgan (eds.), *The Future of Terrorism* (London: Frank Cass, 2000), pp. 170–96.

44. Helene Cooper, "U.S. Weighing Terrorist Label for Iran Guards," *New York Times*, August 15, 2007.

45. James Risen, "Bush Signs Law to Widen Legal Reach for Wiretapping," *New York Times*, August 6, 2007; Eric Lichtblau and Mark Mazzetti, "Broader Spying Authority Advances in Congress," *New York Times*, August 4, 2007.

46. James Adams, *The Financing of Terror* (Sevenoaks, Kent: New English Library, 1986).

47. Full text available at www.un.org/law/cod/finterr.htm (last accessed on August 2, 2008).

48. Nimrod Raphaeli, "Financing of Terrorism: Sources, Methods, and Channels," *Terrorism and Political Violence* 15(4) (2003): 59–82; Trifin Roule, "Follow the Money: Unraveling Al Qaeda's Financial Network," in David A. Charters and Graham F. Walker (eds.), *After 9/11: Terrorism and Crime in a Globalised World* (Fredericton, NB and Halifax, NS: Centre for Conflict Studies, University of New Brunswick, and Centre for Foreign Policy Studies, Dalhousie University, 2004), pp. 357–73; Thomas J. Biersteker and Sue E. Eckert (eds.), *Countering the Financing of Terrorism* (London: Routledge, 2007); Harold Trinkunas and Jeanne Giraldo (eds.), *Terrorism Financing and State Responses: A Comparative Perspective* (Stanford, CA: Stanford University Press, 2007).

49. Joseph M. Myers, "Disrupting Terrorist Networks: The New U.S. and International Regime for Halting Terrorist Funding," *Law and Policy in International Business* 34(1) (2002): 17–24; Bruce Zagaris, "The Merging of the Counter-Terrorism and Anti-Money Laundering Regimes," *Law and Policy in International Business* 34(1) (2002): 45–108.

50. See, for example, Eric Lichtblau and James Risen, "Bank Data Is Sifted by U.S. in Secret to Block Terror," *New York Times*, June 23, 2006.

51. Eric Lichtblau, "Europe Panel Faults Sifting of Bank Data," *New York Times*, September 26, 2006.

52. Lichtblau and Risen, "Bank Data Is Sifted by U.S. in Secret to Block Terror."

53. David Firestone, "F.B.I. Traces Hamas's Plan to Finance Attacks to '93: Eight years ago, electronic eavesdropping provided the first clear indication that the group planned to raise money in the United States for terrorism in Israel," *New York Times*, December 6, 2001.

54. Leslie Eaton, "U.S. Prosecution of Muslim Group Ends in Mistrial," *New York Times*, October 23, 2007.

55. Kurt Eichenwald, "Terror Money Hard to Block, Officials Find: Officials say Al Qaeda's money apparatus is so far-flung and diversified that it could survive even if Osama bin Laden is captured or killed," *New York Times*, December 10, 2001.

56. Ekaterina Stepanova, *Anti-terrorism and Peace-building During and After Conflict* (Stockholm: SIPRI, 2003), at p. 32.

57. Josh Meyer and Eric Lichtblau, "Crackdown on Terror Funding Is Questioned – Finance: U.S. officials say a lack of evidence and fighting among agencies have hampered the drive," *Los Angeles Times*, April 7, 2002.

58. Madeleine Baran, "The Terrorism Case that Wasn't: One Year On, 'Help the Needy' Case Still Shrouded in Mystery, Innuendo," *New Standard*, February 29, 2004. Available at http://newstandardnews.net/content/index.cfm/items/165 (last accessed on August 2, 2008).

59. Michael Chandler and Rohan Gunaratna, *Countering Terrorism: Can We Meet the Threat of Global Violence?* (London: Reaktion Books, 2007), pp. 138–9.

60. Ibid., pp. 146–7.

61. Josh Meyer, "Cutting Money Flow to Terrorists Proves Difficult: Nations at the heart of Al Qaeda's network lack financial safeguards, and the global alliance is weaker. Cells are now deeper underground," *Los Angeles Times*, September 28, 2003.

62. Ronald D. Crelinsten, "The EU–US Partnership in the Area of Counterterrorism: A Multicentric View," in Dan Hansén and Magnus Ranstorp (eds.), *Cooperating Against Terrorism: EU–US Relations Post September 11* (Stockholm: Swedish National Defence College, 2007), pp. 53–98.

63. Rogelio Pardo-Mauer, *The Contras, 1980–1989: A Special Kind of Politics* (New York: Greenwood Publishing, 1990); Christopher Dickey, *With the Contras: A Reporter in the Wilds of Nicaragua* (New York: Simon & Schuster, 1987).

64. Erich Lichtblau and James C. McKinley, Jr., "2 Albany Men are Arrested in Plot to Import a Missile and Kill a Diplomat," *New York Times*, August 6, 2004; Lobe, "From One Blunder to the Next" (n. 14); Mark Santora, "Key Evidence Cast in Doubt On a Claim of Terrorism," *New York Times*, August 18, 2004; Michael Wilson, "Jury Convicts 2 Albany Men in Missile Plot," *New York Times*, October 11, 2006; "2 Men Sentenced in Fictitious Terror Plot," *New York Times*, March 9, 2006.

65. For an analysis of the Bush Administration's privileging of presidential authority in the "war on terror," see Scott Shane, "Behind Power, One Principle," *New York Times*, December 17, 2005. See also Adam Cohen, "Just What the Founders Feared:

An Imperial President Goes to War," *New York Times*, July 23, 2007.

66. Michael Kenney, *From Pablo to Osama: Trafficking and Terrorist Networks, Government Bureaucracies, and Competitive Adaptation* (University Park, PA: The Pennsylvania State University Press, 2007), pp. 191–202. For a comprehensive analysis of the intelligence failures leading up to 9/11, see Amy B. Zegart, *Spying Blind: The CIA, the FBI, and the Origins of 9/11* (Princeton, NJ: Princeton University Press, 2007).

CHAPTER 4. PERSUASIVE COUNTERTERRORISM

1. Ronald D. Crelinsten, "Analysing Terrorism and Counter-terrorism: A Communication Model," *Terrorism and Political Violence*, 14(2) (2002): 77–122, at pp. 83–4.

2. Ronald D. Crelinsten, "Terrorism as Political Communication: The Relationship between the Controller and the Controlled," in Paul Wilkinson and A. M. Stewart (eds.), *Contemporary Research on Terrorism* (Aberdeen: University of Aberdeen Press, 1987), pp. 3–23; Alex P. Schmid and Janny de Graaf, *Violence as Communication: Insurgent Terrorism and the Western News Media* (London: Sage, 1982).

3. See, for example, Paul R. Pillar, *Terrorism and U.S. Foreign Policy* (Washington, DC: Brookings Institution Press, 2001), pp. 104–5.

4. Frank E. Zimring and Gordon. J. Hawkins, *Deterrence: The Legal Threat in Crime Control* (Chicago: University of Chicago Press, 1973), p. 7.

5. Ibid., pp. 74–89.

6. See, for example Charles Krauthammer, "The Unipolar Moment Revisited," in Gus Martin (ed.), *The New Era of Terrorism: Selected Readings* (London: Sage, 2004), pp. 13–23, at p. 16.

7. The literature on suicide terrorism is large and constantly expanding. See, for example, Ami Pedhazur, *Suicide Terrorism* (London: Polity, 2004); Anne Marie Oliver and Paul Steinberg, *The Road to Martyr's Square: A Journey into the World of the Suicide Bomber* (Oxford: Oxford University Press, 2005); Mia Bloom, *Dying to Kill: The Allure of Suicide Terrorism* (New York: Columbia University Press, 2005); Robert Pape, *Dying to Win: The Strategic Logic of Suicide Terrorism* (New York: Random

House, 2005); Ami Pedhazur, *The Root Causes of Suicide Terrorism: The Globalization of Martyrdom* (London: Routledge, 2005); Diego Gambetta (ed.), *Making Sense of Suicide Missions* (Oxford: Oxford University Press, 2005); Mohammed M. Hafez, *Manufacturing Human Bombs: The Making of Palestinian Suicide Bombers* (Washington, DC: United States Institute of Peace Press, 2006); Andrew Silke, "The Role of Suicide in Politics, Conflict, and Terrorism," *Terrorism and Political Violence* 18(1) (2006): 35–46; Berko Anat, *The Path to Paradise: The Inner World of Suicide Bombers and Their Dispatchers* (Westport, CT: Praeger, 2007). Some researchers argue that the term "suicide terrorism" is a misnomer, since the central feature of such terrorism is, in fact, martyrdom, not suicide. See, for example, David Cook and Olivia Allison, *Understanding and Addressing Suicide Attacks: The Faith and Politics of Martyrdom Operations* (Westport, CT: Praeger Security International, 2007); Mohammed M. Hafez, *Suicide Bombers in Iraq: The Strategy and Ideology of Martyrdom* (Washington, DC: United States Institute of Peace Press, 2007); Mohammed M. Hafez, "Martyrdom Mythology in Iraq: How Jihadists Frame Suicide Terrorism in Videos and Biographies," *Terrorism and Political Violence* 19(1) (2007): 95–115; Ivan Strenski, "Sacrifice, Gift and the Social Logic of Muslim 'Human Bombers,'" *Terrorism and Political Violence* 15(3) (2003): 1–34 (see also the responses by Richard D. Hecht and Richard C. Martin, as well as Strenski's reply to Hecht and Martin, all in the same issue).

8. For scholarly analyses of state terrorism, see Michael Stohl and George A. Lopez (eds.), *The State as Terrorist: The Dynamics of Government Violence and Repression* (Westport, CT: Greenwood Press, 1984); Peter Alan Sproat, "Can the State Be Terrorist?" *Studies in Conflict and Terrorism* 14(1) (1991): 19–29.

9. Marc Sageman, *Understanding Terror Networks* (Philadelphia: University of Pennsylvania Press, 2004), esp. ch. 5 : "Social Networks and the Jihad." See also Jessica Stern, *Terror in the Name of God: Why Religious Militants Kill* (New York: HarperCollins, 2003).

10. Roderick A. Macdonald, "Metaphors of Multiplicity: Civil Society, Regimes, and Legal Pluralism," *Arizona Journal of International and Comparative Law* 15(1) (1998): 69–91.

11. Michael Slackman, "Voices Rise in Egypt to Shield Girls from an Old Tradition," *New York Times*, September 21, 2007.

12. For a history and analysis of the headscarf debate in France, see Jane Freedman, "The Headscarf Debate: Muslim Women in Europe and the 'War on Terror,' " in Krista Hunt and Kim Rygiel (eds.), *(En)Gendering the War on Terror: War Stories and Camouflaged Politics* (Aldershot: Ashgate, 2006), pp. 169–89. For Turkey, see Jenny B. White, *Islamist Mobilization in Turkey: A Study in Vernacular Politics* (Seattle: University of Washington Press, 2002), esp. ch. 7: "Islamist Elitism and Women's Choices," pp. 212–41.

13. For some classic discussions, see Herman Kahn, *Thinking About the Unthinkable* (New York: Horizon, 1962); Patrick M. Morgan, *Deterrence: A Conceptual Analysis* (Beverly Hills, CA: Sage, 1977); John J. Mearsheimer, *Conventional Deterrence* (Ithaca, NY: Cornell University Press, 1983); Robert Jervis, Richard Ned Lebow, and Janice Gross Stein, *Psychology and Deterrence* (Baltimore, MD: Johns Hopkins University Press, 1985).

14. Former US Vice-President Dick Cheney, speaking at the Heritage Foundation on October 10, 2003. Cited in Eric Schmitt, "Cheney Lashes Out at Critics of Policy on Iraq," *The New York Times*, October 11, 2003.

15. Ibid.

16. Robert F. Trager and Dessislava P. Zagorcheva, "Deterring Terrorism: It Can Be Done," *International Security* 30(3) (Winter 2005/6): 87–123, at p. 89.

17. George W. Bush, *National Strategy for Combating Terrorism*, ch. V: "Strategy for Winning the War on Terror,"Available at www.whitehouse.gov/nsc/nsct/2006 (last accessed on August 4, 2008). See also Eric Schmitt and Tom Shanker, "U.S. Adapts Cold-War Idea to Fight Terrorists," September 2006. *New York Times*, March 18, 2008. For a similar argument, see Paul K. Davis and Brian Michael Jenkins, *Deterrence & Influence in Counterterrorism: A Component in the War on al Qaeda* (Santa Monica, CA: Rand, 2002), esp. ch. 6, at pp. 59–60.

18. For an overview of Israel's multifaceted approach to CT, see Leonard A. Cole, *Terror: How Israel Has Coped and What America Can Learn* (Bloomington: Indiana University Press, 2007).

19. Martin van Creveld, "Israel's Counterterrorism," in Doron Zimmermann and Andreas Wenger (eds.), *How States Fight*

Terrorism: Policy Dynamics in the West (Boulder, CO: Lynne Rienner, 2007), pp. 157–73, at p. 163.

20. Ibid., p. 165.

21. Bruno S. Frey and Dominic Rohner, "Protecting Cultural Monuments against Terrorism," Institute for Empirical Research in Economics Working Paper No. 257, November 22, 2005, available at Social Science Research Network: http://ssrn.com/abstract=868971 (last accessed on August 7, 2008).

22. For Israel and its emergency response capabilities, see Matthew Kalman, "Israel Offers U.S. Doctors Training in Emergency Response," *San Francisco Chronicle*, November 18, 2007, at www.sfgate.com/cgi-bin/article.cgi?f=/c/a/2007/11/18/MN66T9B6P.DTL (last accessed on August 7, 2008).

23. Ronald D. Crelinsten, "Power and Meaning: Terrorism as a Struggle over Access to the Communication Structure," in Wilkinson and Stewart (eds.), *Contemporary Research on Terrorism*, pp. 419–50; Ronald D. Crelinsten, "Television and Terrorism: Implications for Crisis Management and Policy-Making," *Terrorism and Political Violence* 9(4) (1997): 8–32.

24. BBC World, *World News Today with Mike Embley*, February 8, 2008 broadcast. See also Kirsten E. Schultze, "Indonesia's Approach to Jihadist Deradicalization," *CTC Sentinel*, 7, (8) (July 2008): 8–10; Michael Jacobson, "Why Terrorists Quit: Gaining From Al-Qa'ida's Losses," *CTC Sentinel*, 1(8) (July 2008): 1–4, esp. p. 2 (both available at www.ctc.usma.edu/sentinel/; last accessed on September 13, 2008).

25. Donatella della Porta, "Institutional Responses to Terrorism: The Italian Case," in Alex P. Schmid and Ronald D. Crelinsten (eds.), *Western Responses to Terrorism* (London: Frank Cass), pp. 151–70.

26. Martha Crenshaw, "How Terrorism Declines," *Terrorism and Political Violence* 3(1) (1991): 69–87, at p. 83.

27. BBC News, "Al-Qaeda disowns 'fake letter,' " October 13, 2005, at http://news.bbc.co.uk/2/hi/middle_east/4339912.stm (last accessed on August 7, 2008). See also Combating Terrorism Center, *Harmony and Disharmony: Exploiting al-Qa'ida's Organizational Vulnerabilities* (West Point, NY: Department of Social Sciences, US Military Academy, 2006), available at http://ctc.usma.edu/harmony/harmony_menu.asp (last accessed on August 7, 2008); Combating Terrorism Center, *Cracks in the*

Foundation: Leadership Schisms in Al-Qa'ida From 1989–2006 (West Point, NY: Department of Social Sciences, US Military Academy, 2007), available at http://ctc.usma.edu/harmony/harmony_menu.asp (last accessed on August 7, 2008).

28. David S. Cloud and Jeff Gerth, "Muslim Scholars Were Paid to Aid U.S. Propaganda," *New York Times*, January 2, 2006. For a broader discussion of the US military's propaganda programs, see Jeff Gerth, "Military's Information War is Vast and Often Secretive," *New York Times*, December 11, 2005.

29. Jeff Victoroff et al., "Working Group 2: Preventing Substate Terrorist Groups from Recruiting and Retaining Young Members," in Jeff Victoroff (ed.), *Tangled Roots: Social and Psychological Factors in the Genesis of Terrorism* (Amsterdam: IOS Press, 2006), p. 441.

30. "*Black* propaganda is when the source is concealed or credited to a false authority and spreads lies, fabrications, and deceptions." Gerth S. Jowett and Victoria O'Donnell, *Propaganda and Persuasion, Fourth Edition*. (Thousand Oaks, CA: Sage, 2006), p. 17

31. Associated Press, "Carter Defends his Talks with Hamas after 2 Days of Meetings with Militant Palestinian Group," *International Herald Tribune*, April 17, 2008.

32. Colum Lynch, "The U.N. Insignia Emerges as a Global Target for Al-Qaeda Attacks," *Washington Post*, December 25, 2007.

33. Integrated Regional Information Networks, "N.G.O.'s in Afghanistan Vulnerable to Criminal Violence and Insurgency," November 11, 2007, available at www.worldpress.org/Asia/2986.cfm (last accessed on August 7, 2008).

34. Albert Bandura, "Mechanisms of Moral Disengagement," in Walter Reich (ed.), *Origins of Terrorism: Psychologies, Ideologies, Theologies, States of Mind* (Washington, DC: Woodrow Wilson Center Press, 1990), pp. 161–91; Mohammed M. Hafez, "Moral Agents, Immoral Violence: Mechanisms of Moral Disengagement in Palestinian Suicide Terrorism," in Victoroff (ed.), *Tangled Roots*, pp. 292–307.

35. Schmitt and Shanker, "U.S. Adapts Cold-War Idea to Fight Terrorists."

36. David Cook, *Understanding Jihad* (Berkeley: University of California Press, 2005). See also John C. Zimmerman, "Jihad, Theory and Practice: A Review Essay," *Terrorism and Political Violence* 19(2) (2007): 279–87; Mary Habeck, *Knowing the Enemy:*

Jihadist Ideology and the War on Terror (New Haven, CT: Yale University Press, 2006); John Kelsay, *Arguing the Just War in Islam* (Cambridge, MA: Harvard University Press, 2007); David Bukay, *From Muhammad to Bin Laden: Religious and Ideological Sources of the Homicide Bombers Phenomenon* (New Brunswick, NJ: Transaction Publishers, 2008).

37. Raphael Israeli, "Education, Identity, State Building and the Peace Process: Educating Palestinian Children in the Post-Oslo Era," *Terrorism and Political Violence* 12(1) (2000): 79–94.

38. See, for example, Wayne Nelles (ed.), *Comparative Education, Terrorism and Human Security: From Critical Pedagogy to Peacebuilding?* (New York: Palgrave Macmillan, 2003).

39. Peter Bergen and Swati Pandey, "The Madrassa Myth," *New York Times*, June 14, 2005.

40. Donatella della Porta, "Recruitment Processes in Clandestine Political Organizations: Italian Left-Wing Terrorism," *International Social Movement Research* 1 (1988): 155–69; Rogelio Alonso, "Individual Motivations For Joining Terrorist Organizations: A Comparative Qualitative Study On Members of ETA and IRA," in Victoroff (ed.), *Tangled Roots*, pp. 187–202, esp. pp. 193–8.

41. Anne Speckhard, "Defusing Human Bombs: Understanding Suicide Terrorism," in Victoroff (ed.), *Tangled Roots*, pp. 277–91, at pp. 282–3.

42. Ibid., esp. pp. 283–5; Shaul Kimhi and Shemuel Even, "The Palestinian Human Bombers," in Victoroff (ed.), *Tangled Roots*, pp. 308–23, esp. pp. 314–15; Khapta Akhmedova and Anne Speckhard, "A Multi-Causal Analysis of the Genesis of Suicide Terrorism: The Chechen Case," in Victoroff (ed.), *Tangled Roots*, pp. 324–54, esp. pp. 339–40.

43. Linda O. Valenty et al., "Working Group I: Reducing the Threat of Substate Terrorism: Interventions to Reduce the Efficacy of Committed Terrorists," in Victoroff (ed.), *Tangled Roots*, pp. 431–7, at p. 433.

44. Neil MacFarquhar, "At State Dept., Blog Team Joins Muslim Debate," *New York Times*, September 22, 2007.

45. For a history of the meteoric rise of this all-news channel, see Mohammed el-Nawawy and Adel Iskandar, *Al-Jazeera: How the Free Arab News Network Scooped the World and Changed the Middle East* (Cambridge, MA: Westview Press, 2002).

46. For an insider's critique of the US military's, and, to a lesser extent, the British Army's, media policy in Iraq, see Steve Tatham, *Losing Arab Hearts and Minds: The Coalition, Al Jazeera and Muslim Public Opinion* (London: Hurst and Company, 2006).

47. Hassan M. Fattah, "A New Al Jazeera With a Global Focus," *New York Times*, November 13, 2006; Alessandra Stanley, "The TV Watch; Not Coming Soon to a Channel Near You," *New York Times*, November 16, 2006.

48. Peter Waldmann, "The Radical Community: A Comparative Analysis of the Social Background of ETA, IRA, and Hezbollah," in Victoroff (ed.), *Tangled Roots*, pp. 133–46.

49. Tom Pyszczynski, Abdollhossein Abdollahi, Jeff Greenberg, and Sheldon Solomon, "Crusades and Jihads: An Existential Psychological Perspective on the Psychology of Terrorism and Political Extremism," in Victoroff (ed.), *Tangled Roots*, pp. 85–97, at pp. 89–90.

50. Ibid., pp. 90–1.

51. Howard Davis and Phil Scraton, "Institutionalised Conflict and the Subordination of 'Loss' in the Immediate Aftermath of UK Mass Fatality Disasters," *Journal of Contingencies and Crisis Management* 7(2) (1999): 86–97.

52. David L. Paletz and Alex P. Schmid (eds.), *Perspectives on Terrorism and the Media* (Newbury Park, CA: Sage, 1992); Ronald D. Crelinsten (1994), "The Impact of Television on Terrorism and Crisis Situations: Implications for Public Policy," *Journal of Contingencies and Crisis Management* 2(2): 61–72; Crelinsten, "Television and Terrorism."

53. Brigitte L. Nacos, Robert Y. Shapiro, and Pierangelo Isernia (eds.), *Decisionmaking in a Glass House: Mass Media, Public Opinion, and American and European Foreign Policy in the 21st Century* (Lanham, MD: Rowman & Littlefield, 2000), p. 2. See also Philip M. Taylor, "The Military and the Media," in Stephen Badsey (ed.), *The Media and International Security* (London: Frank Cass, 2000), pp. 177–202, esp. pp. 197–200. For a critique of the power of the media to set the policy agenda, especially in the area of conflict prevention and humanitarian intervention, see Nik Gowing, "Media Coverage: Help or Hindrance in Conflict Prevention?" in Badsey (ed.), *The Media and International Security*, pp. 203–26.

54. Gabriel Weimann, *Terror on the Internet: The New Arena, the New Challenges* (Washington, DC: United States Institute of Peace Press, 2006).

55. Rose McDermott and Philip G. Zimbardo, "The Psychological Consequences of Terrorist Alerts," in Bruce Bongar, Lisa M. Brown, Larry E. Beutler, James N. Breckenridge, and Philip G. Zimbardo (eds.), *Psychology of Terrorism* (Oxford: Oxford University Press, 2007), pp. 357–70.

56. Jeanne Meserve, "Duct Tape Sales Rise amid Terror Fears," CNN, February 11, 2003, available at www.cnn.com/2003/US/02/11/emergency.supplies (last accessed on August 7, 2008).

57. The Associated Press, "States Moderating Response to Upgraded Alerts," *New York Times*, May 24, 2003; Jack Weiss, "Orange Crunch," *New York Times*, January 14, 2004; Stephen E. Flynn, "Color Me Scared," *New York Times*, May 25, 2005.

58. Paul Krugman, "Hired Gun Fetish," *New York Times*, September 28, 2007.

59. For two scathing critiques of the Bush Administration's use of deceptive public relations tactics during the run-up to the Iraq War, see Frank Rich, *The Greatest Story Ever Sold: The Decline and Fall of Truth in Bush's America* (New York: Penguin, 2007); Michael Isikoff and David Corn, *Hubris: The Inside Story of Spin, Scandal, and the Selling of the Iraq War* (New York: Three Rivers Press, 2007).

60. Editorial, "From the Editors: The Times and Iraq," *New York Times*, May 26, 2004.

61. Lorne Manly, "Big News Media Join in Push to Limit Use of Unidentified Sources," *New York Times*, May 23, 2005.

62. World Public Opinion.org, "Misperceptions, the Media and the Iraq War," October 2, 2003, at www.worldpublicopinion.org/pipa/articles/international_security_bt/102.php?nid= &pnt= 102 (last accessed on August 5, 2008). The study was done by the Program on International Policy Attitudes (PIPA), a joint program of the Center on Policy Attitudes and the Center for International and Security Studies at the University of Maryland. The full report is available from a link at this site or directly from http://65.109.167.118/pipa/pdf/oct03/IraqMedia_Oct03_rpt.pdf (last accessed on August 5, 2008). For a discussion of Fox News coverage after the 9/11 attacks, see Jim Rutenberg, "Fox Portrays a War of Good and Evil, and Many Applaud," *New York Times*, December 3, 2001.

63. "Al-Jazeera 'hit by missile,'" BBC News, April 8, 2003. Available at http://news.bbc.co.uk/1/hi/world/middle_east/2927527.stm (last accessed on August 5, 2008).

64. For an interesting case study, see Anneli Botha, "Terrorism in Algeria: The Role of the Community in Combating Terrorism," in Peter Katona, Michael D. Intriligator, and John P. Sullivan (eds.), *Countering Terrorism and WMD: Creating a Global Counter-Terrorism Network* (London: Routledge, 2006), pp. 144–57.

65. Sharon Pickering, David Wright-Neville, Jude McCulloch, and Pete Lentini, *Counter-Terrorism Policing and Culturally Diverse Communities* (Melbourne: Monash University, 2007).

CHAPTER 5. DEFENSIVE COUNTERTERRORISM

1. See, for example, Lawrence Freedman (ed.), *Superterrorism: Policy Responses* (Oxford: Blackwell, 2002).

2. Before the 9/11 attacks, the effectiveness of this measure was disputed by some pilots, who argued that they would open the door if their air crew were threatened with violence. Presumably, this would no longer be the case, though what people do under extreme stress is always unpredictable. See National Commission on Terrorist Attacks Upon the United States, *The 9/11 Commission Report: Final Report of the National Commission on Terrorist Attacks Upon the United States* (New York: W. W. Norton, 2004), at p. 85.

3. Alan Cowell and Raymond Bonner, "4 Held in Scottish Attack as British See Broader Plot," *New York Times*, July 1, 2007.

4. R. Jeffrey Smith, "New Devices May Foil Airline Security," *Washington Post*, July 21, 1996.

5. Simon Reeve, *The New Jackals: Ramzi Yousef, Osama bin Laden and the Future of Terrorism* (Boston: Northeastern University Press, 1999), ch. 4: "The Bojinka Plot," pp. 71–93, at pp. 75, 79; Richard Miniter, *Losing Bin Laden: How Bill Clinton's Failures Unleashed Global Terror* (Washington, DC: Regnery Publishing, 2003), p. 81.

6. Simon Reeve, "Shoe-Bomb Flight – A Trial Run? U.S., British Officials Fear Similar Attacks in the Works," *San Francisco Chronicle*, January 6, 2002.

7. Joe Sharkey, "ON THE ROAD; Turns Out There's a Reason For Those 3-Ounce Bottles," *New York Times*, September 11, 2007.

8. Eric Lipton, "Airport Security Alert for Toys With Remotes," *New York Times*, October 2, 2007.

9. Janet Hessert, "The Gore Commission Demanded Tougher Airline Security, But Airlines and Conservatives Said No," Democrats.com website, at http://archive.democrats.com/view.cfm?id=4532 (last accessed on August 7, 2008).

10. See, for example, Robert W. Hahn, "The Cost of Antiterrorist Rhetoric," *Regulation: The Cato Review of Business and Government* 19(4) (1996), at www.cato.org/pubs/regulation/reg19n4e.html (last accessed on August 7, 2008).

11. For an assessment of airline safety and security written just after the 9/11 attacks, see Daniel Eisenberg, "How Safe Can We Get?" *Time* (2001), at www.time.com/time/covers/1101010924/bsecurity.html (last accessed on August 7, 2008). For a pre-9/11 scholarly look at the issue, see Paul Wilkinson and Brian M. Jenkins (eds.), *Aviation Terrorism and Security* (London: Frank Cass, 1999).

12. Walter Enders and Todd Sandler, *The Political Economy of Terrorism* (Cambridge: Cambridge University Press, 2006).

13. Tim Newburn, *Criminology* (Portland, OR: Willan Publishing, 2007), p. 582.

14. Ibid., p. 583.

15. National Commission on Terrorist Attacks Upon the United States, *The 9/11 Commission Report: Final Report*, p. 391.

16. Editorial, "A Huge Hole in Airport Security," *New York Times*, March 16, 2007.

17. Stephen E. Flynn and Lawrence M. Wein, "Think Inside the Box," *New York Times*, November 29, 2005; Eric Lipton, "Security Effort by Coast Guard is Falling Short," *New York Times*, December 30, 2006.

18. White House Commission on Aviation Safety and Security, *Final Report of White House Commission on Aviation Safety and Security*, ch. 3: "Improving Security for Travelers."

19. M. Victoria Cummock, "Appendix I: Dissent with the Final Report of the White House Commission on Aviation Safety and Security," *Final Report of White House Commission on Aviation Safety and Security*.

20. Ibid.

21. Mike Fish, "Many Warnings over Airport Security Preceded Terrorist Attacks," *Flight Risk. Part Two: Previous Warnings*,

CNN.com In-Depth Specials, 2001, downloaded at www. cnn.com/SPECIALS/2001/trade.center/flight.risk/stories/part2. mainbar.html (last accessed on August 7, 2008).

22. For a comparative analysis of airport security in the USA and in Europe, see Jens Hainmüller and Jan Martin Lemnitzer, "Why Do Europeans Fly Safer? The Politics of Airport Security in Europe and the US," *Terrorism and Political Violence* 15(4) (2003): 1–36.

23. Blake Morrison, "Feds Take Over Airport Screening," *USA Today*, November 19, 2002, available at www.usatoday.com/travel/news/2002/2002-11-18-screeners.htm (last accessed on August 7, 2008).

24. John Tierney, "Fighting the Last Hijackers," *New York Times*, August 16, 2005.

25. See, for example, Bernard E. Harcourt, "Search and Defend," *New York Times*, August 25, 2006.

26. Justin Blum, "Terrorists Have Oil Industry in Cross Hairs," *Washington Post*, September 27, 2004, p. A12, available at www.washingtonpost.com/ac2/wp-dyn/A52810–2004Sep26? language=printer (last accessed on August 7, 2008).

27. Gavin Cameron and Jason Pate, "Covert Biological Weapon Attacks Against Agricultural Targets: Assessing the Impact Against US Agriculture," *Terrorism and Political Violence* 13(3) (2001): 61–82.

28. There is an ongoing debate over whether radical environmentalist movements should be classified as terrorists, since their activities have not resulted in any deaths, or whether they have the potential for engaging in mass-casualty terrorism. See Bron Taylor, "Religion, Violence and Radical Environmentalism: From Earth First! to the Unabomber to the Earth Liberation Front," *Terrorism and Political Violence* 10(4) (1998): 1–42; Stephan H. Leader and Peter Probst, "The Earth Liberation Front and Environmental Terrorism," *Terrorism and Political Violence* 15(4) (2003): 37–58; Gary Ackerman, "Beyond Arson? A Threat Assessment of the Earth Liberation Front," *Terrorism and Political Violence* 15(4) (2003): 143–70. See also the comments on Ackerman, "Beyond Arson?" by Gary Perlstein (pp. 171–2) and Bron Taylor (pp. 173–82), as well as Ackerman's reply (pp. 183–9) in the same issue (15[4]).

29. George W. Bush, "December 17, 2003 Homeland Security Presidential Direction / Hspd-7," available at www.whitehouse. gov/news/releases/2003/12/20031217-5.html (last accessed on August 7, 2008).

30. See, for example, "Chemical Plants, Still Unprotected," *New York Times*, Editorial, September 25, 2006; David Kocieniewski, "Despite 9/11 Effect, Railyards Are Still Vulnerable," *New York Times*, March 27, 2006; Gregory S. McNeal, "The Terrorist and the Grid," *New York Times*, August 13, 2005.

31. Anthony H. Cordesman and Justin G. Cordesman, *Cyber-Threats, Information Warfare, and Critical Infrastructure Protection: Defending the U.S. Homeland* (Westport, CT: Praeger, 2002).

32. Wikipedia.org, Northeast Blackout of 2003, at http://en.wikipedia .org/wiki/2003_North_America_blackout#Sequence_of_events (last accessed on August 7, 2008). See also US–Canada Power System Outage Task Force, *Final Report on the August 14th Blackout in the United States and Canada: Causes and Recommendations*, April, 2004.

33. "Major Power Outage hits New York, other Large Cities," CNN.com, August 14, 2003, available at www.cnn.com/2003/US/ 08/14/power.outage (last accessed on September 14, 2008).

34. Ian Traynor, "Russia Accused of Unleashing Cyberwar to Disable Estonia," *Guardian*, May 17, 2007, available at www.guardian.co. uk/world/2007/may/17/topstories3.russia (last accessed on August 7, 2008).

35. Jeremy Kirk, "Student Convicted in Attack Against Estonian Web Site," *PC World*, January 24, 2008, at www.pcworld.com/article/id,141730-page,1/article.html# (last accessed on August 7, 2008); BBC News, "Estonia Fines Man for 'Cyber War,'" January 25, 2008, at http://news.bbc.co.uk/2/hi/technology/7208511.stm (last accessed on August 7, 2008).

36. David Kocieniewski, "Facing the City, Potential Targets Rely on a Patchwork of Security," *New York Times*, May 9, 2005.

37. Eric Lipton, "Administration to Seek Antiterror Rules for Chemical Plants," *New York Times*, June 15, 2005.

38. Associated Press, "U.S. Won't Override State Rules on Plants," *New York Times*, April 2, 2007.

39. See Public Safety Canada website at www.publicsafety.gc.ca/abt/ index-eng.aspx (last accessed on August 7, 2008).

40. Eric Lipton, "U.S. Terror Targets: Petting Zoo and Flea Market?" *New York Times*, July 12, 2006.

41. Eric Lipton, "Security Cuts for New York and Washington," *New York Times*, June 1, 2006.

42. David Johnston, "A City's Police Force Now Doubts Terror Focus," *New York Times*, July 24, 2008; Eric Schmitt and David Johnston, "States Chafing at U.S. Focus on Terrorism," *New York Times*, May 26, 2008. According to state officials, one quarter of Federal grants in 2008 have to be spent on defending against improvised explosive devices (IEDs) despite the absence of any intelligence suggesting that such a threat exists domestically (as opposed to in Iraq).

43. Ronald V. Clarke and Graeme R. Newman, *Outsmarting the Terrorists* (Westport, CT: Praeger Security International, 2006).

44. Ibid., ch. 5: "Suicide Bombings, Step by Step," pp. 53–69.

45. C. Christine Fair and Bryan Shepherd, "Research Note: Who Supports Terrorism? Evidence from Fourteen Muslim Countries," in Jeff Victoroff (ed.), *Tangled Roots: Social and Psychological Factors in the Genesis of Terrorism* (Amsterdam: IOS Press, 2006), pp. 162–86; C. Christine Fair, "Who Are Pakistan's Militants and Their Families?" *Terrorism and Political Violence* 20(1) (2008): 49–65.

46. Daniel Benjamin, Aidan Kirby, and Julianne Smith, *Currents and Crosscurrents of Radical Islamism: A Report of the Transatlantic Dialogue on Terrorism* (Washington, DC: Center for Strategic and International Studies (CSIS), April 2006), p. 7. See also Neil MacFarquhar, "Pakistanis Find U.S. an Easier Fit Than Britain," *New York Times*, August 21, 2006.

47. Benjamin et al., *Currents and Crosscurrents*, pp. 6–7.

48. David Johnston and Don Van Natta, Jr., "Traces of Terror: The F.B.I. Memo; Ashcroft Learned of Agent's Alert Just After 9/11," *New York Times*, May 21, 2002.

49. Associated Press, "Student Visa Fraud Ring Broken by 58 Arrests, Government Says," *New York Times*, May 8, 2002.

50. For a comment from the left, see Jörg Victor, "The Netherlands: Xenophobic Campaign Follows Theo Van Gogh Murder," *World Socialist Website*, November 23, 2004, at www.wsws.org/articles/2004/nov2004/gogh-n23.shtml (last accessed on August 7, 2008). For a comment from the right, see Michael Ledeen, "The Killers: The Dutch Hit Crisis Point," *National Review Online*, November 10, 2004, at www.nationalreview.com/ledeen/ledeen200411101620.asp (last accessed on August 7, 2008).

51. Matthew Tempest, "Clarke Reveals Terror Deportation Rules," *Guardian*, August 24, 2005.

52. John F. Burns, "British Muslim Leaders Propose 'Code of Conduct,'" *New York Times*, November 30, 2007.

53. David A. Charters, "'Defence Against Help': Canadian–American Cooperation in the War on Terrorism," in David A. Charters and Graham F. Walker (eds.), *After 9/11: Terrorism and Crime in a Globalised World* (Fredericton, NB and Halifax, NS: Centre for Conflict Studies, University of New Brunswick, and Centre for Foreign Policy Studies, Dalhousie University), pp. 288–305, at p. 290.

54. Eric Schmitt and David E. Sanger, "Pakistan Rebuffs Secret U.S. Plea for C.I.A. Buildup," *New York Times*, January 27, 2008; David E. Sanger and David Rohde, "In Pakistan Quandary, U.S. Reviews Stance," *New York Times*, October 21, 2007.

55. BBC News, "UN Rules against Israeli Barrier," July 9, 2004, at http://news.bbc.co.uk/2/hi/middle_east/3879057.stm (last accessed on August 7, 2008); Scott Wilson, "Israeli Court Orders Rerouting of Barrier," *Washington Post*, September 5, 2007, p. A16.

56. Arie Farnam, "Czechs Try to Cap Plastic Explosives Sales," *Christian Science Monitor*, February 26, 2002, at www.csmonitor.com/2002/0226/p07s02-woeu.html (last accessed on August 7, 2008).

57. Wikipedia.org, "DMDNB," at http://en.wikipedia.org/wiki/DMDNB (last accessed on August 7, 2008).

58. Tim Weiner, "U.S. Increases Fund to Outbid Terrorists for Afghan Missiles," *New York Times*, July 24, 1993.

59. Mats Berdal and Mónica Serrano, "Transnational Organized Crime and International Security: The New Topography," in Mats Berdal and Mónica Serrano (eds.), *Transnational Organized Crime and International Security: Business As Usual?* (Boulder, CO: Lynne Rienner, 2002), pp. 197–207, esp. pp. 201–2.

60. Cited by Sandia National Laboratories' Principal Scientist, Gerry Yonas, in Sandia News Release, May 17, 2005.

61. John Mueller, *Overblown: How Politicians and the Terrorism Industry Inflate National Security Threats, and Why We Believe Them* (New York: Free Press, 2006).

62. Cited in J. Bowyer Bell, *A Time of Terror: How Democratic Societies Respond to Revolutionary Violence* (New York: Basic Books, 1978), p. 124.

63. Andrew Buncombe and Omar Waraich, "British Police to Help Investigate Bhutto Murder," *Independent*, January 3, 2008.

64. See, for example, H. V. Savitch, *Cities in a Time of Terror: Space, Territory, and Local Resilience* (Armonk, NY: M. E. Sharpe, 2008).

65. Marc Coester, Klaus Bott, and Hans-Jürgen Kerner, *Prevention of Terrorism: Core Challenges for Cities in Germany and Europe* (Tübingen: Institut für Kriminologie der Universität Tübingen, 2007).

66. Ibid., p. 29.

67. Leonard A. Cole, *The Anthrax Letters: A Medical Detective Story* (Washington, DC: National Academy of Science, 2003). See also Scott Shane and Eric Lichtblau, "F.B.I. Presents Anthrax Case, Saying Scientist Acted Alone," *New York Times*, August 6, 2008.

68. David Shukman, "Problems Mount from 9/11 Fallout," BBC News, April 12, 2006, at http://news.bbc.co.uk/2/hi/science/nature/4904188.stm (last accessed on August 5, 2008).

69. Barry S. Levy and Victor W. Sidel (eds.), *Terrorism and Public Health: A Balanced Approach to Strengthening Systems and Protecting People* (Oxford: Oxford University Press, 2002).

70. Andreas Wenger and Reto Wollenmann (eds.), *Bioterrorism: Confronting a Complex Threat* (Boulder, CO: Lynne Rienner Publishers, 2007); Ceci Connolly, "Readiness for Chemical Attack Criticized: Most States' Public Health Labs Lack Equipment and Expertise, Group Reports," *Washington Post*, June 4, 2003, p. A11.

71. Susan Kim, "Sociologists Study Disasters," *Disaster News Network*, October 28, 2003, at www.disasternews.net/news/article.php?articleid=1609 (last accessed on August 5, 2008).

72. Gina Kolata and Lawrence K. Altman, "A National Challenged [*sic*]: The Bioterror Threat; Smallpox Vaccine Stockpile Is Larger Than Was Thought," *New York Times*, March 29, 2002; Tom Jefferson, "Bioterrorism and Compulsory Vaccination," *BMJ* 329 (September 4, 2004): 524–5, at www.bmj.com/cgi/content/full/329/7465/524 (last accessed on August 5, 2008).

73. Associated Press, "WHO: Pandemic Vaccine Stockpile Would Help Poor Nations," *USA Today*, March 2, 2007, at www.usatoday.com/news/health/2007-03-02-bird-flu_N.htm (last accessed on August 5, 2008).

74. CNN.com, "Bush Orders Smallpox Vaccine for Military, Himself," CNN.com, January 30, 2004, at http://archives.cnn. com/2002/HEALTH/12/13/bush.smallpox/index.html (last accessed on August 5, 2008).

75. Associated Press, "Pentagon Suspends Mandatory Anthrax Vaccine," MSNBC.com, October 27, 2004, at www.msnbc.msn.com/id/6348898 (last accessed on August 5, 2008).

76. Anita Manning, "Smallpox Vaccination Plan 'Ceased,'" *USA Today*, October 15, 2003, at www.usatoday.com/news/health/2003-10-15-smallpox_x.htm (last accessed an August 5, 2008); Ray Moynihan, "Health Professionals Challenge US Smallpox Vaccination Plan," *BMJ* 326 (January 25, 2003): 179, at www.bmj.com/cgi/content/full/326/7382/179?etoc (last accessed on August 5, 2008).

77. The CRTI website is at www.css.drdc-rddc.gc.ca/crti/index-eng.asp (last accessed on August 5, 2008).

78. E. Alison Holman, Roxane Cohen Silver, Michael Poulin, Judith Andersen, Virginia Gil-Rivas, Daniel N. McIntosh, "Terrorism, Acute Stress, and Cardiovascular Health," *Archives General of Psychiatry* 65(1) (2008): 73–80.

79. Ronald Crelinsten, *The Dimensions of Victimization in the Context of Terroristic Acts*, Final Report of an international seminar (Montreal: Centre international de criminologie comparée, Université de Montréal, 1977).

80. For a recent review, see Lisa D. Butler, Leslie A. Morland, and Gregory A. Leskin, "Psychological Resilience in the Face of Terrorism," in Bruce Bongar, Lisa M. Brown, Larry E. Beutler, James N. Breckenridge, and Philip G. Zimbardo (eds.), *Psychology of Terrorism* (Oxford: Oxford University Press, 2007), pp. 400–17.

81. The English-language version of Impact's website is at www.impact-kenniscentrum.nl/?userlang=en (last accessed on August 7, 2008).

82. Ernest B. Abbot and Otto J. Hetzel (eds.), *A Legal Guide to Homeland Security and Emergency Management for State and Local Governments* (Chicago: ABA Publishing, 2005), pp. 121–2.

83. James N. Rosenau, *Turbulence in World Politics: A Theory of Change and Continuity* (Princeton: Princeton University Press, 1990), pp. 298–305.

84. Anthony Shadid and Kevin Sullivan, "Anatomy of the Cartoon Protest Movement," *Washington Post*, February 16, 2006, p. A01; Rosalind Ryan, "How the Muhammad Cartoons Row Escalated," *Guardian*, February 12, 2008, at www.guardian.co.uk/world/2008/feb/12/muhammadcartoons.islam (last accessed on August 7, 2008).

85. Rosalind Ryan, "Danish Newspapers Reprint Muhammad Cartoon," *Guardian*, February 13, 2008, at www.guardian.co.uk/world/2008/feb/13/muhammadcartoons (last accessed on August 7, 2008).

86. Ewen MacAskill and Fred Atewill, "New Bin Laden Message Attacks EU over Cartoons," *Guardian*, March 20, 2008, at www.guardian.co.uk/world/2008/mar/20/alqaida.eu (last accessed on August 7, 2008).

87. Roxanne Escobales, "Denmark Evacuates Embassies after 'Concrete' Terror Threat," *Guardian*, April 23, 2008, at www.guardian.co.uk/world/2008/apr/23/muhammadcartoons.afghanistan (last accessed on August 7, 2008).

CHAPTER 6. LONG-TERM
COUNTERTERRORISM

1. Richard A. Clarke, *Against All Enemies: Inside America's War on Terror* (New York: The Free Press, 2004); Steve Coll, *Ghost Wars: The Secret History of the CIA, Afghanistan, and bin Laden, From the Soviet Invasion to September 10, 2001* (New York: The Penguin Press, 2004); National Commission on Terrorist Attacks Upon the United States, *The 9/11 Commission Report: Final Report of the National Commission on Terrorist Attacks Upon the United States* (New York: W. W. Norton, 2004), pp. 198–214.

2. David C. Rapoport, "The Four Waves of Rebel Terror and September 11," in Charles W. Kegley, Jr. (ed.), *The New Global Terrorism: Characteristics, Causes, Controls* (Upper Saddle River, NJ: Prentice Hall, 2003), pp. 36–52.

3. Jacques Batigne, *Nous sommes tous des otages* [We are all hostages] (Paris: Plon, 1973).

4. David C. Rapoport, "Fear and Trembling: Terrorism in Three Religious Traditions," *American Political Science Review* 78(3) (1984): 658–77.

5. The findings were subsequently published in Tore Bjørgo (ed.), *Root Causes of Terrorism: Myths, Reality and Ways Forward* (London: Routledge, 2005).

6. Tore Bjørgo, *Root Causes of Terrorism: Findings from an International Expert Meeting in Oslo, 9–11 June 2003* (Oslo: The Norwegian Institute of International Affairs, 2003).

7. Ibid.
8. James J. F. Forest (ed.), *The Making of a Terrorist: Recruitment, Training, and Root Causes*, vol. III: *Root Causes* (Westport, CT: Praeger Security International, 2006).
9. Rune Henriksen and Anthony Vinci, "Combat Motivation in Non-State Armed Groups," *Terrorism and Political Violence* 20(1) (2008): 87–109.
10. See, for example, John C. Zimmerman, "Sayyid Qutb's Influence on the 11 September Attacks," *Terrorism and Political Violence* 16(2) (2004): 222–52; John C. Zimmerman, "Roots of Conflict: The Islamist Critique of Western Values," *Journal of Social, Political and Economic Studies* 30(4) (2005): 425–58.
11. Neil Harvey, *The Chiapas Rebellion: The Struggle for Land and Democracy* (Durham, NC: Duke University Press, 1998).
12. Reuters, "Brazil Plans Vast Amazon Reserve to Stem Logging," ABC News Online, February 18, 2005, at www.abc.net.au/news/news items/200502/s1306089.htm (last accessed on August 7, 2008).
13. BBC News, "Shell Admits Fuelling Corruption," June 11, 2004, at http://news.bbc.co.uk/2/hi/business/3796375.stm (last accessed on August 7, 2008).
14. Michael Klare, *Blood and Oil: The Dangers and Consequences of America's Growing Petroleum Dependency* (New York: Metropolitan Books, 2004).
15. Peter Goodspeed, "Food Crisis Being Felt Around the World," *National Post*, April 2, 2008, at www.financialpost.com/story. html?id=412984 (last accessed on August 7, 2008); Margaret Munro, "As Food Shortages Swell, Doubts Surface on Biofuel Policies," *Vancouver Sun*, May 2, 2008, at www.canada.com/ vancouversun/news/story.html?id=598b159d-e9ff-4013-9cfa-131bd2d68d55 (last accessed on August 7, 2008).
16. The most well-known case is that of French farmer and anti-globalization activist José Bové. See Suzanne Daly, "Montredon Journal; French See a Hero in War on 'McDomination,'" *New York Times*, October 12, 1999; Suzanne Daly, "French Farmer Is Sentenced to Jail for Attack on McDonald's," *New York Times*, September 14, 2000.
17. Thomas L. Friedman, "Better Late Than . . .: President Bush's speech on Thursday announcing a big increase in foreign aid for poor countries is a breakthrough for this administration," *New York Times*, March 17, 2002.

18. Ibid.
19. Richard Rosecrance, *The Rise of the Trading State: Commerce and Conquest in the Modern World* (New York: Basic Books, 1986); Bruce Russett and John R. Oneal, *Triangulating Peace: Democracy, Interdependence, and International Organizations* (New York: W. W. Norton, 2001). See also Dale C. Copeland, "Economic Interdependence and War: A Theory of Trade Expectations," *International Security* 20(4) (1996): 5–41; Michael Mousseau, Håvard Hegre, and John R. Oneal, "How the Wealth of Nations Conditions the Liberal Peace," *European Journal of International Relations* 9(2) (2003): 277–314.
20. Bob Deacon, with Michelle Hulse and Paul Stubbs, *Global Social Policy: International Organizations and the Future of Welfare* (London: Sage, 1997), p. 1.
21. Ibid.
22. SIPRI, *SIPRI Yearbook 2005: Armaments, Disarmament and International Security* (London/Stockholm: Oxford University Press / SIPRI, 2005), p. 280, n. 128.
23. Michael Mousseau, "Terrorism and Export Economies: The Dark Side of Free Trade," in Forest (ed.), *The Making of a Terrorist*, vol. III: *Root Causes*, p. 194.
24. Ibid., p. 201.
25. Ann Hironaka, *Neverending Wars: The International Community, Weak States and the Perpetuation of Civil War* (Cambridge, MA: Harvard University Press, 2005).
26. Mark Duffield, *Global Governance and the New Wars: The Merging of Development and Security* (London: Zed Books, 2001).
27. Ahmed Rashid, *Descent Into Chaos: The United States and the Failure of Nation Building in Pakistan, Afghanistan, and Central Asia* (New York: Penguin, 2008).
28. Joanne Wright, "The Importance of Europe in the Global Campaign Against Terrorism," *Terrorism and Political Violence* 18(2) (2006): 281–99, at p. 295.
29. Ibid.
30. OSCE – Organization for Security and Cooperation in Europe; ASEM – Asia–Europe Meeting.
31. Wright, "The Importance of Europe," p. 296.
32. Edward Newman, "Weak States, State Failure, and Terrorism," *Terrorism and Political Violence* 19(4) (2007): 463–88, at p. 484.

33. Nicholas Thompson, "A War Best Served Cold," *New York Times*, July 31, 2007.
34. Fahed Fanek, "No More Reports on Human Development in the Arab World," *Jordan Times*, May 5, 2003, accessed at www.aljazeerah.info/Opinion%20editiorials/2003%20Opinion% 20Editorials/May/5%20o/No%20more%20reports%20on%20h uman%20development%20in%20the%20Arab%20world,%20F ahed%20Fanek.htm (last accessed on August 7, 2008).
35. UN News Service, "Top UN Envoy Sergio Vieira de Mello Killed in Terrorist Blast in Baghdad," UN News Centre, August 19, 2003, at www.un.org/apps/news/story.asp?NewsID=8023&Cr=iraq&Cr1 (last accessed on August 7, 2008).
36. For a discussion of the role of the military in complex emergencies, see Robert Kaplan, "Next: A War Against Nature," *New York Times*, October 12, 2005.
37. Sharon Lafraniere, "Europe Takes Africa's Fish, and Boatloads of Migrants Follow," *New York Times*, January 14, 2008.
38. Paul Collier, *The Bottom Billion: Why the Poorest Countries are Failing and What Can Be Done About It* (Oxford: Oxford University Press, 2007).
39. Robin Kirk, "Colombia and the 'War' on Terror: Rhetoric and Reality," *World Today* 60(3) (2004), Chatham House's monthly magazine, available at Human Rights Watch website, at www.hrw.org/english/docs/2004/03/04/colomb7932.htm (last accessed on August 7, 2008). For a broader look, see Mario A. Murillo and Jesus Rey Avirama, *Colombia and the United States: War, Unrest, and Destabilization* (New York: Seven Stories Press, 2003).
40. Juan Forero, "Bush's Aid Cuts on Court Issue Roil Neighbors," *New York Times*, August 19, 2005. The Bush Administration began to reconsider this policy as the Defense Department realized that it was having a negative impact on military cooperation with key allies. See Steven R. Weisman, "U.S. Rethinks Its Cutoff of Military Aid to Latin American Nations," *New York Times*, March 12, 2006.
41. Howard W. French, "China Confirms Protests by Uighur Muslims," *New York Times*, April 3, 2008.
42. See, for example, Nancy Chang, *Silencing Political Dissent: How Post-September 11 Anti-Terrorism Measures Threaten Our Civil Liberties* (New York: Open Media, 2002); Benjamin R. Barber, *Fear's Empire: War, Terrorism, and Democracy* (New York: W. W.

Norton, 2003); Cynthia Brown (ed.), *Lost Liberties: Ashcroft and the Assault on Personal Freedom* (New York: The New Press, 2003); David Cole, *Enemy Aliens: Double Standards and Constitutional Freedoms in the War on Terrorism* (New York: The New Press, 2003); Nat Hentoff, *The War on the Bill of Rights and the Gathering Resistance* (New York: Seven Stories Press, 2003); Richard C. Leone and Greg Anrig, Jr. (eds.), *The War on Our Freedoms: Civil Liberties in an Age of Terrorism* (New York: A Century Foundation Book / PublicAffairs, 2003). See also Philip B. Heymann, *Terrorism, Freedom, and Security: Winning Without War* (Cambridge, MA: The MIT Press, 2003); Michael Ignatieff, *The Lesser Evil: Political Ethics in an Age of Terror* (Toronto: Penguin Canada, 2004); Philip B. Heymann and Juliette N. Kayyem, *Protecting Liberty in an Age of Terror* (Cambridge, MA: The MIT Press, 2005); Magnus Ranstorp and Paul Wilkinson (eds.), *Terrorism and Human Rights* (London: Taylor & Francis, 2006); Eric Lichtblau, *Bush's Law: The Remaking of American Justice* (New York: Pantheon, 2008); Philippe Sands, *Torture Team: Rumsfeld's Memo and the Betrayal of American Values* (New York: Palgrave Macmillan, 2008); Jane Mayer, *The Dark Side: The Inside Story of How The War on Terror Turned into a War on American Ideals* (New York: Doubleday, 2008).

43. For an analysis of the issue of the outright banning of anti-democratic political parties, see John Finn, "Electoral Regimes and the Proscription of Anti-democratic Parties," *Terrorism and Political Violence* 12(3 & 4) (2000): 51–77.

44. Michael Taarnby, "Understanding Recruitment of Islamist Terrorists in Europe," in Magnus Ranstorp (ed.), *Mapping Terrorism Research: State of the Art, Gaps and Future Direction* (London: Routledge, 2007), pp. 164–86, at p. 172.

45. Sharon Pickering, David Wright-Neville, Jude McCulloch, and Pete Lentini, *Counter-Terrorism Policing and Culturally Diverse Communities* (Melbourne: Monash University, 2007), p. 17.

46. Sushi Das, "State and Federal Police Rift on Terror: Report Warns Against the Hard Line," *Age* (Melbourne), October 15, 2007, p. 3; Sushi Das, "Good Cop, Bad Cop?" *Age* (Melbourne), October 15, 2007, p. 11.

47. Samuel P. Huntington, *The Clash of Civilizations and the Remaking of World Order* (New York: Simon & Schuster, 1996).

48. Alliance of Civilizations website, at www.unaoc.org (last accessed on August 7, 2008).

49. Amartya Sen, *Identity and Violence: The Illusion of Destiny* (New York: W. W. Norton, 2006), p. 83.

50. International Conference on Counter Terrorism, Melbourne, October 2007, organized by the Victoria Police, Monash University, and the Australian Multicultural Foundation.

51. Theo Van Boven, "The European Context for Intercultural Education," paper presented at the conference "Social Diversity and Discrimination in the Common Curriculum," Bergen, The Netherlands, January 27–30, 1993.

52. Otto Nathan, Heinz Norden, and Albert Einstein, *Einstein on Peace* (New York: Simon & Schuster, 1960), p. 253.

53. Tom Pyszczynski, Abdollhossein Abdollahi, Jeff Greenberg, and Sheldon Solomon, "Crusades and Jihads: An Existential Psychological Perspective on the Psychology of Terrorism and Political Extremism," in Jeff Victoroff (ed.), *Tangled Roots: Social and Psychological Factors in the Genesis of Terrorism* (Amsterdam: IOS Press, 2006), pp. 85–97, at p. 93.

54. Pickering, et al., *Counter-Terrorism Policing and Culturally Diverse Communities*, pp. 19–21.

55. Valerie M. Hudson and Andrea M. den Boer, *Bare Branches: The Security Implications of Asia's Surplus Male Population* (Boston: MIT Press, 2004).

56. BBC World (2008), *Looking for China Girl*, television documentary produced by Sophie Todd and Frank Smith, broadcast on March 1 and 2 as part of "Inside China" series. First broadcast on BBC2 in 2005.

57. Ronald D. Crelinsten, "In Their Own Words: The World of the Torturer," in Ronald D. Crelinsten and Alex P. Schmid (eds.), *The Politics of Pain: Torturers and Their Masters* (Boulder, CO: Westview Press, 1995), pp. 35–64.

58. See, for example, Martha Ainsworth, Kathleen Beegle, and Andrew Nyamete, "The Impact of Women's Schooling on Fertility and Contraceptive Use: A Study of Fourteen Sub-Saharan African Countries," *World Bank Economic Review* 10(1) (1996): 85–122.

59. Choe Sang-Hun, "South Korea, Where Boys Were Kings, A Shift Toward Baby Girls," *New York Times*, December 23, 2007.

60. CNN World Report, January 2, 2008.

61. UNDP, Regional Bureau for Arab States (RBAS), *The Arab Human Development Report 2005: Towards the Role of Women in the Arab World* (New York: UNDP/RBAS, 2006), at p. 6.

62. Ibid., p. 8.

63. Nicholas D. Kristof, "It Takes a School, Not Missiles," *New York Times*, July 13, 2008. For a personal account of this school-building program, see Greg Mortenson and David Oliver Relin, *Three Cups of Tea: One Man's Mission to Fight Terrorism and Build Nations . . . One School at a Time* (New York: Viking, 2006).

64. Neil MacFarquhar, "Heavy Hand of the Secret Police Impeding Reform in Arab World," *New York Times*, November 14, 2005.

65. David C. Rapoport and Leonard Weinberg, "Elections and Violence," *Terrorism and Political Violence* 12(3 & 4) (2000): 15–50.

66. Jeffrey Gettleman, "Kenya Topples Into Post-Election Chaos," *New York Times*, January 3, 2008.

67. Victor T. Le Vine, "Violence and the Paradox of Democratic Renewal: A Preliminary Assessment," *Terrorism and Political Violence* 12(3 & 4) (2000): 261–92. For a case study of the structural conditions that produce a culture of violence, see Peter Waldmann, "Is There a Culture of Violence in Colombia?" *Terrorism and Political Violence* 19(4) (2007): 593–609.

68. Andrew Gumble, *Steal This Vote: Dirty Elections and the Rotten History of Democracy in America* (New York: Nation Books, 2005), ch. 10. For the 2004 election, see ch.13.

69. For a trenchant critique of the American approach to democratization, both generally and in the "war on terror" and Iraq in particular, see Benjamin R. Barber, *Fear's Empire: War, Terrorism, and Democracy* (New York: W. W. Norton, 2003), Part Two, especially chs. 7 and 8. For an alternative approach, see his ch. 9 (pp. 218–32).

70. William Crotty, "International Terrorism: Causes and Consequences for a Democratic Society," in William Crotty (ed.), *Democratic Development and Political Terrorism: The Global Perspective* (Boston: Northeastern University Press, 2005), pp. 523–32, at p. 524.

71. The Report is available at www.ipcc.ch/ (last accessed on August 6, 2008).

72. The Report is available at http://hdr.undp.org/en/reports/global/hdr2007-2008 (last accessed on August 6, 2008).

73. BBC News, " 'Over 11,000' Dead in French Heat," August 29, 2003, at http://news.bbc.co.uk/1/hi/world/europe/3190585.stm (last accessed on August 7, 2008); Australian Broadcasting Corporation, "Heatwaves, Floods Torment Europe," ABC News, June 28, 2007, at www.abc.net.au/news/stories/2007/06/28/1964084.htm (last accessed on August 7, 2008).

74. Elisabeth Rosenthal, "As Earth Warms Up, Tropical Virus Moves to Italy," *New York Times*, December 23, 2007.

75. IPCC, "Summary for Policymakers," in M. L. Parry, O. F. Canziani, J. P. Palutikof, P. J. van der Linden, and C. E. Hanson (eds.), *Climate Change 2007: Impacts, Adaptation and Vulnerability. Contribution of Working Group II to the Fourth Assessment Report of the Intergovernmental Panel on Climate Change* (Cambridge: Cambridge University Press, 2007), pp. 7–22, at p. 12. For a crisis management perspective, see Patrick Lagadec, "Understanding the French 2003 Heat Wave Experience: Beyond the Heat, a Multi-Layered Challenge," *Journal of Contingencies and Crisis Management* 12(4) (2004): 160–9.

76. See, for example, Thomas F. Homer-Dixon, *Environment, Scarcity and Violence* (Princeton, NJ: Princeton University Press, 2001); Hans Günter Brauch, P. H. Liotta, Antonio Marquina, Paul F. Rogers, and Mohammed El-Sayed Selim (eds.) *Security and Environment in the Mediterranean: Conceptualising Security and Environmental Conflicts* (New York: Springer-Verlag, 2003); Editorial, "Warming and Global Security," *New York Times*, April 20, 2007.

77. Michael Thompson, "Security and Solidarity: An Anti-Reductionist Analysis of Environmental Policy," in Frank Fischer and Maarten A. Hajer (eds.), *Living with Nature: Environmental Politics as Cultural Discourse* (Oxford: Oxford University Press, 1999), pp. 135–50, at p. 135.

78. Al Gore, *An Inconvenient Truth: The Planetary Emergency of Global Warming and What We Can Do About It* (New York: Rodale, 2006).

79. Alex P. Schmid, "Terrorism and Human Rights: A Perspective from the United Nations," *Terrorism and Political Violence* 17(1–2) (2005): 25–35, at p. 32.

80. For more on the role of the United Nations in counterterrorism, see Jane Boulden and Thomas G. Weiss (eds.), *Terrorism and the UN: Before and After September 11* (Bloomington: Indiana University Press, 2004).

81. Ronald D. Crelinsten, "The EU–US Partnership in the Area of Counterterrorism: A Multicentric View," in Dan Hansén and Magnus Ranstorp (eds.), *Cooperating Against Terrorism: EU–US Relations Post September 11* (Stockholm: Swedish National Defence College, 2007), pp. 53–98.

82. Marianne van Leeuwen (ed.), *Confronting Terrorism: European Experiences, Threat Perceptions and Policies* (The Hague: Kluwer Law International, 2003).

83. Judy Dempsey, "Poland Signals Doubt About Planned U.S. Missile-Defense Bases on Its Territory," *New York Times*, January 7, 2008; "Poland Firm on U.S. Missile Defense Opposition," cnn.com, July 7, 2008, at http://edition.cnn.com/2008/WORLD/europe/07/07/missile.defense/index.html?iref=newssearch (last accessed on August 7, 2008).

   In August 2008, Poland finally agreed to the deal, triggered in large part by Polish fears of Russia's intentions in the region in the wake of the Russian military incursion into Georgia that same month. As a result of Russia's actions in Georgia, Poland was even able to extract further security guarantees from the USA. See Thom Shankar and Nicholas Kulish, "U.S. and Poland Set Missile Deal," *New York Times*, August 14, 2008.

84. David Rohde, "Al Qaeda Finds Its Center of Gravity," *New York Times*, September 10, 2006; Eric Schmitt, "Militant Gains in Pakistan Said to Draw More Fighters," *New York Times*, July 10, 2008.

85. Steven Lee Myers, David E. Sanger, and Eric Schmitt, "U.S. Considers New Covert Push Within Pakistan," *New York Times*, January 6, 2008. In July 2008, President Bush secretly approved orders allowing US Special Operations forces to carry out ground assaults inside Pakistan without the prior approval of the Pakistani government. In September, Pakistani troops fired at US helicopters that had entered Pakistani airspace from Afghanistan, forcing them to turn back and presumably aborting an attempted airstrike in South Waziristan. See Eric Schmitt and Mark Mazzetti, "Bush Said to Give Orders Allowing Raids in Pakistan," *New York Times*, September 10, 2008; Saeed Shah, "War on Terror: Pakistani Troops Fire on US Helicopters Trying to Enter Lawless Tribal Region," *Guardian*, September 16, 2008, available at www.guardian.co.uk/world/2008/sep/16/pakistan.usa (last accessed on September 17, 2008).

86. Robert Wolfe, "Rendering unto Caesar: How Legal Pluralism and Regime Theory Help in Understanding Multiple Centres of Power," in Gordon Smith and Daniel Wolfish (eds.), *Who Is Afraid of the State? Canada in a World of Multiple Centres of Power* (Toronto: University of Toronto Press, 2001), pp. 259–309, at p. 262.

87. See, for example, Anne-Marie Slaughter, *A New World Order* (Princeton, NJ: Princeton University Press, 2004); David Coleman, "The United Nations and Transnational Corporations: From an Inter-nation to a 'Beyond-state' Model of Engagement," *Global Society* 17(4) (2003): 339–57.

CONCLUSION. A COMPREHENSIVE COUNTERTERRORISM STRATEGY

1. Peter C. Sederberg. "Global Terrorism: Problems of Challenge and Response," in Charles W. Kegley, Jr. (ed)., *The New Global Terrorism: Characteristics, Causes, Controls* (Upper Saddle River, NJ: Prentice Hall, 2003), pp. 267–84, at p. 273.

2. Ronald D. Crelinsten and Alex P. Schmid, "Western Responses to Terrorism: A Twenty-Five Year Balance Sheet," in Alex P. Schmid and Ronald D. Crelinsten (eds.), *Western Responses to Terrorism* (London: Frank Cass, 1993), pp. 307–40, at p. 332.

3. Boaz Ganor, *The Counter-Terrorism Puzzle: A Guide for Decision Makers* (New Brunswick, NJ: Transaction Publishers, 2005).

4. See also Margaret P. Karns and Karen A. Mingst, *International Organizations: The Politics and Processes of Global Governance* (Boulder, CO: Lynne Rienner, 2004), esp. Part 3: "The Need for Global Governance."

Select bibliography

Abbot, Ernest B., and Otto J. Hetzel (eds.), *A Legal Guide to Homeland Security and Emergency Management for State and Local Governments* (Chicago: ABA Publishing, 2005).

Alexander, Yonah, and Seymour Finger (eds.), *Terrorism: Interdisciplinary Perspectives* (New York: John Jay, 1977).

Anat, Berko, *The Path to Paradise: The Inner World of Suicide Bombers and Their Dispatchers* (Westport, CT: Praeger, 2007).

Angstrom, Jan, and Isabelle Duyvesteyn (eds.), *Understanding Victory and Defeat in Contemporary War* (New York: Routledge, 2007).

Aydinli, Ersel, and James N. Rosenau (eds.), *Globalization, Security, and the Nation-State: Paradigms in Transition* (Albany: State University of New York Press, 2005).

Ayoob, Mohammed, *The Third World Security Predicament: State Making, Regional Conflict and the International System* (Boulder, CO: Lynne Rienner, 1995).

Baer, Robert, *See No Evil: The True Story of a Ground Soldier in the CIA's War on Terrorism* (New York: Crown, 2002).

Bailes, Alyson J. K., and Isabel Frommelt (eds.), *Business and Security: Public–Private Sector Relationships in a New Security Environment* (Oxford: Oxford University Press, 2004).

Barber, Benjamin R., *Fear's Empire: War, Terrorism, and Democracy* (New York: W. W. Norton, 2003).

Bell, J. Bowyer, *A Time of Terror: How Democratic Societies Respond to Revolutionary Violence* (New York: Basic Books, 1978).

Berdal, Mats, and Mónica Serrano (eds.), *Transnational Organized Crime and International Security: Business As Usual?* (Boulder, CO: Lynne Rienner, 2002).

Biersteker, Thomas J. and Sue E. Eckert (eds.), *Countering the Financing of Terrorism* (London: Routledge, 2007).

Bjørgo, Tore (ed.), *Root Causes of Terrorism: Myths, Reality and Ways Forward* (London: Routledge, 2005).

(ed.), *Terror from the Extreme Right* (London: Frank Cass, 1995).

Bloom, Mia, *Dying to Kill: The Allure of Suicide Terrorism* (New York: Columbia University Press, 2005).

Bongar, Bruce, Lisa M. Brown, Larry E. Beutler, James N. Breckenridge, and Philip G. Zimbardo (eds.), *Psychology of Terrorism* (Oxford: Oxford University Press, 2007).

Booth, Ken, and Tim Dunne (eds.), *Worlds in Collision: Terror and the Future of Global Order* (New York: Palgrave Macmillan, 2002).

Boulden, Jane, and Thomas G. Weiss (eds.), *Terrorism and the UN: Before and After September 11* (Bloomington: Indiana University Press, 2004).

Brown, Cynthia (ed.), *Lost Liberties: Ashcroft and the Assault on Personal Freedom* (New York: The New Press, 2003).

Bukay, David, *From Muhammad to Bin Laden: Religious and Ideological Sources of the Homicide Bombers Phenomenon* (New Brunswick, NJ: Transaction Publishers, 2008).

Buzan, Barry, *People, States and Fear: An Agenda for International Security Studies in the Post-Cold War Era, Second Edition* (Boulder, CO: Lynne Rienner, 1991).

Buzan, Barry, and Ole Waever, *Regions and Powers: The Structure of International Security*, Cambridge Studies in International Relations (Cambridge: Cambridge University Press, 2004).

Buzan, Barry, Ole Waever, and Jaap de Wilde, *Security: A New Framework for Analysis* (Boulder, CO: Lynne Rienner Publishers, 1998).

Caraley, Demetrios James (ed.), *September 11, Terrorist Attacks and U.S. Foreign Policy* (New York: The Academy of Political Science, 2002).

Chandler, Michael, and Rohan Gunaratna, *Countering Terrorism: Can We Meet the Threat of Global Violence?* (London: Reaktion Books, 2007).

Chang, Nancy, *Silencing Political Dissent: How Post-September 11 Anti-Terrorism Measures Threaten Our Civil Liberties* (New York: Open Media, 2002).

Charters, David A., and Graham F. Walker (eds.), *After 9/11: Terrorism and Crime in a Globalised World* (Fredericton, NB and Halifax, NS: Centre for Conflict Studies, University of New Brunswick, and Centre for Foreign Policy Studies, Dalhousie University, 2004).

Chesterman, Simon, *Just War or Just Peace? Humanitarian Intervention and International Law* (Oxford: Oxford University Press, 2001).

Chomsky, Noam, and Edward S. Herman, *The Washington Connection and Third World Fascism* (Boston: South End Press, 1979).

Clapham, Christopher, *Africa and the International System: The Politics of State Survival* (Cambridge: Cambridge University Press, 1996).

Clarke, Richard A., *Against All Enemies: Inside America's War on Terror* (New York: The Free Press, 2004).

Clarke, Ronald V., and Graeme R. Newman, *Outsmarting the Terrorists* (Westport, CT.: Praeger Security International, 2006).

Cline, Ray S. and Yonah Alexander, *Terrorism: The Soviet Connection* (New York: Crane Russak, 1984).

Clutterbuck, Richard, *Terrorism in an Unstable World* (London: Routledge, 1994).

Cole, David, *Enemy Aliens: Double Standards and Constitutional Freedoms in the War on Terrorism* (New York: The New Press, 2003).

Cole, Leonard A., *Terror: How Israel Has Coped and What America Can Learn* (Bloomington: Indiana University Press, 2007).

The Anthrax Letters: A Medical Detective Story (Washington, DC: National Academy of Science, 2003).

Coll, Steve, *Ghost Wars: The Secret History of the CIA, Afghanistan, and bin Laden, From the Soviet Invasion to September 10, 2001* (New York: The Penguin Press, 2004).

Collier, Paul, *The Bottom Billion: Why the Poorest Countries are Failing and What Can Be Done About It* (Oxford: Oxford University Press, 2007).

Collins, John, and Ross Glover (eds.), *Collateral Language: A User's Guide to America's New War* (New York: New York University Press, 2002).

Commonwealth Human Rights Initiative, *Stamping Out Rights: The Impact of Anti-Terrorism Laws on Policing* (New Delhi: Commonwealth Human Rights Initiative, 2007).

Cook, David, and Olivia Allison, *Understanding and Addressing Suicide Attacks: The Faith and Politics of Martyrdom Operations* (Westport, CT: Praeger Security International, 2007).

Cordesman, Anthony H., and Justin G. Cordesman, *Cyber-Threats, Information Warfare, and Critical Infrastructure Protection: Defending the U.S. Homeland* (Westport, CT: Praeger, 2002).

Crelinsten, Ronald D., Danielle Laberge-Altmejd, and Denis Szabo, *Terrorism and Criminal Justice* (Lexington, MA: Lexington Books, D. C. Heath, 1978).

Crelinsten, Ronald D., and Alex P. Schmid (eds.), *The Politics of Pain: Torturers and Their Masters* (Boulder, CO: Westview Press, 1995).

Crelinsten, Ronald D., and Denis Szabo, *Hostage-Taking* (Lexington, MA: Lexington Books, D. C. Heath, 1979).

Crenshaw, Martha (ed.), *Terrorism in Context* (Philadelphia: University of Pennsylvania Press, 1995).

Crotty, William (ed.), *Democratic Development and Political Terrorism: The Global Perspective* (Boston: Northeastern University Press, 2005).

Dalgaard-Nielsen, Anja, and Daniel S. Hamilton (eds.), *Transatlantic Homeland Security: Protecting Society in an Age of Catastrophic Terrorism* (London: Routledge, 2006).

Davis, Paul K., and Brian Michael Jenkins, *Deterrence & Influence in Counterterrorism: A Component in the War on al Qaeda* (Santa Monica, CA: Rand, 2002).

Deflem, Mathieu (ed.), *Terrorism and Counterterrorism: Criminological Perspectives* (Amsterdam: Elsevier, 2004).

Duffield, Mark, *Global Governance and the New Wars: The Merging of Development and Security* (London: Zed Books, 2001).

Dunlop, John B., *The 2002 Dubrovka and 2004 Beslan Hostage Crises: A Critique of Russian Counter-Terrorism*, Soviet and Post-Soviet Politics and Society 26 (Stuttgart: ibidem-Verlag, 2006).

Dyer, Gwynne, *The Mess They Made: The Middle East After Iraq* (Melbourne: Scribe, 2007).

Elshtain, Jean Bethke, *Just War Against Terror: The Burden of American Power in a Violent World* (New York: Basic Books, 2003).

Enders, Walter, and Todd Sandler, *The Political Economy of Terrorism* (Cambridge: Cambridge University Press, 2006).

Finn, John E., *Constitutions in Crisis: Political Violence and the Rule of Law* (New York: Oxford University Press, 1991).

Forest, James J. F. (ed.), *The Making of a Terrorist: Recruitment, Training, and Root Causes*, vol. III: *Root Causes* (Westport, CT: Praeger Security International, 2006).

Freedman, Lawrence (ed.), *Superterrorism: Policy Responses* (Oxford: Blackwell, 2002).

Gambetta, Diego (ed.), *Making Sense of Suicide Missions* (Oxford: Oxford University Press, 2005).

Ganor, Boaz, *The Counter-Terrorism Puzzle: A Guide for Decision Makers* (New Brunswick, NJ: Transaction Publishers, 2005).

Habeck, Mary, *Knowing the Enemy: Jihadist Ideology and the War on Terror* (New Haven, CT: Yale University Press, 2006).

Hafez, Mohammed M., *Suicide Bombers in Iraq: The Strategy and*

Ideology of Martyrdom (Washington, DC: United States Institute of Peace Press, 2007).

Manufacturing Human Bombs: The Making of Palestinian Suicide Bombers (Washington, DC: United States Institute of Peace Press, 2006).

Hansén, Dan, and Magnus Ranstorp (eds.), *Cooperating Against Terrorism: EU–US Relations Post September 11* (Stockholm: Swedish National Defence College, 2007).

Heinz, Wolfgang S., and Hugo Frühling, *Determinants of Gross Human Rights Violations by State and State-Sponsored Actors in Brazil, Uruguay, Chile, and Argentina 1960–1990* (The Hague: Kluwer Law International, 1999).

Hentoff, Nat, *The War on the Bill of Rights and the Gathering Resistance* (New York: Seven Stories Press, 2003).

Herman, Edward S., *The Real Terror Network: Terrorism in Fact and Propaganda* (Boston: South End Press, 1982).

Hewitt, Christopher, *The Effectiveness of Anti-Terrorist Policies* (New York: University Press of America, 1984).

Heymann, Philip B., *Terrorism, Freedom, and Security: Winning Without War* (Cambridge, MA: The MIT Press, 2003).

Heymann, Philip B., and Juliette N. Kayyem, *Protecting Liberty in an Age of Terror* (Cambridge, MA: The MIT Press, 2005).

Hironaka, Ann, *Neverending Wars: The International Community, Weak States and the Perpetuation of Civil War* (Cambridge, MA: Harvard University Press, 2005).

Hoffman, Bruce, *Inside Terrorism* (New York: Columbia University Press, 1998).

Homer-Dixon, Thomas F., *Environment, Scarcity and Violence* (Princeton, NJ: Princeton University Press, 2001).

Hudson, Valerie M., and Andrea M. den Boer, *Bare Branches: The Security Implications of Asia's Surplus Male Population* (Boston: MIT Press, 2004).

Hunt, Krista and Kim Rygiel (eds.) *(En)Gendering the War on Terror: War Stories and Camouflaged Politics* (Aldershot: Ashgate, 2006).

Ibrahim, Raymond (ed.), *The Al Qaeda Reader* (New York: Broadway Books, 2007).

Ignatieff, Michael, *The Lesser Evil: Political Ethics in an Age of Terror* (Toronto: Penguin Canada, 2004).

International Commission on Intervention and State Sovereignty (ICISS), *The Responsibility to Protect: Report of the International*

Commission on Intervention and State Sovereignty (Ottawa:
    International Development Research Centre for ICISS, 2001).
Isikoff, Michael, and David Corn, Hubris: The Inside Story of Spin,
    Scandal, and the Selling of the Iraq War (New York: Three Rivers
    Press, 2007).
Jackson, Robert H., Quasi-States: Sovereignty, International Relations
    and the Third World (Cambridge: Cambridge University Press,
    1993).
Jenkins, Brian, Janera Johnson, and David Ronfeldt, Numbered Lives:
    Some Statistical Observations from 77 International Hostage Episodes
    (Santa Monica, CA: Rand, 1977).
Jones, Seth G., and Martin C. Libicki, How Terrorist Groups End:
    Lessons for Countering al Qa'ida (Santa Monica, CA: Rand, 2008).
Kaldor, Mary, New and Old Wars: Organized Violence in a Global Era,
    Second Edition (Cambridge: Polity, 2006).
Katona, Peter, Michael D. Intriligator and John P. Sullivan (eds.),
    Countering Terrorism and WMD: Creating a Global Counter-Terrorism
    Network (London: Routledge, 2006).
Kegley, Jr., Charles W. (ed.), The New Global Terrorism: Characteristics,
    Causes, Controls (Upper Saddle River, NJ: Prentice Hall, 2003).
Kelsay, John, Arguing the Just War in Islam (Cambridge, MA: Harvard
    University Press, 2007).
Kenney, Michael, From Pablo to Osama: Trafficking and Terrorist Networks,
    Government Bureaucracies, and Competitive Adaptation (University
    Park, PA: The Pennsylvania State University Press, 2007).
Khanna, Parag, The Second World: Empires and Influence in the New
    Global Order (New York: Random House, 2008).
Kirchheimer, Otto, Political Justice: The Use of Legal Procedure for
    Political Ends (Westport, CT: Greenwood Press, 1980).
Klare, Michael T., Resource Wars: The New Landscape of Global Conflict
    (New York: Metropolitan Books, Henry Holt, 2001).
    (ed.), World Security: Challenges for a New Century. Third Edition
    (New York: St. Martin's Press, 1998).
Kurth Cronin, Audrey, and James M. Ludes (eds.), Attacking Terrorism:
    Elements of a Grand Strategy (Washington, DC: Georgetown
    University Press, 2004).
Laqueur, Walter, The New Terrorism: Fanaticism and the Arms of Mass
    Destruction (Oxford: Oxford University Press, 1999).
Lawrence, Bruce (ed.), Messages to the World: The Statements of
    Osama bin Laden, trans. James Howarth (London: Verso, 2005).

Le Billon, Phili, *The Geopolitics of Resource Wars* (London: Routledge, 2008).

Leone, Richard C., and Greg Anrig, Jr. (eds.), *The War on Our Freedoms: Civil Liberties in an Age of Terrorism* (New York: A Century Foundation Book / PublicAffairs, 2003).

Lesser, Ian O., Bruce Hoffman, John Arquilla, David Ronfeldt, and Michele Zanini, *Countering the New Terrorism* (Santa Monica, CA: Rand, 1999).

Levy, Barry S., and Victor W. Sidel (eds.), *Terrorism and Public Health: A Balanced Approach to Strengthening Systems and Protecting People* (Oxford: Oxford University Press, 2002).

Lia, Brynjar, *Globalization and the Future of Terrorism: Patterns and Predictions* (London: Routledge, 2005).

Litchblau, Eric, *Bush's Law: The Remaking of American Justice* (New York: Pantheon, 2008).

Livingstone, Neil C., and Terrell E. Arnold (eds.), *Fighting Back: Winning The War Against Terrorism* (Lexington, MA: Lexington Books, 1986).

Lustgarten, Laurence, and Ian Leigh, *In From the Cold: National Security and Parliamentary Democracy* (Oxford: Clarendon Press, 1994).

Lustick, Ian S., *Trapped in the War on Terror* (Philadelphia: University of Pennsylvania Press, 2006).

Marks, John, and Igor Beliaev (eds.), *Common Ground on Terrorism: Soviet–American Cooperation Against the Politics of Terror* (New York: W. W. Norton, 1991).

Martin, David C., and John Walcott, *Best Laid Plans: The Inside Story of America's War Against Terrorism* (New York: Simon & Schuster, 1988).

Martin, Gus (ed.), *The New Era of Terrorism: Selected Readings* (London: Sage, 2004).

Marx, Gary T., *Undercover: Police Surveillance in America* (Berkeley: University of California Press, 1988).

Mayer Jane, *The Dark Side: The Inside Story of How The War on Terror Turned into a War on American Ideals* (New York: Doubleday, 2008).

McAdams, A. James (ed.), *Transitional Justice and the Rule of Law in New Democracies* (Notre Dame, IN: University of Notre Dame Press, 1997).

McRae, Rob, and Don Hubert (eds.), *Human Security and the New Diplomacy: Protecting People, Promoting Peace* (Montreal: McGill-Queen's University Press, 2001).

Miniter, Richard, *Losing Bin Laden: How Bill Clinton's Failures Unleashed Global Terror* (Washington, DC: Regnery Publishing, 2003).

Mortenson, Greg, and David Oliver Relin, *Three Cups of Tea: One Man's Mission to Fight Terrorism and Build Nations . . . One School at a Time* (New York: Viking, 2006).

Mueller, John, *Overblown: How Politicians and the Terrorism Industry Inflate National Security Threats, and Why We Believe Them* (New York: Free Press, 2006).

Murillo, Mario A. and Jesus Rey Avirama, *Colombia and the United States: War, Unrest, and Destabilization* (New York: Seven Stories Press, 2003).

Nadelmann, Ethan A., *Cops Across Borders: The Internationalization of U.S. Criminal Law Enforcement* (University Park, PA: The Pennsylvania State University Press, 1993).

National Commission on Terrorist Attacks Upon the United States, *The 9/11 Commission Report: Final Report of the National Commission on Terrorist Attacks Upon the United States* (New York: W. W. Norton, 2004).

Nicander, Lars, and Magnus Ranstorp (eds.), *Terrorism in the Information Age – New Frontiers?* (Stockholm: Swedish National Defence College, 2004).

O'Kane, Rosemary H. T. (ed.), *Terrorism*, 2 vols. (Northampton, MA: Edward Elgar Publishing, 2005).

Oliver, Anne Marie, and Paul Steinberg, *The Road to Martyr's Square: A Journey into the World of the Suicide Bomber* (Oxford: Oxford University Press, 2005).

Paletz, David L. and Alex P. Schmid (eds.), *Perspectives on Terrorism and the Media* (Newbury Park, CA: Sage, 1992).

Pape, Robert, *Dying to Win: The Strategic Logic of Suicide Terrorism* (New York: Random House, 2005).

Parenti, Christian, *The Soft Cage: Surveillance in America from Slavery to the War on Terror* (New York: Basic Books, 2003).

Parry, M. L., O. F. Canziani, J. P. Palutikof, P. J. van der Linden, and C. E. Hanson (eds.), *Climate Change 2007: Impacts, Adaptation and Vulnerability. Contribution of Working Group II to the Fourth Assessment Report of the Intergovernmental Panel on Climate Change* (Cambridge: Cambridge University Press, 2007).

Pedhazur, Ami, *The Root Causes of Suicide Terrorism: The Globalization of Martyrdom* (London: Routledge, 2005).

Suicide Terrorism (London: Polity, 2004).

Phythian, Mark, and Peter Gill, *Intelligence in an Insecure World* (Cambridge: Polity, 2006).

Pickering, Sharon, David Wright-Neville, Jude McCulloch, and Pete
    Lentini, *Counter-Terrorism Policing and Culturally Diverse
    Communities* (Melbourne: Monash University, 2007).
Pillar, Paul R., *Terrorism and U.S. Foreign Policy* (Washington, DC:
    Brookings Institution Press, 2001).
Podhoretz, Norman, *World War IV: The Long Struggle Against
    Islamofascism* (New York: Doubleday, 2007).
Ranstorp, Magnus (ed.), *Mapping Terrorism Research: State of the Art,
    Gaps and Future Direction* (London: Routledge, 2007).
Ranstorp, Magnus, and Paul Wilkinson (eds.), *Terrorism and Human
    Rights* (London: Taylor & Francis, 2006).
Rapoport, David C., and Yonah Alexander (eds.), *The Morality of
    Terrorism: Religious and Secular Justifications* (New York: University
    of Columbia Press, 1982).
Rapoport, David C., and Leonard Weinberg (eds.), *The Democratic
    Experience and Political Violence* (London: Frank Cass, 2000).
Rashid, Ahmed, *Descent Into Chaos: The United States and the Failure
    of Nation Building in Pakistan, Afghanistan, and Central Asia* (New
    York: Penguin, 2008).
Reeve, Simon, *The New Jackals: Ramzi Yousef, Osama bin Laden and the
    Future of Terrorism* (Boston: Northeastern University Press, 1999).
Reich, Walter (ed.), *Origins of Terrorism: Psychologies, Ideologies,
    Theologies, States of Mind* (Washington, DC: Woodrow Wilson
    Center Press, 1990).
Reinares, Fernando (ed.), *European Democracies Against Terrorism:
    Governmental Policies and Intergovernmental Cooperation* (Aldershot:
    Ashgate, 2000).
Rejali, Darius, *Torture and Democracy* (Princeton, NJ: Princeton
    University Press, 2007).
Rich, Frank, *The Greatest Story Ever Sold: The Decline and Fall of Truth
    in Bush's America* (New York: Penguin, 2007).
Robinson, Paul (ed.), *Just War in Comparative Perspective* (Aldershot:
    Ashgate, 2003).
Rosen, Jeffrey, *The Naked Crowd: Reclaiming Security and Freedom in an
    Anxious Age* (New York: Random House, 2004).
Rosenau, James N., *Along the Domestic–Foreign Frontier: Exploring
    Governance in a Turbulent World* (Cambridge: Cambridge University
    Press, 1997).
    Turbulence in World Politics: A Theory of Change and Continuity
    (Princeton: Princeton University Press, 1990).

Russett, Bruce, and John R. Oneal, *Triangulating Peace: Democracy, Interdependence, and International Organizations* (New York: W. W. Norton, 2001).

Sageman, Marc, *Leaderless Jihad: Terror Networks in the Twenty First Century* (Philadelphia: University of Pennsylvania Press, 2007).
    Understanding Terror Networks (Philadelphia: University of Pennsylvania Press, 2004).

Sands, Philippe, *Torture Team: Rumsfeld's Memo and the Betrayal of American Values* (New York: Palgrave Macmillan, 2008).

Satloff, Robert, *The Battle of Ideas in the War on Terror: Essays on US Public Diplomacy in the Middle East* (Washington, DC: The Washington Institute, 2004).

Savitch, H. V., *Cities in a Time of Terror: Space, Territory, and Local Resilience* (Armonk, NY: M. E. Sharpe, 2008).

Schafer, Stephen, *The Political Criminal: The Problem of Morality and Crime* (New York: Free Press, 1974).

Schmid, Alex P., and Ronald D. Crelinsten (eds.), *Western Responses to Terrorism* (London: Frank Cass, 1993).

Schmid, Alex P., and Janny de Graaf, *Violence as Communication: Insurgent Terrorism and the Western News Media* (Beverly Hills, CA: Sage, 1982).

Sederberg, Peter C., *Terrorist Myths: Illusion, Rhetoric, and Reality* (Englewood Cliffs, NJ: Prentice-Hall, 1989).

Sen, Amartya, *Identity and Violence: The Illusion of Destiny* (New York: W. W. Norton, 2006).

Slaughter, Anne-Marie, *A New World Order* (Princeton, NJ: Princeton University Press, 2004).

Smith, Dan, and Janani Vivekananda, *A Climate of Conflict: The Links Between Climate Change, Peace and War* (London: International Alert, 2007).

Stepanova, Ekaterina, *Anti-terrorism and Peace-building During and After Conflict* (Stockholm: SIPRI, 2003).

Sterling, Claire, *The Terror Network: The Secret War of International Terrorism* (New York: Henry Holt & Co., 1981).

Stern, Jessica, *Terror in the Name of God: Why Religious Militants Kill* (New York: HarperCollins, 2003).

Tan, Andrew, and Kumar Ramakrishna (eds.), *The New Terrorism: Anatomy, Trends and Counter-strategies* (Singapore: Eastern University Press, 2002).

Tatham, Steve, *Losing Arab Hearts and Minds: The Coalition, Al*

Jazeera and Muslim Public Opinion (London: Hurst and Company, 2006).

Taylor, Max, and John Horgan (eds.), *The Future of Terrorism* (London: Frank Cass, 2000).

Temple-Raston, Dina, *The Jihad Next Door: The Lackawanna Six and Rough Justice in an Age of Terror* (New York: PublicAffairs Books, 2007).

Trinkunas, Harold, and Jeanne Giraldo (eds.), *Terrorism Financing and State Responses: A Comparative Perspective* (Stanford, CA: Stanford University Press, 2007).

Tucker, Jonathan B. (ed.), *Toxic Terror: Assessing Terrorist Use of Chemical and Biological Weapons* (Cambridge, MA: MIT Press, 2000).

van Leeuwen, Marianne (ed.), *Confronting Terrorism: European Experiences, Threat Perceptions and Policies* (The Hague: Kluwer Law International, 2003).

Victoroff, Jeff (ed.), *Tangled Roots: Social and Psychological Factors in the Genesis of Terrorism* (Amsterdam: IOS Press, 2006).

Vidino, Lorenzo, *Al-Qaeda in Europe: The New Battleground for International Jihad* (Amherst, NY: Prometheus Books, 2006).

Walzer, Michael, *Just and Unjust Wars: A Moral Argument With Historical Illustrations* (New York: Basic Books, 1977).

Wardlaw, Grant, *Political Terrorism: Theory, Tactics, and Counter-measures. Second edition* (Cambridge: Cambridge University Press, 1989).

Weimann, Gabriel, *Terror on the Internet: The New Arena, the New Challenges* (Washington, DC: United States Institute of Peace Press, 2006).

Wenger, Andreas, and Reto Wollenmann (eds.), *Bioterrorism: Confronting a Complex Threat* (Boulder, CO and London: Lynne Rienner Publishers, 2007).

Wilkinson, Paul, *Terrorism and the Liberal State* (London: Macmillan, 1977).

Wilkinson, Paul, and Brian M. Jenkins (eds.), *Aviation Terrorism and Security* (London: Frank Cass, 1999).

Wilkinson, Paul, and A. M. Stewart (eds.), *Contemporary Research on Terrorism* (Aberdeen: University of Aberdeen Press, 1987).

Wilson, Richard Ashley (ed.), *Human Rights in the "War on Terror"* (Cambridge: Cambridge University Press, 2005).

Wittes, Benjamin, *Law and the Long War: The Future of Justice in the Age of Terror* (New York:Penguin Press, 2008).

Zegart, Amy B., *Spying Blind: The CIA, the FBI, and the Origins of 9/11* (Princeton, NJ: Princeton University Press, 2007).

Zimmermann, Doron, and Andreas Wenger (eds.), *How States Fight Terrorism: Policy Dynamics in the West* (Boulder, CO: Lynne Rienner, 2007).

Index